Memoirs of the Countess de Valois de la Motte; containing a compleat justification of her conduct and an explanation of the intrigues relative to the diamond necklace

Jeanne de Saint-Remy

Memoirs of the Countess de Valois de la Motte; containing a compleat justification of her conduct, and an explanation of the intrigues ... relative to the diamond necklace; also the correspondence between the Queen and the Cardinal de Rohan ... Translated
La Motte, Jeanne de Saint-Rémy de Valois, comtesse de
ESTCID: T142432
Reproduction from British Library
With a half-title. Pp.260 and 261 misnumbered 230, 231. Includes 'Justificatory pieces' With separate pagination and register. Apparently bearing the signature of the author on p.231 [i.e.261].
London : printed for the author, and sold by J. Ridgway, 1789.
viii,231[i.e.261],[3],48p. ; 8°

ECCO
ECCO
Eighteenth Century
Collections Online
Print Editions

Gale ECCO Print Editions

Relive history with *Eighteenth Century Collections Online*, now available in print for the independent historian and collector. This series includes the most significant English-language and foreign-language works printed in Great Britain during the eighteenth century, and is organized in seven different subject areas including literature and language; medicine, science, and technology; and religion and philosophy. The collection also includes thousands of important works from the Americas.

The eighteenth century has been called "The Age of Enlightenment." It was a period of rapid advance in print culture and publishing, in world exploration, and in the rapid growth of science and technology – all of which had a profound impact on the political and cultural landscape. At the end of the century the American Revolution, French Revolution and Industrial Revolution, perhaps three of the most significant events in modern history, set in motion developments that eventually dominated world political, economic, and social life.

In a groundbreaking effort, Gale initiated a revolution of its own: digitization of epic proportions to preserve these invaluable works in the largest online archive of its kind. Contributions from major world libraries constitute over 175,000 original printed works. Scanned images of the actual pages, rather than transcriptions, recreate the works *as they first appeared.*

Now for the first time, these high-quality digital scans of original works are available via print-on-demand, making them readily accessible to libraries, students, independent scholars, and readers of all ages.

For our initial release we have created seven robust collections to form one the world's most comprehensive catalogs of 18th century works.

Initial Gale ECCO Print Editions collections include:

> ***History and Geography***
> Rich in titles on English life and social history, this collection spans the world as it was known to eighteenth-century historians and explorers. Titles include a wealth of travel accounts and diaries, histories of nations from throughout the world, and maps and charts of a world that was still being discovered. Students of the War of American Independence will find fascinating accounts from the British side of conflict.

Social Science
Delve into what it was like to live during the eighteenth century by reading the first-hand accounts of everyday people, including city dwellers and farmers, businessmen and bankers, artisans and merchants, artists and their patrons, politicians and their constituents. Original texts make the American, French, and Industrial revolutions vividly contemporary.

Medicine, Science and Technology
Medical theory and practice of the 1700s developed rapidly, as is evidenced by the extensive collection, which includes descriptions of diseases, their conditions, and treatments. Books on science and technology, agriculture, military technology, natural philosophy, even cookbooks, are all contained here.

Literature and Language
Western literary study flows out of eighteenth-century works by Alexander Pope, Daniel Defoe, Henry Fielding, Frances Burney, Denis Diderot, Johann Gottfried Herder, Johann Wolfgang von Goethe, and others. Experience the birth of the modern novel, or compare the development of language using dictionaries and grammar discourses.

Religion and Philosophy
The Age of Enlightenment profoundly enriched religious and philosophical understanding and continues to influence present-day thinking. Works collected here include masterpieces by David Hume, Immanuel Kant, and Jean-Jacques Rousseau, as well as religious sermons and moral debates on the issues of the day, such as the slave trade. The Age of Reason saw conflict between Protestantism and Catholicism transformed into one between faith and logic -- a debate that continues in the twenty-first century.

Law and Reference
This collection reveals the history of English common law and Empire law in a vastly changing world of British expansion. Dominating the legal field is the *Commentaries of the Law of England* by Sir William Blackstone, which first appeared in 1765. Reference works such as almanacs and catalogues continue to educate us by revealing the day-to-day workings of society.

Fine Arts
The eighteenth-century fascination with Greek and Roman antiquity followed the systematic excavation of the ruins at Pompeii and Herculaneum in southern Italy; and after 1750 a neoclassical style dominated all artistic fields. The titles here trace developments in mostly English-language works on painting, sculpture, architecture, music, theater, and other disciplines. Instructional works on musical instruments, catalogs of art objects, comic operas, and more are also included.

bibliolife
old books. new life.

The BiblioLife Network

This project was made possible in part by the BiblioLife Network (BLN), a project aimed at addressing some of the huge challenges facing book preservationists around the world. The BLN includes libraries, library networks, archives, subject matter experts, online communities and library service providers. We believe every book ever published should be available as a high-quality print reproduction; printed on-demand anywhere in the world. This insures the ongoing accessibility of the content and helps generate sustainable revenue for the libraries and organizations that work to preserve these important materials.

The following book is in the "public domain" and represents an authentic reproduction of the text as printed by the original publisher. While we have attempted to accurately maintain the integrity of the original work, there are sometimes problems with the original work or the micro-film from which the books were digitized. This can result in minor errors in reproduction. Possible imperfections include missing and blurred pages, poor pictures, markings and other reproduction issues beyond our control. Because this work is culturally important, we have made it available as part of our commitment to protecting, preserving, and promoting the world's literature.

GUIDE TO FOLD-OUTS MAPS and OVERSIZED IMAGES

The book you are reading was digitized from microfilm captured over the past thirty to forty years. Years after the creation of the original microfilm, the book was converted to digital files and made available in an online database.

In an online database, page images do not need to conform to the size restrictions found in a printed book. When converting these images back into a printed bound book, the page sizes are standardized in ways that maintain the detail of the original. For large images, such as fold-out maps, the original page image is split into two or more pages

Guidelines used to determine how to split the page image follows:

• Some images are split vertically; large images require vertical and horizontal splits.
• For horizontal splits, the content is split left to right.
• For vertical splits, the content is split from top to bottom.
• For both vertical and horizontal splits, the image is processed from top left to bottom right.

MEMOIRS

OF THE

COUNTESS DE VALOIS DE LA MOTTE.

MEMOIRS

OF THE

COUNTESS DE VALOIS DE LA MOTTE;

CONTAINING A COMPLEAT

JUSTIFICATION OF HER CONDUCT, AND AN EXPLANATION OF THE INTRIGUES AND ARTIFICES USED AGAINST HER BY HER ENEMIES, RELATIVE TO

THE DIAMOND NECKLACE,

ALSO

THE CORRESPONDENCE BETWEEN

THE QUEEN AND THE CARDINAL DE ROHAN

AND CONCLUDING WITH

AN ADDRESS TO THE KING OF FRANCE,

SUPPLICATING A RE-INVESTIGATION OF THAT APPARENTLY MYSTERIOUS BUSINESS.

TRANSLATED FROM THE FRENCH, WRITTEN BY HERSELF,

" If little faults, proceeding on distemper,
" Shall not be wink'd at—how shall we stretch our eyes
" When capital crimes, chew'd, swallow'd and digested,
" Appear before us? SHAKESPEAR.

LONDON

PRINTED FOR THE AUTHOR,
AND SOLD BY J RIDGWAY, YORK-STREET, ST. JAMES'S-SQ.
MDCCLXXXIX
[Entered at Stationers Hall.]

PREFATORY ADDRESS

TO those who know the worth and conscious dignity of Virtue, the following Memoirs containing the vindication of *injured Innocence*, will require no apology, since all of that description, will FEEL the necessity of their publication.

Is there that *Monster of Virtue* existing, who can point the finger of scorn at *foibles*, which I candidly confess to be my lot, in common with my fellow creatures, foibles which have perhaps been the primary and unfortunate means of rendering me the dupe to crafty policy, and designing artifice. The DIAMOND NECKLACE, which was the fatal spring of all my misfortunes, the source of all my miseries, has afforded matter of public speculation to almost every rank of persons, in almost every kingdom in Europe.

[vi]

What various sentiments have been entertained of that dark transaction, what reports have been disseminated, what infinite pains have been bestowed, to make innocence wear the face of guilt, and to conceal the blackest turpitude under the mask of purity.

Too fatally have the artifices of powerful guilt hitherto prevailed, too successfully has chicanery and deception influenced the general opinion of mankind, and too long have they united to slander and stigmatize with infamy the name of the *Countess de Valois de la Motte*.

Many circumstances, which I have made known in a previous publication have concurred to delay the appearance of these Memoirs. The time is at length arrived, when I shall endeavour to vindicate my injured fame.

Seated, as I am, in that happy kingdom, where Liberty stretches forth her hand to the distressed, and affords a welcome asylum from the vindictive terrors of oppressive tyranny, I now proceed to remove the veil which has so long obscured this mysterious transaction, and expose to public view, Characters, whose crimes receive additional force from their elevated situation. In prosecuting this intention, I shall

" Nothing extenuate, nor set down aught in malice,"

Rescuing

Refcuing myfelf from unmerited opprobrium, if I am neceffarily driven to drag to light the views of thofe, who would have deftroyed me, without claiming the privilege of the law of retaliation, I fhall furely ftand acquitted in the minds of the candid and impartial.

I flatter myfelf, that independent of my own vindication, thefe Memoirs will not prove unentertaining. The Moral and Philofophic Reader, will therein find frefh room for reflexion, and obfervation, on the depravity of human nature, the Courtly and Political Reader will probably find a fatisfaction in developing the myfterious intrigues which were in agitation, at the period of the tranfactions, and the Curfory Reader will, I hope, be amply gratified, in finding thofe matters explained, which have probably much excited curiofity.

From a mind long ufed to affliction, every literary defect will be excufed. To addrefs myfelf to the Public is not a matter of choice, but of neceffity. If I have given vent to my feelings, where the fting of injury moft feverely affected me, let it it be remembered, that I have feverely fuffered, that I am ftill fmarting under my griefs---that I am a woman!---If I fpeak forcibly, it is not premeditated diction, but the language of the heart.

Impreffed

Impressed with a due sense of the liberality of the English nation, I chearfully submit my vindication to their candour. In that Supreme Power, who knows our inmost thoughts, I trust, that I shall yet be rescued from the obloquy I have not merited; in His name, I pledge myself for the veracity of my assertions---let the circumstances impartially be weighed, and then let me stand, either acquitted with honour, or condemned to lasting reproach.

COUNTESS DE VALOIS DE LA MOTTE.

MEMOIRS

OF THE

COUNTESS DE VALOIS DE LA MOTTE.

WRITTEN BY HERSELF.

MUST I,----Oh! painful task! must I inevitably resume that pen, which twenty times has fallen from my unwilling hand?----Must I suppress those remorseful agitations of a mind, which yet full of the once loved images I am about to wound, startles at the fatality that compels me to it? I must, the convulsive pangs, the agonies which I experience at the idea, yield at this instant to the imperious claims of wounded honour, to the keen inspirations of sad despair, for the preservation of a fame, more outrageously injured by my silence, than it can have been by my fancied guilt, and the barbarous punishment inflicted it

I am anxious to proclaim wherein I have been *faulty*, because having ventured on the word *honour*, I expect, even in the recess of solitude, the attacks of malignity,----let the acknowledgement of being *faulty*, soften the rigour of those who would carp at the claim of *honour*. Alas! drenched with my own tears, loaded with humiliations, overwhelmed with imputed igno-

B miny,

mony, I shall not make a vain display of pride, what I call charge of *honour* is no more than that feeble portion, which unfortunate persons still preserve, who, though oppressed with calumny, are assured of the rectitude of their own intentions.

Daily prostrated before him, who alone can penetrate into the inmost recesses of the heart, I am practised in the avowal of my *imprudences*. I shall not seek to disguise them to the public, and I expect from that *second judge*, a consolation which the goodness of the former encourages me yet to hope.

Yes, I have committed faults, I confess it----but should not the punishment be proportioned to the guilt? If, from the exposure of my errors, they should appear to be but accessories to crimes infinitely more weighty, in which I found myself involved by a series of events arising from each other----if the most inexcusable of my offences, be only that of rendering myself an accomplice with personages too mighty for my weakness to resist,----her once engaged, can the difference of rank which chance has placed between three culprits, alone ascertain the degrees of their respective guilt, and must that be the just standard of their chastisement? Alas! have I been so fortunate as to be ignorant of this truth? and I the first victim however, of the weak being sacrificed to the strong? Oh no!----but the records of human wickedness afford few instances similar to mine. Those who consider my defence with the slightest attention, will not be able, that it was not a direct chastisement which crushed me, and that neither the ——— nor the Cardinal de ROHAN had contrived ——— to prevent the iniquitous conflict of their dependant,

dependant interests, that precipitated me into distress and misery.

Have I then uttered their names?---Those personages whom I asserted to be once dear to me? That generous Prince to whom I had vowed a gratitude, which my very disasters have not been able to impair, that beguiling Sovereign, whom I may be said to have idolized, and whose image I must at this moment remove from my " mind's eye," that I may retain sufficient fortitude to proceed. Yes, I have declared *that I must*, I have assigned the reason, but I have not yet said any thing of my forbearance, of my moderation, or the struggles I have had to shake off the galling yoke of that necessity. It is the criminal craftiness of those, who at the time of my sad catastrophe, prevented the Queen from holding out to me the hand of comfort and relief, which has kept from her the knowledge of the weapons I am provided with, to wrest from fear, what I should have been happy to owe to justice, to humanity, to the remains of past regard.

Ever since (by a kind of miracle) I set my foot on this protecting land, where freedom smiles alike on unhappiness and prosperity, nothing has been left untried to acquaint her Majesty, that I am possessed of a correspondence, the publication of which would produce the effect of extenuating my guilt, though at the painful expence of exposing her, of interesting the public in my fate, and substituting pity, for that ignominy, which has hitherto been my torment. I have found all avenues blocked up by despotic favourites, who envelope a Princess, devoted, at once, to the cravings of their insatiable covetousness, and to the tyranny of their intriguing ambition.

In

In the affecting memorials which I have endeavoured to submit to her Majesty's clemency, I recalled to view, without complaint, the evils, the horrors of every kind I have undergone, and proved to her, that my discretion and the fidelity of my attachment, were the only causes of my calamities. I offered, even, to sacrifice the means of my justification, on terms which equity or common justice must approve, in a word, I only demanded the restitution, or rather an equivalent for the losses, consequent to my unhappy prosecution. In every one of my letters I repeated, that " Since it had pleased " Providence I should survive those shocking barba- ' rities, since it had rescued me from my own fury; " its intention, doubtless, was not, that I should perish " for want of a subsistance, that in the condition I was " reduced to, I was allowed to hope, that the Queen " would, at least, cause to be restored to me, what the " confiscation of my property had poured into the ' KING'S EXCHEQUER.'

Those memorials which contained a too faithful report of the destitute condition, under which the victim of duty and affection laboured, which echoed the cries, of suffering humanity, have undoubtedly not reached the ear of Majesty. Her eyes have not beheld those mournful characters, drawn with a trembling hand, upon the paper moistened with affliction's tears, nothing has induced the recollection of me to the most humane of Princesses, all, all have been intercepted!—Let those devouring fiends, therefore, take to themselves the mischief that may ensue ——upon their own heads be the necessary consequences of that despair to which I am reduced.

I have

I have taken up my pen, and foregoing sleep, foregoing the importunate cares of a body brought to decay, that is no longer of any concern to me, I will not lay it down, till I have eased my soul of its overwhelming load, by pouring forth all the secret horrors it conceals.

It has been my wish, to save the honour of the Queen; but in the abyss, into which I am more and more deeply plunged, can I at this day turn my thoughts to any thing, besides the shattered remains of my own honour? The public must at length pronounce between HER MAJESTY and *the atom she has crushed.*

My mind is too much agitated to regard my style, I am unused to writing, and my husband's military education, places him in point of literature, nearly on a level with myself.----No matter, truth has its force, grief has its eloquence, the sentiments of sorrow will flow with rapidity, and despair possesses energy amidst disorder, with these incitements an author may claim a perusal. I shall therefore write.

Alas, that I could dispense with the mention of my birth! My judges made no account of it, can I then reckon it as something? No, but it were, perhaps, a piece of pride, to dissemble that my father died at the *Hotel-Dieu*, in Paris. If the reader will please to cast an eye on No. I. of the annexed papers, he will there find his sad genealogy. I shall not, surely be suspected of vanity in such an invitation, but it appears a necessary document, in as much as it accounts for the first acts of my life, justifies the deviations of a natural ambition, and gives a conception why, scarce emerged from obscurity

scurity and indigence, J... DE St. Remy de Valois courted it our, in order to recover the rank, to which she was by birth entitled.

My father, it is true, had just ended his deplorable career in the arms of charity, but the very register of his funeral told me, that the blood of the Valois flowed in my veins. Could I then, implicitly, resign myself to the idea, of tamely submitting that honoured name, to sink into the grave in obscurity. Perhaps had Heaven endowed me with that resignation, it would have been a gift more precious to me than existence: but I received it not in my birth, and unfortunately did not imbibe the sentiments from the tuition of my *second* mother.

The tenderness of the Marchioness de Boulainvilliers, who protected me in my childhood, would not permit her to counteract the early symptoms of ambition, which appeared in me, and which she looked upon as the noble failing of great souls; on the contrary she had encouraged me in the intention of putting in my claims, the nature of which are as follow.

In the perusal of my genealogy, it may have been observed, that my progenitors, possessed in right of his lady, the estate of Fontette, and that from him to me and his children, that estate had regularly devolved. All my ancestors had been born upon, and almost all had been entombed in it. My father alone, by means of a natural propensity to quiet and extravagance, and the consequent accumulated distresses, had first parcelled out, and afterwards compleatly alienated that demesne. It passed for a fact, and was indeed but too true, that he had not received a sixth part of the value of the various inheritances, when he had successively mortgaged.

Peo-

People were incessantly telling me, I heard it from every quarter, that, with a small degree of favour, it might be easy to regain possession of that estate.

Madame de Boulainvilliers, whose kindness induced her to take some measures to obtain that object, was the first to advise me to repair to the place, and to ascertain how far my hopes might probably be realized. It was, therefore, not only with her consent, but by her express advice, that in 1779 I repaired to Bar-sur-Aube, where the information I gained, confirmed me in the opinion, that had determined my journey. It appeared to me evident, that *with favour* I might recover part of the possessions of my house. Impressed with this idea, my imagination could not entertain a thought, which had not for its object the accomplishment of my favourite wish, to obtain the necessary support, but from that moment, I may venture to date the origin of my ruin.

During my first abode at Bar-sur-Aube I became acquainted with Count de la Motte, but as it is not a novel I am writing, I shall pass over the circumstances which brought him to a proposal of marriage, as well as the motives that determined me to accept it. It will be enough to say, that our union being approved of by M. de la Luzerne, Bishop of Langres, on the overtures he was pleased to make, M.^d de Boulainvilliers, my excellent mother, yielded her consent, and a few days after the nuptial band was tied.

My husband was then in the Gens d'Armes, in which corps his father had run an honourable career, gloriously terminated at the battle of Minder, where he was killed at the head of his company.

Mon-

[8]

Monsieur de la Motte thought that upon the circumstance of his marriage he might hope for some military promotion.

Marshal de Castries commanded the Gens d'Armes which was then quartered at Luneville, M. de la Motte proposed my joining the garrison with him, which I only accepted, on condition I should pass in a convent the whole time his stay should require. We therefore fixed upon one about three leagues from Luneville, to which I retired, but was doomed not to enjoy long the tranquility which was afforded me by that asylum. The affairs of the navy department, entrusted to the Marshal de Castries, not permitting him to revisit his corps, the intended solicitations could not take place.

Here the reader will be presented with a clew to my misfortunes, which, if he will take hold of, I will lead him step by step through the labyrinth in which I was bewildered.

Never was woman less vain than myself of personal charms, I know not by what fatality my youth, that healthful look which is called freshness, that vivacity, the appendage of juvenility, supplied in me the want of beauty, so far as to lay me open to the importunities of presuming men.

The Marquis d'Autichamp, who commanded in the absence of the Marshal de Castries, is the being, to whom I was first beholden for that distrust which all my life after I conceived of the over-pressing civilities of his sex. He employed the most ardent zeal to serve us. He strove to persuade us we should do nothing at Luneville, that there was a necessity of going to Paris, where,

exclu-

exclusive of the good offices we had to expect from the Marshall, and of those, which the maternal fondness of Madame de Boulainvilliers infused to us, he would exert his interest with his own private friends to get my husband into place. He found no difficulty in persuading us that his advice was rational, but when the time came for our departure, for the metropolis, it appeared that I, alone, was to solicit, under the auspices of the Marquis; who condescended to take the journey with me. He pretended that my husband, having already twice had leave of absence, could not hope for a third, and accordingly he refused it him, the indispensible consequence of which refusal was, Count de la Motte quitted the corps ---- These were the first fruits of *favour with the great* ---- This resolution intimated and fixed upon, we immediately took the road to Strasburg; where the Marquis de Boulainvilliers and his lady then were, but on the very day we reached that place, they had left it, to go to Saverne, at which place we joined them the next day.

It was there, for the first time, I saw the Cardinal de Rohan. To him I was presented, and but too well recommended by the Marchioness, who, a few days after, set off on her return to Paris, inviting me, together with the Count, my husband, to accept of an apartment in her hotel in that city. It was not long before I followed her, and my husband, detained at Bar-sur-Aube by family concerns, joined me shortly after, but when he arrived, my dear protectress was no more; death having just robbed me of the only support I had left in the world.

[10]

A second time become an orphan, by this unfortunate incident, deprived of the wife counsels and examples which had hitherto directed my conduct, I cast my eyes on all around me, and saw nothing but a frightful void, a vast solitude, where apprehensions, since, too fully verified, suggested to me, that if I deviated from the path of rectitude, I should perhaps be lost -----The Marquis de Boulainvilliers remained, but of him I had formed so unfavourable an opinion, that my first determination was to quit his hotel. He guessed my intentions, to prevent which he assured me, that he should consider it as his duty to stand in the place of the Marchioness, that in him I should find a father. Accordingly, for some time, he seemed to continue towards us the kindness with which we had been honoured by his Lady. Soon, however, I discovered that this kindness was not wholly disinterested, and I comprehended his motives as fully, as if he had imparted to me his intention. He had just lost a wife, but chance had placed another woman under his roof, and the situation was become a matter of *convenience*, which he pretended was *reciprocal*, at least that was the light in which he represented it to me, and without much hesitation made me a downright proposal.

Alas! said I to myself, are such the characteristics of men? they are still far from being restored to my good opinion; yet I think, for the credit of their sex, that few of them are capable of such meanness, not to say baseness of behaviour, as that I have experienced on this occasion.

The moment M. de Boulainvilliers was convinced of the futility of his designs, all his assiduous attentions

were

were converted into harsh and uncivil treatment. Indeed, it is not without a blush, I shall here produce some instances of it. It will scarce be credited, for example, that not chusing openly to propose our quitting his house, he took the resolution of rendering it gradually insupportable to us; causing every day some necessary article to be retrenched, and using every mean substitution that could be made, in those which he allowed. I know not whether the mention of such trivial circumstances should be admitted into a serious narrative, but as it concerns me to prove, that my existence has been a series of misfortunes, more or less afflicting or humiliating, I thought it necessary to shew that passing from under the protection of Mad. de Boulainvilliers to that of her husband, was no small one.

My readers will readily conceive, that such conduct soon occasioned a separation. Nearly about the same time I resumed the fatal idea of seeking by powerful patronage, to recover part of the possessions alienated by my father, and especially the estate of Fontette. I had several acquaintances, amongst them were some, whom I styled friends, being simple enough, too readily to confide in friendship. The hopes of prevailing on these to interfere drew me to Versailles, where my time was spent in fruitless solicitations, during the successive administrations of Messrs. Joly de Fleury and d'Ormesson, which passed away like a shadow, afterwards under that of Mr de Calonne, which, on the contrary, appeared so long to France. Whoever is acquainted with his insinuating assiduities, can form an idea of the graces he displayed on the first reception. I thought I could perceive the moment when he would propose to share with me the treasure entrusted to Madame d'Arveley (*).

The ancient fabulist has whimsically described the agitation of the mountain, which was at length delivered of a mouse, I cannot help comparing to it the labour of Mr de Calonne, who undertook to augment to fifteen hundred livres, the mighty pension of eight hundred, granted me at the time of my recognition, to enable me to support worthily the name of Valois. Justly incensed at the Comptroller General, I secretly purposed to use compulsive means, and to recover my estate of Fontette independent of his assistance, and the step which appeared to me best calculated to effect this purpose, was to ingratiate myself into the favour of a *** An opportunity soon after presented itself, wherein the success of my stratagem would have been tried, but my situation did not permit me to embrace it, which will be amply explained, when my connexions with the Cardinal are known, this circumstance,

how-

*** was, at that period, wife to the keeper of the Royal Treasury, during the administration of M. C*** who had the *** to be in the *** of the ***, previous to his exaltation. Mons. d'Arveley at his death, left her a considerable fortune *** but of a *** propensity to be *** (free he was no longer permitted ***) prevailed is uncertain, but *** *** *** from the Continent, he has *** the management of the widow's concerns, and has *** *** with the name of C***

however, is not the less remarkable, as it determined my fate, by opening to me the way, which afterwards brought me to her Majesty's feet.

I have already protested against all pretensions to beauty, but were I to carry humility as far as a confession of homeliness, I could not reverse what has been; or counteract the circumstance of his Royal Highness the Count d'Artois, who saw me at the parish church of Versailles, having honoured me with a distinction which I did not endeavour to obtain. The steps taken by that Prince to acquaint me with the generosity of his disposition, reached the ear of the Princess, his consort, who, satisfied with my behaviour, vouchsafed to receive me with kindness, and took me under her protection, placing me ostensibly under that of her royal sister, Madame. To conceive the motives of that precaution, it is only necessary to recollect, that a very short time before that period, Madame the Countess d'Artois, had found herself in very delicate circumstances, which made her extremely circumspect.

Although the point was thus settled between the two Princesses respecting me, I experienced equal effects of their goodness towards me. One day as I was paying my court to them at Madam's, I was seized with a sudden indisposition that occasioned some stir in the palace. The Queen being informed of it, was graciously pleased to express some concern. Her Majesty even sent for Mrs. Pitt, first waiting-woman to Madame, to know the particulars of that accident, an instance of regard which her Majesty continued for some days after.

Nothing escapes the notice of courtiers, they observed, that, from that moment her Majesty honoured me with

a graa gracious condescension whenever I came into her presence, some speculations were even hazarded on the subject, but the man at Court who carried them the farthest, was the Cardinal de Rohan.

I have hitherto only mentioned that Prince, in reference to the incident which first procured me the honor of seeing him. During the interval between that period, and the one I am now adverting to, I must own I had not lost sight of him. I had received kindnesses from him, gratitude, justly due inviolably attached me to him, I had no secrets concealed from him, he, none from me. We mutually read in each other's mind, our respective ambition. His, it is well known to every one, was, to have become, at any rate, Prime Minister; mine had no further views, than to be Lady of the Manor of *Fontette*.

Obstacles almost insurmountable, and arising from the same cause, thwarted both our views. The Cardinal some years before, had the misfortune to incur the Queen's displeasure (*). The first step towards supreme power, was of consequence, to recover her Majesty's favor, and as long as he could do nothing in his own behalf, he had as little power to do any thing for me. It may be remembered, in that letter to which I have referred the reader, that at the time I am speaking of, he had made various attempts, all equally unsuccessful, either from his backwardness with which they were attended, or from the weak offices of the Princess de Guémenée, who, whilst she seemed to have undertaken his reconciliation with the Queen, had removed him from it infinitely more contrary, than he had been at the period she undertook to exert herself on his account.

Matters

Matters were thus circumstanced, when that feeble ray of favour which he saw shine upon my head, revived his hopes, and re-animated his ambition. Nothing can equal the astonishment into which he threw me, one day, when happening to be in the royal gallery, her Majesty vouchsafed me one of those smiles, which it is so difficult to appear insensible of. Having, a moment after, by chance, raised my eyes up to him, I saw joy sparkle in his countenance, and a desire at the same time to speak to me. This desire I fulfilled, and the words which he addressed me with, will never be effaced from my remembrance. " Do you know, Countess," said he, " that my fortune is in your hands, as well as your own?"---His fortune! oh Heavens! I shudder when I think that his misfortunes are not even yet drawn to a conclusion, that I am perhaps going to fill up the measure of them. As to my own fortune, thank Heaven, I now see it drawing nigh, I behold it in the tomb, half open to receive me, but at the moment the Cardinal was then speaking to me, my ideas were not so melancholy.

Though I had seen neither his fortune nor my own in the Queen's enchanting smile, yet my heart was full of it. When the first surprise had subsided, I asked the Prince whether he was jesting or in earnest?---" A man
" cannot be more in earnest than I am," answered he,
" sit down and hear me attentively. In the first place,
" convince yourself thoroughly of a truth, which, as it
" admits, in general, of very few exceptions in the
" world, so at Court it admits of none. It is this: It
" is not in the power of human wisdom to chain down
" Fortune, blindfolded, and ever led by chance, the
" fickle

"fickle deity holds out her hand to all who stand ready
"to grasp it on her rapid passage, but if not seized
"upon that very instant, opportunity never more re-
"turns----The moment of your good fortune is arriv-
"ed----I have not been the only person who has ob-
"served it, but having more interest than any other in
"its consequence, my observation has been more atten-
"tive, and I have discovered to a certainty, that the
"Queen has taken a fancy to you"----" A fancy,"
ced I, " you mean she feels a benevolent compassion
" towards me'---" You may give" answered he,
" what name you please, to the sentiments she honours
" you with, all that is necessary for you to know is,
" that there is something in your *form pleasing to her*, and
" that you must not let the happy dispositions she has
" shewn towards you for some time past, grow cool
" You see that all favour centers in her, that every
" where else there is nothing to be done. that Madame
" and the Countess d'Artois are not only devoid of in-
" fluence, but that their very protection stamps the seal
" of reprobation   Attach yourself then solely to the
" Queen   and confider, (I tell you so again) that your
" fortune and fame are in your hands."

The Cardinal concluded by desiring me to write to
the Marchioness de Polignac, but he could not
have given a worse advice   Though the Polignacs
were then possessed of the almost exclusive right of presentation to the Queen, they had such mighty interests
to manage, they were assailed by so many fears, tormented by so many jealousies, that it was necessary they
should be well assured of their creatures, before they
bring them forward   I was not suited to their purpose

pose, they by no means found their account in introducing me, nor indeed did they give it the least countenance. They refused me the requested interview, and confined their answer to this: "That Mr DE CALONNE "having given the Queen an account of the addition "lately made to my pension, her Majesty thought that "I ought to rest satisfied." Soon afterwards I learnt there was not one word of truth in this bold assertion, and that they had not so much as mentioned my name to the Queen.

During the short interval, between the moment I am now speaking of, and that, wherein I had the honour to approach the Queen, I had daily opportunities of observing, that all the methods I took to effect my purpose, were counteracted by the Polignacs, and that they had so thoroughly obstructed all the avenues to an access, that I one day said to the Cardinal with ill-humour, I would hear no more about seeing the Queen ---
"*Why, you are a child,*" said he, "*at the first obstacle, 'you are for giving up the point, but remember,* "He that 'stays in the valley will never get over the hill." *The* "*gale is propitious, you must sail into harbour. I am* "*going to propose a course to you, the only one you have* "*left to pursue. I forewarn you, it is a* COUP D'ECLAT "*that I shall advise you to adopt.*"

Seeing me perplexed and confused, before I knew what the business was, he made an end, by explaining to me what he meant by *a coup d'eclat.* He told me, I must not hesitate to throw myself at the Queen's feet, but that he thought, in order to overawe our common enemies the more, I should seize the occasion to do it, at the time of the procession of the Blue Ribbands,

which

which was to take place on the second of February. Accustomed implicitly to follow his advice, I promised to act as he should dictate.

The great day at length arrived. Furnished with the petition I was to present, and the most ample instructions to govern my conduct by, in every possible situation, I repaired, full dressed, to the Castle, and waited in one of the saloons till the procession returned. As the Queen passed by, I fell at her feet, and delivered my petition, told her, in few words, that I was lineally descended from the Valois, that I was acknowledged as such by Lewis the Sixteenth, that the fortune of my progenitors, not having been transmitted to me with their name, I had no resource but in the King's munificence, his Majesty being in possession of the major part of the estates they had enjoyed, that having found every avenue to her Majesty's presence shut against me, despair had determined me to take this step.

The Queen raised me up with kindness, received my petition with her usual complacency, and seeing me tremble, condescended to bid me hope. She then passed on, telling me to make myself easy, and promised to pay regard to the object of my request.

I withdrew, my limbs tottering under me, and had scarcely reached home, when I received a note from the Cardinal, in consequence of which I went to him. After acquainting him with what had passed, in pursuance of his advice, I immediately wrote to Madame de Misery, first Lady of the Bed-chamber, and waiting-woman to the Queen, desiring her to deliver to her Majesty an enclosed letter, which I took the liberty of addressing to her.

The

The same evening I received an answer from that lady, containing an invitation to her apartment, at half an hour past seven. When I saw her, she told me she had laid my letter on the Queen's mantle-piece, that she believed her Majesty was at that very moment talking to Madame respecting me, and added, that her Majesty had not been to church that afternoon, on account of the agitation my letter had thrown her into.

In the first moment of our conversation, Madame de Misery hinted to me, "that the honour I was going to "have conferred on me, by being presented to her Ma- "jesty, must be a secret to all the world, not excepting "*Madame*, warning me, that the smallest indiscretion "would ruin me past recovery." (*)

Our conversation continued till eleven o'clock, when the presence of her Majesty at length put an end to it --- How beauteous did she appear! I had always considered her so, when I beheld her, but the affability with which she received me at that instance, added to the charms of her person. I was again seized with a palpitation, when her Majesty was pleased, a second time, to encourage me, requesting my confidence, and ordered me to speak to her with an open heart, respecting whatever concerned myself. At length I took courage, and after setting forth the nature of my claims, the steps I had taken with the Ministers, and with the Princesses her sisters in-law, I concluded, by complaining with some asperity, of the harsh treatment I had received from the *Polignacs*. Her Majesty smiled, and her looks at that

moment

---

* The reader is particularly requested not to lose remembrance of this positive injunction, through the course of these Memoirs.

moment, indicated to me many things, the explanation of which is found in her letters to the Cardinal (*)

After a short recollection, her Majesty spoke to me nearly in these terms: ' I have perused your memorial " with attention and concern. I perceive that its object " is to urge the Minister to the restitution of some ' estates, which have belonged to your house. I have ' peculiar reasons for not complying with your request, ' which shall be made known to you, they being such " as regard you personally. I cannot reconcile the de- " sire I feel of seeing you publicly, with that I expe- " rience of seeing you familiarly; but I may *indirectly* " do you the good offices you desire of me. Send for " your brother, (*) who being now the head of your " house, it is more natural that he should personally " follow the honours to which it has a claim. I promise " you I will strongly support his solicitations, there- " fore make yourself easy."---Her Majesty terminated the conversation, by presenting me with a purse, and honoured me with a first salute, enjoining me to remain at Versailles, TO SPEAK TO NO PERSON WHATEVER OF THIS INTERVIEW, or of the success of my petition, then quitted me saying, ' *Adieu, we shall meet again.*"

It is material to observe, that in this first interview, her Majesty talked to me concerning MADAME, in terms extremely unfavourable; that above all, she insisted much on the duplicity of that Princess, recommending to me,

to

---

* See No VII.

* The Baron de Valois, at that time a Lieutenant in the N---. It is well known both in England and France, how much he distinguished himself on board the Surveillante.

to beware of her, not to say a word to her about my affairs, and advising me, even, not to see her any more, which I could not but deem an express prohibition

It was said that "*we should meet again.*" Accordingly, a few days after, I received a note, written by the hand of Mademoiselle Dorvat, one of her Majesty's women, containing an order for me to repair, between eleven and twelve that night, to the little Trianon. Having attended punctually to the appointed hour, I was introduced into her Majesty's closet by Mademoiselle Dorvat. I received an explanation of what the Cardinal meant to intimate, when he spoke to me of "*fancy*" and of there being "*something in my* FORM, *pleasing to her Majesty*"--- Good Heaven! thought I, how charming is the Queen! what affability! what an effusion of goodness!---indeed, I also felt myself at that moment something more than mortal

Her Majesty put an end to our long conference, by evincing her munificence to me, in the gift of, pocket book, containing to the amount of ten thousand livres, in bills upon the Caisse d'Escompte. The last words were, as in the first interview "*Adieu, we shall meet again*"----We did so, both frequently and with long interviews, and upon the same footing.

This confession weighs down my soul, my heart trembles, the pen drops from my hand---O my august Sovereign! It is to you alone I now address myself! Recall to your mind those charming moments, which I scarced are reflect on recall to your memory, those places in which they were passed, and those in which I expiated a guilt attributed to me, in consequence of my concealment of them. Whatever be the contumely with which it has since pleased your Majesty to overwhelm me, you will nevertheless find it imprinted on your memory, that you then raised me up to you, that you placed yourself on an equality with me. But in vain did you condescend, before me, to divest yourself of the awfulness of Majesty, in the very manner of laying it aside, your dignity appeared, and inwardly I exclaimed, it is the goddess Flora, who, derobing herself of her dignity, deigns to amuse herself with an humble floweret. You are sensible, Madam, that in the first interview, and those of the same kind which succeeded, I never departed from that respect, with which you even obligingly upbraided me---and yet, it is that unhappy being, whom the bare approach of your lips, ought to render an object ever sacred. it is the woman, whom you had honoured with the name of "*dear friend,*" it is that unfortunate De Valois, whom you have forsaken, given up into the hands----shall I say of executioners?----ah, no!---Let me recall the word----But to return to the Cardinal

From what I have already related, it is manifest, that it was the unbounded ambition of that unhappy Prince, which had conveyed, nay almost dragged me into the Queen's closet. I have also said, that I had concealed nothing from her. As soon as he was able to applaud himself on the success of his speculation, when from the nature of the benefits I received from her Majesty, he knew how to appreciate the degree of beneficence she honoured me with, he repeated with warmth what he had already told me of his fortune and mine, which he pretended were in my hands, and prevailed on me to watch for, to seize upon the first opportunity that offered,

of

of recalling him, without affecting to do it, into the Queen's remembrance. It was not long before an occasion offered, as favourable as it was possible to wish.

One day, when her Majesty had added a fresh favour to the many which had so justly ensured her my tender and respectful duty, she accidentally asked me how I had been able to support myself before I approached her person. Then was the moment for naming my benefactor, without appearing to do it with a premeditated design. I, however, used a good deal of artifice, pretending ignorance of the footing on which the Cardinal stood with her Majesty. I avoided an air of constraint and reserve, which, had it been the least discernible, might have created a suspicion, that I was deeper in the Prince's confidence, than I ought to appear. I therefore spoke of him in general terms, as a man of feeling, benevolent and generous, who, by those various good qualities, had probably acquired the esteem and the favour of her Majesty, and I warmly enumerated the good offices he had done me. The Queen listened to me with such attention, and regarded me with so inquisitive an eye, that I felt the necessity of weakening the first idea, that visibly offered itself to her mind, by hinting, that this munificence of the Prince was far from being confined personally to me. As this was the first time I had uttered the Cardinal's name before the Queen, so it was the first time I had observed how much her Majesty's aversion to him, exceeded the idea he had given me. She was for some time silent, seemingly wrapt in profound reflection, and with the accent of a person who is just awakened, she said to me " What I have just " heard is pleasing to me, but *surprises me!* I did not
" think

" think the Cardinal capable of such actions, he is said
" to be of quite a different disposition."

The Cardinal's name being once introduced, in the frequent and familiar conferences I had with the Queen, I forefaw, that in introducing it again, I should no longer have the same difficulties to surmount. I imparted my idea to the Prince, who conjured me not to omit any opportunity of speaking of him, he even prepared me with instructions, as to the purport of my discourse, suggested to me various introductions, and applied himself to train me up for the performance of my part. The task, however, was not so easy as we had imagined. The Queen never uttered the Cardinal's name, nor spoke of any thing that had the least reference to him; all my instructions were therefore entirely thrown away, as I found no opportunity to introduce the smallest mention of him.

At length an incident occurred, which enabled me to execute my purpose. The Cardinal, having received two hundred thousand livres as a *pot de vin*, for renewing the contract for foraging the cavalry in Alsace, made me a present of twenty thousand. I thought myself bound not to let the Queen remain ignorant of this fresh act of generosity, with which her Majesty seemed affected. I did not lose so favourable an opportunity of expressing to her my gratitude, and the Cardinal's merits; but at this time I proceeded farther than the rest. It was natural, that upon my having recourse to the Prince, in my first conversation with the Queen on his account, he should at least have entrusted me with his troubles. I owned it to her Majesty, and
                                                             represented

represented him as pining away, preyed upon by sorrow, consumed with vexation, and as the victim of envy and detraction. She suffered me to utter, without interruption, all that zeal and gratitude, at that instant, suggested; but when awe and discretion induced me to be silent, she made no direct answer to any thing she had heard, and I read in her eyes that her prejudices were deeply rooted. I even caught some glances expressive of anger, and might, even then, have perceived, that under the deceitful embers of an affected tranquillity, lay the fatal spark that afterwards kindled the conflagration in which I was involved.

It cannot be too early to apprize the reader, that all the tender, all the passionate things he will see in the correspondence I am going to produce, were nothing but dissimulation on both sides. The Queen, who had vowed his ruin, long before I brought the Cardinal into her recollection, was still contriving it in her mind, and when her attachment to the Emperor, her brother, made her yield herself up at Trianon, and elsewhere, to the *studied transports* of the unhappy Prince, (it is shocking to reveal, but I know it to be a fact,) she used to cast upon him the same piercing looks, with which she eyed him on the day when she demanded his head of the King. Such, also, were they, at the moment of the conversation, which I now describe. Nevertheless, she would listen to me with condescension. I incessantly resumed the subject, and sometimes the aukward manner in which I introduced it, would raise a smile in her Majesty's countenance.

The Cardinal exhorted me to perseverance, to which I myself was inclined, from a false notion that I rather gained ground daily. Emboldened by that confidence, I one day advised the Cardinal to venture on a letter, promising him to be the bearer of it myself, to seize on the first occasion, for delivering it, that should offer, and to create one, if none spontaneously occurred. Three days after, the most favourable one presented itself, and from that period begins the correspondence, of which, what I have been able to save, will find a place in these Memoirs, and every one of the letters will be found connected with the various facts, that I am going to set down in regular succession, in point of time.

Number II of this collection, is a literary copy of that first letter written, it is true, by my advice, but not in the manner that I suggested to the Cardinal. I wished him to express no more than his wish to exculpate himself; yet it will be seen, that according to his usual practice, he was already impatient to disclose sentiments, which, had he experienced them, he ought to have suppressed, and which, not experiencing, it was an unpardonable falshood in him to utter. Behold him, at the very commencement already talking of the " *rays of* " *hope shining on his heart,*" of her Majesty's " *beauteous* " ...." and of his own " *flames.*" The Reader will moreover please to observe in it, as a proof of what I have already advanced, that as I had been the instrument, the Cardinal had made use of, to put the Queen in mind of his existence, so I became the pretence, which sanctioned, as I may say, his claims to her returning favour. My advice had been, not to mention me, but to begin with a written justification of himself, knowing that the Queen desired nothing farther of him. But he was wont to treat me as a child, and to this me-discretion he added the folly of assuming the title, which he ever after retained, of her Majesty's "*slave*." Though I highly disapproved of such inconsistencies, I was forced to submit, and delivered the letter.

The subsequent letter, (No. III.) sufficiently points out, what answer the Queen charged me to give to the first. The only observation I have to make upon it, is this, that his communicating the contents of it to me, very much offended me. It is observable, that at the very beginning, it contains a doubt, injurious to me, concerning the degree of confidence with which the Queen might honour me. I thought I discovered that his object was to leave to her Majesty the choice of any other intermediate person, and of course, to sacrifice me, as soon as that other person, no matter whom, should offer, provided only, their situation enabled them to finish the work which I had begun.

The instant the Cardinal appeared to distrust me, that distrust naturally became mutual, and I resolved to watch his proceedings. Though he could not, handsomely, forbear communicating the letters he committed to my charge, I felt I should but imperfectly understand the correspondence, unless I also had a sight of all those I conveyed to him from the Queen. I therefore determined not only to read, but even to take copies of all that passed through my hands on both sides. One motive that particularly stimulated me to this resolution, shall be more fully laid open in the sequel of these Memoirs, all that I can now say of it is, that, notwithstanding the general confidence the Cardinal placed in me, he had some intrigue, concerning which, he shewed something more than mere reserve. I saw couriers arrive

arrive, with whom he was clofetted, and the packets he received, or thofe he delivered, paffed out of one hand into another with the greateft fecrecy, and I have often heard the noife of the ftrong-box, where he no doubt depofited them. If I ventured to put a queftion to him, I faw ferioufnefs, and a tincture of ill-humour overfhade his countenance. Certainly, If I could have furmifed, what I only came to the knowlege of afterwards, that all that myfterioufnefs had a relation to politics, I fhould not have been fo unjuft as to complain of his difcretion, but in general, I knew the Cardinal not to be difcreet, and I little fufpected him of meddling in politics, fo that, I muft own, I thought quite another fort of intrigue was on foot, and I thank Heaven that I yielded to the impulfe of my curiofity, and got the better of the reluctance I experienced when I came to the execution. To that precaution, blameable in fome refpects, but juftified by the event, I am indebted for the only weapons I have left, againft the obduracy of injuftice, and the vindictivenefs of oppreffive power.

It is doubtlefs to be lamented, that out of near two hundred letters, which the collection of this correfpondence would have contained, had I been able to bring them together, only thirty-one have fallen into my power, but I atteft the truth, that I fupprefs none, that they are all I could poffibly copy, becaufe moft of the others, being of little or no confequence, were burnt almoft as foon as received. Thofe from the Queen, which the Cardinal would frequently perufe with rapture, were not depofited in his *ftrong box*, but in his Efcutore, where it was eafy for me to find the means of looking over, and tranfcribing them. As to thofe from the Prince, he
always

always sent them to me under a single wafer, so that, excepting the breach of trust, which I have explained the motive of, I could copy them at leisure, but I did not take that trouble, when they were of no signification, and this proved to be the case four times out of five.

From this exposition, it will easily be conceived, that the extract I present to the Reader is not the most indifferent part of the beforementioned correspondence. Previous to resuming the thread of my narration, may I be allowed to observe, that as I never announced to the public any thing more than the possession of those copies, the conduct of certain idle individuals, and senseless pamphleteers, must appear very extraordinary, who have, for some time past, been obstinately bent upon advertising a *libel*, said to be written by me, grounded on a correspondence, of which I was said to have pretended that the *originals* were in my possession. The originals! How was it possible I should possess them? Was I not obliged to deliver, to the respective parties, all the letters and writings they mutually transmitted to each other through my means? Had I intercepted a single line, would not my infidelity have been discovered at their next meeting? Two words of explanation would have accelerated my ruin. No---I never had the folly to pretend that I possessed the originals, to promise an impossibility; but I have said, in general terms, that I would print letters from the Queen to the Cardinal. I at length fulfil my engagement.

It may be seen, by the second letter of the Cardinal, that the Queen had absolutely refused the interview solicited in his first, and left no hope that it would be granted, unless he should be able to exculpate himself, *in writing*.

..., from an accumulation of heavy charges brought against him. Her Majesty, when she commanded me to return that answer, had expressed herself, as if she imagined it to be an utter impossibility that he could ever ... himself. "I have proofs against him, said she, " which it is not in his power to invalidate." I did not disguise from the Cardinal, that her Majesty appeared but little disposed to alter her mind respecting him, and as I repeated to him the Queen's own words, he said something to me, wrapt in great obscurity, this, however, gave me a little knowledge of the nature of that political intrigue, of which I have said a few words, and concerning which I had been so egregiously mistaken.

He gave me to understand, that the Queen was not such an absolute mistress of her own actions, as I imagined, that she stood as much in need of him, as he did of her; that if ever he should owe his elevation to her, she would be indebted to him for the exercise of sovereignty, the only object, not only of her own personal ambition, but of that of the Emperor, her brother.

That single word was the key to all the mysterious transactions between him and the various agents I frequently saw arriving, and who, I supposed, were Germans. I understood he was in correspondence with the Emperor, and that, probably, it was the wish of the Queen, that the Cardinal should be at the head of affairs, in which supposition I was perfectly right. However, as that idea could not efface the impressions made on me by the Queen's last words relative to the Cardinal, I told him, not adding I hoped I was mistaken, that her Majesty seemed more disposed to injure him, than to exert herself to obtain his elevation, and that I saw no way to
remove

remove her prepossessions, but his vindicating himself by a *written justification*, since she required it. The note No. IV. was the immediate effect of my advice. "*The slave*" said he obeyed, and announced part of his defence for the next day.

The article No. V. is extremely interesting, and deserves to be read with that attention, which the Cardinal at his first setting out requests of the Queen. It contains the defence, announced the day before, and refers to facts, prior in point of date, which few of my readers would suspect the nature of. I think it necessary, therefore, to explain to them, whatever in that long narration might be unintelligible, as I have now bid adieu to all manner of restraint ---That same Cardinal, so profuse of words, in order to prove to the Queen, that all the charges laid against him were so many falsities, and mere slanderous accusations, has repeatedly informed me, that her Majesty's resentments were unfortunately well grounded. He has entrusted me with the secret, that at the time of his embassy to Vienna, when the Queen was yet Archduchess, emboldened by the levity of her behaviour, he had presumed to pay his addresses to her, which had not been rejected; that his expected happiness had, however, passed away like a dream, that the pointed preference which a German officer had obtained before his eyes, had so enraged and distracted him, as to make him hazard indiscreet speeches, that he did not doubt but the Queen had preserved the remembrance of that imprudence, to which he attributed the disgrace he had languished under, ever since her Majesty's accession to the throne. He mentioned to me, one day, that when the Archduchess passed through Saverne, on

her

her way to Versailles, a ray of hope animated his heart, and encouraged him to hasten thither to receive her, in the palace of the Old Cardinal his uncle, where, having thrown himself at her feet, to kiss the hem of her robe, she had kindly raised him up, and, blushing, held out her hand, which he saluted with the most exquisite sensation!——" But," added he, " that was the
" last look of tenderness I ever experienced from the
" Princess. Hurried into the vortex of the court, she
" saw herself surrounded with so many adorers, that I
" was no longer distinguished in the crowd The Count
" d'Artois eclipsed them all, yet the Count d'Artois
" was but an object of coquetry "

This confidential communication necessarily gave birth to another, which must also be imparted to the public We see by the Cardinal's own defence, that he was something more than suspected of having fabricated, at Madame Dubarry's, the letters to which I have alluded He has told me they were the produce of his jealousy, that the Empress Queen, who loved him, having heard of the errors imputed to her daughter, had applied to him, in order to gain the information she desired that attributing to the intrigue of the Count d'Artois, the dislike the Dauphiness expressed for him, he had related the truth, without the least disguise, that those fatal letters being found among the papers of the Empress, after her death, had been returned to the Queen, by the Emperor.

Thunderstruck at this confession " How! cried I, has the Queen such papers in her hands, and you charge me to assure her of your innocence!" He still drew his

arguments

arguments from political considerations, which must influence the Queen's conduct "The Emperor, said he, " will have at the head of affairs a Minister devoted to " him, there is no resentment but must give way." He conversed like a man acquainted with the spirit of courts, and it will shortly be seen, that accordingly her Majesty, though furnished with such proofs of his perfidy, carried her policy to that inconceivable length, as to deny to him her having those proofs in her possession.

I must recommend the most serious attention to this circumstance, it is of infinite consequence to me to evince to the world, that excess of dissimulation of which the Queen was capable. A striking instance of it occurs in the letter No VI It is manifest, by the manner in which the Cardinal there expresses himself, that the verbal answer I had conveyed to him, from the Queen, bespoke an approaching pardon, that consequently her Majesty had affected to be in a great measure satisfied with that defence, although she had in her escrutore all that was requisite to convict the Cardinal. Accordingly it is seen that *the slave* writes with confidence to his *dear master*, and you behold him already suing for kisses, talking of fair hands, and of her charming mouth,---the Queen suffers it all!----She does yet more, she permits me to give hopes of the return of her good graces, nor is that enough, she must write *herself*, her own hand must confirm the assurances I had given in her name, and above all, she must affirm, that she never had knowledge of those letters, which the Cardinal himself knew had been transmitted to her by the Emperor. ----What refinement of dissimulation in so amiable a

F

Princess?

[34]

Princess? In a word, the Queen passes a spunge over past transactions, and asserts that all unfavorable impressions are obliterated (*)

The Emperor's instructions must have been very positive, he must have been heartily tired of the Count de Vergennes, and highly incensed against that Minister, to induce the Queen his sister, to act a part so unworthy, both of her disposition and her rank.

We are come to the moment, when in order to palliate in some respects, the Queen's conduct, it is necessary to shew, that nearly about this time, the correspondence, which, as I have already had occasion to say, had commenced between the Emperor and the Cardinal, was extended to the Queen, and that the grand negociations, I shall have to speak of hereafter, were at the eve of been entered upon. It is to those considerations, infinitely more than to the small ascendancy I had over her Majesty, that the meeting must be attributed, which was thought to be my work, and at which I was myself astonished, yet it would appear, that the Queen wished me to believe, that the Cardinal owed all to me, my influence seeming to increase, in proportion as the Cardinal conceived hopes of recovering that which he had lost. Her Majesty continued to shower benefits upon me, and each succeeding day seemed to add to the confidence with which she honoured me. I in reality was become an important personage, for surrounded as the Queen was with the Cardinal's enemies, since she had

reasons

---

* See No. VII

reasons to treat him with regard, and secretly to favour him, she could not have found a person more proper than myself to second her views, as they so perfectly coincided with my own, being directed to nothing but the Cardinal's elevation.

Her Majesty ceased not to recommend secrecy to me, but so frequent were the personal intercourses, that in spite of all my caution, I was sometimes subject to discovery, and the number of persons who sought after me, made me sufficiently sensible, that I had many self-created confidants, to whom my confidence had never been imparted. I was obliged to be ever on the wing, so fast were letters multiplied on both sides, I have seen the Cardinal write *four* in a day.

I have already noticed, that I only took copies of whatever appeared to me in any way remarkable for instance, I did not miss the letter No VIII. It proves how far those of my hireling detractors swerved from truth, who have dared to assert, that I caused to be forged the letters that I conveyed to the Cardinal from the Queen. Not to advert to the absurdity of supposing, that the Prince did not know her Majesty's hand-writing, it will be allowed, at least, that if I could, in that particular, so grossly impose upon him, I could not possibly make him believe that the Queen "*smiled upon him*" and "*publicly made him signals of intelligence.*" This is the language of the letter referred to, I cannot have dictated it to him,---I cannot have written for him ---I cannot have fascinated his eyes, so far as to make him believe that the Queen "*smiled on him,*" if she actually did not smile, that she "*publicly made him*

F 2 *signals*

"*signals of intelligence,*" if no such signals were publicly made, if he says, that "*he is the happiest of mortals* for "having seen those "*smiles,*" and "*signals of intelligence,*" it is, because he has seen them with his own eyes.

It is well known that I had no kind of intercourse with that mountebank Cagliostro, and that, consequently, I did not record the impostions by which he sported with the Cardinal's credulity. The Queen had smiled, and put on a gracious countenance, the Queen therefore, at the period I am speaking of, was, or pretended to be, freed from her prejudices, I had not, consequently, deceived the Cardinal, when I first gave him hopes, and afterwards assurance, of that revolution in his favour. I had access to the Queen——I had a share in her confidence, and long before she vouchsafed to *smile* on the Cardinal, and *publicly make him signals of intelligence,* I had apprized him that such was her intention, but that she wished to maintain an appearance of reserve, to cover the reconciliation she consented to. Those who have said that I feigned to have influence, that I forged writings, that I had no access to the Queen's person, were therefore slanderers; and what was she herself, the proud Austrian, when at the very moment of her overwhelming the Cardinal with all the awfulness of incensed Majesty, she denied to him in presence of the King, that ever she had known me? I hope that when I come to that melancholy part of my narration, the reader will please to recollect this observation, which my impatience has forced me to anticipate.

Notes

Notes and letters passed in rapid succession to and fro; but the parties did not personally meet. The Cardinal was urgent, I became impatient with the Queen. At length, on the 15th of May, I obtained from her the note numbered (IX.) It will there be seen, that her Majesty promised " shortly to gratify his desire of seeing " her, and *that she found no fault with it* "---Most assuredly that part of the note will not be perused with indifference, where her Majesty condescends to read a lecture on circumspection and prudence to the man, whom in her first letter she styled, " *the most indiscreet of men.*" It must be owned, it was singularly curious that her Majesty should take upon herself the task of instructress to so elevated a religious dignitary.

The paper No X requires no explanation. Every body understands that the impersonal " on," is the *King*, who, already informed of the " *smiles* and *signals of intel-* " *ligence,*" had urged some ambiguous interrogatories. We must not anticipate by any hints the unravelling of the " *scheme which will surely give pleasure.*" I shall frequently have occasion to speak of *Trianon*.

The letter No XI conveys at once an idea both of the Cardinal's style of gallantry, and of the indulgent acquiescence with which her Majesty received a *formal declaration of love.* The Cardinal had not mentioned one word to me of all he pretends to have said, but in love, as in war, stratagems are allowable. However importunate I must often have appeared to the Queen in the Cardinal's behalf, I certainly never should have taken upon me to retail such senseless stuff to her Majesty. nay, I had taken special care, every time that the Prince's

name

name was mentioned in conversation, to avoid all expressions that could attribute to his earnest solicitations, any other motive than that of dutiful respect. It is true, the Queen had even more than hinted to me, that she was not ignorant of the motive which influenced the Cardinal to court the return of her good graces. But, (I cannot too frequently repeat it) as her Majesty was herself swayed by political consideration, she did not think it extraordinary, much less was she offended, that the Cardinal's proceedings should have ambition for their leading principle. But whatever motive might have induced them, I made my representations, which, according to custom, proved unavailing, and I fulfilled my mission, that is I delivered the letter, of the contents of which I had taken the liberty to express my disapprobation. While the Queen was perusing it, I carefully observed her countenance, and was astonished at the serenity with which she went through all the trifling nonsense it contained, but her Majesty has since taught me to wonder at nothing.

Having embarked in this strange correspondence, it will be imagined that my intention is to pursue it to the moment when, for the first time, mention is made of the fatal Necklace. That valuable bauble, which has given birth to such universal conversation and conjecture, will commonly be supposed to be the principal object of these Memoirs. To that subject alone I should have confined myself, had it not appeared to me essential, that I should previously relate the circumstances which preceded that affair, and brought on the total catastrophe that followed. For it is evident, that for being ignorant
of

of the concatenation of those circumstances, nine out of ten persons who have sought to form an idea of that intricate and unhappy affair, have either found themselves led into a labyrinth of confusion, or have formed the most unfavourable impressions of my conduct, in consequence of the various libels published against me by the hirelings of the house of Rohan.

I shall for the reasons alledged, I hope, stand excused, if I continue to diffuse, over the particulars of this correspondence, all the light that is requisite, and it will be found that those circumstances, which at the first sight might appear of trivial consequence in themselves, become of importance as they relate to me, and, of course, to all those who feel an interest in, and seek after the truth of that mysterious transaction.

The paper No. XII. gives rise to reflexions of a very singular nature. A note from a nobleman of the highest rank, from the *Lord High Almoner of France*, commences with the following words, which the Queen is supposed to understand "THE SAVAGE!"---Now, as none but the Queen, the Cardinal the *Savage*, and myself are acquainted with the meaning of that term, it is not foreign to the purpose to inform the non-initiated, that this appellation was the nickname of an obscure man, known but to few, under the title of *Baron de Planta*, the Cardinal's *toad-eater*, not to name him after Voltaire, "*the Prince's friend*." It will appear in the sequel, that he shared with the Cardinal in his perilous adventures.

On the perusal of this note, is it possible to repress a sentiment, if not of indignation, at least of the utmost astonishment?---To see a mighty Queen, some re-

spects

spects so haughty, doomed through a guilty policy to bear with impunity such indecorums, not to say indecencies. Nevertheless, fulsome as the language of this note is, it is evident that the Queen perfectly knew, that this Baron de Planta was in the secret as well as myself, and that she was so little offended at it, that she even vouchsafed to shew him a gracious countenance, or, as the Cardinal expresses it, "*signals of intelligence*." Indeed, it must be owned, her Majesty was very lavish of those signals. I understood them well, and thought them truly enchanting, I do not wonder they turned the poor Baron's brain, less favour from such a quarter, was surely sufficient to bewilder the imagination of any man.

Keeping to the order of dates, I now come to an æra which I cannot possibly pass without more minute attention to it than I have paid to those which have preceded. I earnestly intreat the reader, before he proceeds a line further, to read attentively the paper (No XIII) which is a literal copy of a letter, written by the Cardinal to the Queen, immediately after the scene, in which Mademoiselle Oliva acted the part so much talked of in the proceedings on my trial.

When my relation draws to a conclusion, when the various stratagems are developed and exposed to view, which have been used to prevent my communicating any circumstances which might reflect on the Queen, it will then be understood, why, what I am now going to relate concerning that strange incident, differs so essentially from whatever was said, at that juncture, upon the trial.

The

The reason of that difference is thus accounted for. At that time they laboured to persuade me, that speaking the truth was endangering my life; and now, I am convinced, my honour must be sacrificed, if I do not speak truth. I must therefore solemnly assert and declare to the world, that as well respecting the fatal jewel, as concerning other subsequent matters, I do protest against all that has been said, against all that I myself said before my judges, trusting that this declaration will not be deemed extraordinary, when it is considered as being the result of a mind, now, not fettered by oppression, and which had in the former instance been actuated by fear and apprehension, and trembling under the sword of tyranny and injustice.

One day that the Cardinal and myself were cross examined on a delicate point, which neither of us intended to clear up, from a respect for the Queen, I said something inconsistent with the truth. "Ah, Countess (said "the Prince) how can you confess what you know to "be false?" "Like all the rest, my Lord, answered I, "ever since these gentlemen have put interrogatories to "us, you know that neither you nor I have told them "a single word of the truth."

Nor was it possible we should, the questions to be put to us were ready prepared, nay, often the answers to them, and we were obliged to frame our replies in the manner prescribed, or expect death, in the Bastille. This our counsel incessantly represented to us. Let any one judge of the reliance to be had on a chain of evidence, in which each interrogatory was calculated to bring forth the reply that had been previously attached to it! In a word, all that I, at this period, and

G   when barrassed,

unembarrassed, have to say, concerning the part acted by the Queen in the whole of this unfortunate transaction, I was not permitted to state at the time of my trial. Hence the false notions which the public have imbibed, hence the difficulty of making truth counteract falshood, hence the advantage my detractors will have, by accusing me of being falsified, either at the time of my trial, or at the present period.

With one word, I hope, however, I can resist their malice. I was then compelled to falshood, or death, by the hand of an executioner, to day I *must* speak the truth, or die by my own, for I am made desperate, by imputed ignominies. There is no alternative left me, but non-existence or the clearest justification.

I have sufficiently exposed the ambitious views, the political considerations, that had brought together two beings, who, in the main, mutually despised and detested each other; there remains for me to observe, that as witness to all that passed, confidant to both the personages, I manifestly saw that the demon of politics prevented their proceeding to open extremities. It has been but too well known how little reserved the Cardinal was, in his speeches concerning the Queen, and his restraint was still less with me. On the other hand, the Queen intimated to me from time to time, that she was made acquainted with his indiscretions, past and present Madame de Guémenée had filled her Majesty's mind with prejudices almost unconquerable, and had nearly persuaded her that the object of the Cardinal's proceedings, and of all his contrivances, was to expose her Majesty.

The

The Queen, one day in conversation, said to me, speaking of the Cardinal "Would you believe it? this very morning a person worthy of credit and well acquainted with him, has assured me, he was my bitterest enemy." I heard with attention, and felt concern; for, from thence, I rather despaired of ever being able to establish between two beings, so ill disposed towards each other, that cordiality, that harmony, so necessary to their respective views. Meanwhile the Cardinal was very urgent with me, and I took notice, that for some time past, the Queen did not wait for my mentioning him to her, but often was before-hand with me, by asking questions, which, though seemingly indifferent, had an evident tendency to lead the conversation to that particular subject.

Before any mention was made of the girl *Oliva*, the Queen repeatedly introduced the delicate topic, which I had always sought to elude It is manifest she wanted to bring me to an absolute explanation, on the nature of the sentiments I supposed the Cardinal entertained, or that I might have observed, in his discourse, in his confidential communications Sensible that I had conveyed letters to her Majesty, which contained sentiments, however foreign to those the Cardinal in reality possessed, yet were couched in such language they could not be misunderstood, and having noticed, as I have already observed, that her Majesty perused them without any tokens of disapprobation, I thought I might venture, at length, to hint, that I believed the Prince was *possessed with the most lively passion for her person* One day, therefore, when she was urging me on that head, upon

my telling her that I would warrant the Cardinal's sincerity, on penalty of losing her Majesty's favour. "Ven-
"ture nothing rashly, said she,---sincere or not, the
"Cardinal wants me to credit his professions of since-
"rity.---Suppose I do? pray, tell me what are eventu-
"ally his views? He ought never to have hoped for one
"favourable look, yet I have granted him his pardon.
"He writes to me---I answer him---scarce have I had lei-
"sure, in some degree, to divest myself of the unfavour-
"able sentiments which I have been forced to entertain
"of him, but he obstinately demands a private interview
"---Is it in order to revive the stories he forged about
"his residence at Vienna?---Do you know what he has
"to say to me?---Does he still see the Duke de Lauzun,
"the Prince de Luxembourg?---Is he yet on good terms
"with Madame de Brionne?---Does he still visit at Ma-
"dame de Marigny's?---They say he sees a young lady
"of the name of St. Leger, who is reckoned very hand-
"some?"

After a number of other questions nearly of the same
tendency, her Majesty seemed for an instant to recollect herself, and then resuming her discourse, she proceeded thus---" I have sufficiently signified to you, on
"various occasions, how much reason I have had to
"complain of the Cardinal. Though I have pardon-
"ed, I have not been able to forget his past misicon-
"duct of which I have told you that I have proofs
"irrefragable nor can I shut my eyes on the recent evi-
"dence he has given of a culpability, highly deserving
"reprobation. From what you have been telling me
"yourself, he takes upon him to affect towards me sen-
"timents, the more offensive in proportion as they are

the

" the lefs encouraged. You are not the only one he
" entertains with his idle dreams; the Duke de Lauzun,
" and the Prince de Luxembourg, whom I juft now
" mentioned defignedly, make it the fubject of their
" merriment. I have often had my name very unbe-
" comingly brought in queftion at the Hotel de Sou-
" bife, and I know that numbers who are deceived, by
" his public converfation, think that I admit private
" meetings. How!---would you have me expofe my-
" felf by receiving privately a man of fuch notorious
" indifcretion? Who having prefumed to write roman-
" tic letters to me, would add to his folly by greater
" extravagances, by cafting himfelf at my feet, talking
" of love, and by carrying perhaps ftill farther his rafh-
" nefs and his frenzy? I tell you again that I fufpect
" him, that I cannot impute fo extraordinary a beha-
" viour, but to a fettled fcheme to expofe my charac-
" ter, and that if I had not *some particular reasons* for
" concealing from him my real fentiments, I would for-
" bid you ever to mention him to me, and especially
" charging yourfelf with his letters, I would moreover
" command you to let him know my will"

To thefe circumftances, I reflected I was no ftranger;
but the Queen had particular reafons to keep upon good
terms with him, and I was aware of the cogency of
them ---" If your Majefty, anfwered I, would permit
" me to plead the caufe of the abfent, I would take the
" liberty to obferve, that from the moment you have
" had the goodnefs to pardon what is paft, it is con-
" fiftent with your natural generofity to lofe remem-
" brance of it. Your Majefty's cenfure is not in con-
" fequence

" sequence of your own feelings, but is imitated by the
" envenomed stings of envy and malice. If I have pre-
" sumed to give your Majesty an idea of the nature of
" those sentiments which I attribute to the Cardinal, I
" have taken care to make them consistent with the
" most profound respect. Reason and reflection render
" this latter sentiment, superior to every other, in his
" mind, the former is involuntary, and such as all men who
" have the happiness of seeing you, must feel themselves
" inspired with. The reports respecting his pretended
" imprudences cannot but be slanderous, I would ven-
" ture to take the most sacred assurances of it, and for
" this reason, that I never heard him speak of your
" Majesty but in terms of admiration, and certainly he
" puts on no constraint with me."

Here the Queen took a few turns in her closet, and
coming back to me, with a thoughtful look. " An idea
" occurs to me, said she,----Pray, what female ac-
' quaintances have you got? Tell me the names of
' some of your intimates.-----I have my reasons for
' asking you this question."

After I had named various persons with whom I
was more or less connected, she said to me: " Do you
" think you have so much influence over any one of
" those women, as to prevail on her to comply with
" what I am going to propose?----You will absolutely
" persuade me to grant the Cardinal an interview----
" but I have my reasons for dreading an interview----
' I shall not be without uneasiness till I have made
" trial of him. I will condescend *to see him, without
' seeing him.*-----I know not whether you perfectly understand

"derstand my meaning?----I could wish to be satisfied
"of his behaviour to me, the first time I should really
"grant him an interview. Were it not possible, under
"favour of the darkness, to substitute some other wo-
"man in my stead, with whom the Cardinal might
"converse, while he, at the same time concludes, he is
"addressing himself to me? I could be near enough to
"overhear their conversation. I should then know
"how to act with respect to the real interview, and
"would resolve upon granting or denying it, according
"as his behaviour should appear, either to deserve it or
"not. Among the ladies you have been mentioning,
"do you know of none who would willingly fall in with
"this little piece of deceit, which is suggested by pru-
"dence? The matter, however, may perhaps require
"greater consideration than I have had time to bestow
"upon it.----Come to-morrow, we will talk more fully
"on the subject."

Returning the next day, in compliance with her Majesty's command, I found her determined on the execution of her project. The business seemed to wear so
pleasant an appearance, that it drew from her, when
alone, involuntary peals of laughter. She singled out
for the actress, in the farce, that is, for her representative, the *Lady Baroness of Crussol*, whom I was frequently
with, and who, in reality, had a capacity to favour the
deception, but I represented, that however universal
the desire must be of performing any thing pleasing to
her Majesty, I questioned whether Madame de Crussol
would comply with the proposal, without previously consulting her husband, a circumstance which could not be
agreeable.

agreeable. I observed, besides, that the very natural fear of being discovered by the Cardinal, and detected in the performance of such an imposition on him, appeared to me an insuperable bar ---" In that case," said the Queen, interrupting me, ' I would make my ap-
" pearance, and extricate the Lady out of her diffi-
" culty. You may tell her, that such an act of com-
" plaisance will very much oblige me."

This manner of expressing herself was equivalent to a command, I no longer insisted, but quitted her Majesty, promising my utmost endeavour to procure her satisfaction.

At that period of time, my husband had no knowledge of the political intrigue between the Queen and the Cardinal, he only knew that I was admitted to her Majesty, and that it was to her liberality I owed the affluence of which he was a partaker. The Cardinal, from motives which I never searched into, continually recommended to me *difcretion* with regard to Mr. de la Motte. Hitherto I had scrupulously followed his advice, but the reflections I had made on the Queen's design and whimsical plan, on the fickleness of disposition of the person she had pitched upon, together with a multitude of other prevailing considerations, determined me to consult him in so delicate a conjuncture, and I disclosed to him the whole affair. He turned pale while he listened to me, and his peremptory refusal of being concerned in an intrigue, which he called dangerous, put me greatly out of temper. I urged the matter forcibly, and by dint of perseverance and persuasion, I made him at length understand that his happiness and mine

depended

depended on the Queen, and that we muſt yield a blind compliance to all that ſhe deſired. I recollect our paſſing the whole night in conſidering whether or not I ſhould venture on the ſtep I was commiſſioned to take with regard to Madame de Cruſſol. All circumſtances duly weighed, we agreed it was dangerous for ourſelves to introduce her into the ſcheme. That her family being very ambitious, might avail themſelves of the opportunity to ſupplant us.---Ways might be found, ſaid M de la Motte, to ſatisfy the Queen, without expoſing any one, but I will not explain my meaning before we agree that the Cardinal be let into the ſecret. I aſſented, and gave him an account of all that had paſſed, and of what we were planning. I told him, it was a trial he muſt go through, or give up all hopes of a farther interview. After pauſing a while, he burſt into a loud laugh-----
" How, then, ſays he, can the Queen really think that
" I can be ſo groſsly impoſed on?----Well, no matter,
" I will comply with every thing If ſhe is fond of a
" farce, we muſt give her one You may reſt aſſured,
" *ſhe ſhall never know that I was forewarned,* and I will
" play my part in ſuch a manner as ſhall leave her no
" ſuſpicion of my not acting it in earneſt."

Every thing being thus agreed upon with the Cardinal, the only remaining point was, to meet with a woman who would anſwer our views My huſband took upon him to find one, who ſhould be induced to do, for a pecuniary conſideration, what it was intended another ſhould do from a motive of ambition. Chance, on this occaſion, ſerved him better than all his enquiries could have done The very next day, coming out of the Pa-

H lais-

lais-Royal Gardens, up a flight of steps, which lead from a very narrow, dark paffage into the ftreet, he obferved a woman, decently dreffed, holding a child of five or fix years old by the hand. Seeing her pufhed about by the croud afcending and defcending, he offered his hand, which fhe refufed, however, he helped the child up to the top of the ftairs, where he again proferred to fee the mother fafe home. This propofal, with fome apparent reluctance, fhe accepted. He therefore proceeded with her to the ready furnifhed hotel where fhe refided, and was not long before he difcovered by her converfation, that fhe was pretty nearly fuch a machine as he was looking for. Slight intimations which fhe gave of her fituation not being the moft comfortable, fufficiently declared fhe would not turn a deaf ear to offers of a pecuniary nature. From the account he gave me of his difcovery, I prevailed on him to go to her again, and to make fure of her by a prefent. Accordingly he did fo, and having renewed the former converfation relative to her little difficulties, he difcovered that a fum of three or four hundred livres was for the prefent the object of her wifhes. He embraced this opportunity to tell her, that he would not only lend her that fum, but would procure her a more confiderable one, provided fhe would take an active part, in a trick that was to be put upon a certain perfon. Upon her enquiring what the bufinefs was, he told her that he was a married man, that the Queen fhewed great confidence and kindnefs to his wife, that her Majefty was defirous of playing a trick upon one of the Ladies at Court, which fhe had imparted to his wife, charging her with the management of the whole,

that

that in order to bring it about, she had need of a female, whom she could substitute in her Majesty's place, that she, *Mademoiselle Oliva*, seemed perfectly well calculated for acting the part, and that, if she had no objection, he would that very evening bring his wife to her, with whom she might converse on the subject. She appearing to be disposed to do whatever was required of her, he left her observing to her, that the least imprudence on her part would be attended with her ruin.

That same evening, therefore, according to agreement, I repaired with my husband to the young woman's lodgings, to whom I gave some instructions concerning what she had to do, and we quitted her, leaving a bag of 400 livres upon her drawers. The next day the Count went in his carriage, and conveyed her to Versailles. I preceded them early in the morning; they arrived at the close of day, but I apprized them that the Queen, not having had timely notice, her Majesty had appointed the next night at half past twelve. I had scarce had a minute's talk with her Majesty, whose presence was then rendered by etiquette indispensable elsewhere, so that I had said to her but these two words, as well as I can remember: "*All's ready.*" "*To-morrow,*" answered she, "*at the same hour.*" But the next day I had the honour to see her again in the forenoon, and to acquaint her with our fortunate encounter with *Oliva*; at which she laughed heartily. She then settled with me the scene of action, but as I was infinitely less acquainted than her Majesty with the situation of the ground, I went to reconnoitre it, and prevailed on the Cardinal to accompany me, in order to determine the respective positions, so that the Queen might hear all from the spot which she had chosen for that purpose. To render the scene intelligible, we must necessarily delineate the theatre on which it was exhibited. This was the arbour at the lower end of the grass-plat. The arbour on the left hand path to it, is encompassed with a hedge of horn beam, supported by a strong wooden lattice work; at the distance of three feet is another, before you come to the inward part of the arbour; so that the space intervening between the two quicksets, forms a walk that leads you round the inclosure, without letting you into the arbour itself. Each of the inclosures has its distinct passage, and their entrances are at opposite sides. The Queen had taken her station in the walk between the two lattices, which in that place close together in such a manner, that no passage or communication is left between the two hedges. Her Majesty was attended by *Mademoiselle Dorsat*. The Cardinal who had reconnoitered the ground, had placed himself close to the hedge, whither my husband conducted Mademoiselle O—, concerning whom, I must here say a few words to relieve the reader's attention.

The poor girl was as fine as hands could make her, and had spared no cost to dress herself in the most exquisite taste. From the questions she had asked me, from her cool and artful replies, it was easy to perceive that she expected some great adventure, and had prepared herself accordingly.——" But," said she to me, " what will the nobleman say to me?——If he should " put such and such a question, what shall I answer " him? If he offers to salute me, must I let him?"——
‘ Without

"Without doubt," answered I.----" If he should re-
" quire any thing more?" --" I don't think he will."---
Nothing could be more comic than the creature's embarassment, who in the main was only solicitous for the
unravelling of the plot, because she knew the Queen
would be a spectatress of it.

At the appointed hour I brought the signal, by giving
to Mademoiselle Oliva the rose which the Queen had
charged me to have delivered by her to the Cardinal.
Having placed her in a proper situation, I withdrew. I
was not ten steps distant from the Queen, when Oliva's
timidity put me greatly in pain for her conduct, no
doubt the Queen experienced the same sensation, for in
spite of all her reserve and caution, she could restrain
herself no longer, but cried out to her, " Courage,
" don't be afraid." (This Oliva confessed in her depositions.) The Cardinal being arrived, the conversation
commenced. He, who was quite unconcerned, since
he was in the secret, gave the poor girl every encouragement, by only asking her trifling questions, and making his
conversation meer matter of compliment. What disconc-
certed her most was, his talking to her of "*past faults
" being forgiven,*" of his gratitude, and his making fair
promises for the time to come, all which she could not
possibly understand the meaning of, and therefore answered at random with the monosyllables *yes* or *no*.
The Cardinal made the most he could of those monosyllables, to express his happiness, uttering the prettiest
things imaginable but took no other liberty but that,
of gently raising her foot, which he most respectfully
kissed. It was then that Mademoiselle Oliva delivered
him

[54]

him the rose, which he laid upon his heart, saying "He
"should preserve that pledge as long as he lived,"
calling it "The rose of happiness." (*) Here I recollected the Queen's instructions. All explanations were
over, nothing remained but insipid chit chat, when I
rushed forth and announced the approach of Madame,
and Madame Countess d'Artois, the conference was
broken off as quick as lightning, Oliva making her way
back to the bench where my husband was waiting for
her, the Cardinal joining the Baron de Planta, whom
he had left at a small distance to watch, came up with
her to my post, and prevailed on me to follow him beyond the avenue, behind which he squeezed himself up
to see the Queen go by. Catching a glance of her at
the instant she turned off the grass-plat, up the walk that
leads to the terrace, he desired me to go after her Majesty, and endeavour to speak to her, to know whether
she was satisfied. I accordingly tripped along after
her, and overtaking her at her entrance into the Castle,
she took me up stairs with her, told me in substance,
that she had been highly entertained, paid me a few
compliments, and forbid me to tell the Cardinal that I
had seen her that night. I had no need to tell him of
it, since it was at his request I had followed the Queen,
and

---

* The Cardinal has since had a case made for the
Rose, and some time after, changed the name of a
favourite walk of his at Saverne, into that of "The
Way of the Rose."

and it would have been hard for me to conceal it from him, as he was waiting for me with the Baron de Planta at the foot of the little ſtair-caſe, a circumſtance the Baron mentioned in his croſs examination, intending to prove that I had admiſſion to the Queen.

God both ſees and hears me. I in his preſence take this ſolemn oath, that, were I in my laſt moments, I would repeat all that I have here written as being the genuine truth, yes, in my laſt dying will, I would not alter a letter of this declaration, the firſt it has been in my power to make with freedom ----But, perhaps, ſome perſons will ſay, is it probable that a Queen of France ſhould entertain herſelf with ſuch low contrivances? If the Queen of France was indeed what ſhe ought to be, or rather, was not what ſhe is, theſe memoirs would not have been written---I ſhould not have the painful taſk to accuſe her of the blackeſt ingratitude, of the moſt ſhocking inſenſibility If the Queen of France were not what ſhe is, ſhould I have been to her what a defenceleſs bird is in the hands of a froward child, who, after being amuſed with it for a few moments, ſtrips it of its feathers, one by one, and then throws it into the deſtructive talons of a devouring animal? Were not the Queen of France what ſhe is, would that kingdom have become a ſcene of anarchy? Would an ignorant pedagogue of an Abbé, (*) a troubleſome babbler, the brother of an obſcure *accoucheur*, turn the ſtate upſide down, and ſubvert

its

---

* The Abbé de Vermont

its constitution? (*) It would be truly an excellent argument to advance, that any act of criminality whatever is improbable, because attributed to Majesty! Whoever is versed in history must know, that thrones are no protection against even the blackest crimes by which humanity is too frequently degraded. I have made this observation meerly to oppose such an argument as I have mentioned being advanced against the circumstances I have related, especially as there are still more improbable matters to succeed.

After having given way to the natural severity, which unavoidably rises on the recollection of my enemies, I am myself again. I must be just---I have been guilty of foibles, and of very great ones in this adventure, romantic as it is. I do not dissemble with my own heart, that in giving the Cardinal a fore-knowledge of the Queen's project, was a breach of confidence to her Majesty, but I therein yielded to my husband's representations, to the suggestions of my own ambitious views. I frankly acknowledged

---

* It would require a long note on this article, but I am too full of my own subject to enter into political discussions. I shall only tell those of my English readers, who may be ignorant of it, that when the Dauphin was to be married to the Archduchess, Mr de Choiseul applied to the Archbishop of Toulouse (now of Sens) to have a tutor. The Archbishop gave him the Abbé de Vermont, whose gratitude, seconded by the Queen's all-prevailing power, has signalized itself by getting his benefactor appointed Prime Minister.

knowledged that I was guilty, and endeavoured to atone for it in the first pages of these Memoirs, but I at the same time submitted, whether there ought not to be a proportion between the guilt and the punishment? and whether it was just, that the least criminal of three complices, should alone undergo the punishment of a crime common to them all?

In the circumstance I have just alluded to, I confess that I ought to have refused my compliance with the Queen's whimsical desire; or, if I did yield to it, to have kept her secret. But what sort of a character in the same scene do those persons fill, whom I may justly call my accomplices? *A Queen*, who after telling me all the horrible things I have related, against a man, who n " *she has reasons to keep upon terms with*," descends to make herself sport, by contriving a mock intrigue between him and an insignificant girl, humiliating herself so much as to submit herself, as she imagined, to be the subject of those fooleries that very man was guilty of towards the girl! *A Prince*, who knows that he has kissed that same girl's slipper, and then writes to the Queen to thank her for *her favors*. Such are however the personages who (as I have already observed) by the junction of their unequal and discordant powers, have crushed me to atoms.

The farce was over. The Cardinal was pleased with himself for the dexterity with which he had taken advantage of the pretext to write fooleries to the Queen, and her Majesty had been *entertained*, without seeming yet, to have formed any intention of permitting *real* interviews, postponing them under various pretences, and

I evading

evading a compliance with the Cardinal's earneft and continued folicitations. Her anfwers hitherto conveyed by me were generally, " That fhe was bufied in feeking " fome plaufible means, which, without giving a hold " to fcandal, might open to him an eafy accefs to her " perfon " A circumftance which is explained in Letter XIV. ferved the Cardinal to his wifh. That circumftance he availed himfelf of, to write the letter alluded to. The obfervations to be made upon that letter are fo apparent, that it would be needlefs to point them out to the intelligent reader Still lefs fhall I offer any on No. XV that letter alfo fufficiently fpeaking for itfelf

I have already taken notice, that *the Savage* was the Baron de Planta, and that the Baron de Planta was the Cardinal's *fhadow* On that day, or to fpeak more properly, that night, which was the fcene of action in the garden, the *fhadow* had followed the *body* to Trianon. As to the reft the reader will form what conclufions he pleafes With regard to No XVI fome furprize will naturally be created by the words " *Thou---thine---thee*" which in this letter are for the firft time ufhered into the correfpondence and I may again be accufed of producing improbabilities, but thofe who may accufe me muft be ftrangers to what a degree Sovereigns, of either fex, relax their dignity, when once they have thrown off the dull etiquette which they are obliged to maintain, however irkfome But a truce to matters of fuch trifling import, I fhall proceed to bufinefs of more confequence

A certain COMPANY had prefented to the Cardinal, through the medium of my application, a plan for the
Regulation

Regulation of the Finances. The nature of it was, as nearly as I can recollect, a suppression of the custom of farming the Revenues, the Aids, the Land-Tax, the Twentieths, the Tenths, &c.----The Company engaged, provided those suppressions took place, to bring into the King's coffers annually FORTY MILLIONS of livres more than the usual receipts produced, and to pay one year in advance. The QUEEN, in consideration of this plan being adopted, was to receive " four millions," MR. DE CALONNE " one million," and one other million was allotted to me, with " fifty thousand livres per annum. The scheme the Company had planned, was to raise upon all inheritances, a certain sum, instead of all the taxes with which the estates stood charged. The heir, it was intended, should pay, upon taking possession of his inheritance, *ten per cent* on the value of all the property he became possessed of, and this sum should liberate him, for life, from any future tax. By this plan there would certainly, in a short time, have been no taxes subsisting throughout France. The Cardinal had several times mentioned this project to the Queen, and it was after receiving the memorial, and the particulars concerning it, that her Majesty wrote the letter now under the reader's consideration. That, from the Cardinal, to which this is an answer, contained reflexions on the Comptroller General, who at that time was Mr. de Calonne. I recollect the nature of them. He was apprehensive, lest the Minister, whose avarice, lust for power, and craftiness, was perfectly known to him, would, after having investigated the matter, *affect* a disapprobation of the scheme, and lay it aside,

aside, in order to bring it forwards at a subsequent period, under some other appellation. To corroborate this, it is a fact, the Cardinal never did present it to Mr de Calonne; and when I urged him to it, he would answer, "*I will not make advances towards any man whom I shall shortly be in a capacity to command.*" As to what regards me in that letter, the case is briefly this. When Mr de Calonne was called to the administration of the finances, he received me with that specious kind of civility, which is so frequently substituted for friendship, but which is only a mask for deceit. He, indeed, attended to my claims, the justice of which he could not but acknowledge, and for a long time buoyed me up, with the sanguine hopes he had flattered me with on the very first audience. All that apparent courtesy, terminated as I have before mentioned, in the vast augmentation of *seven hundred* livres, to my existing pension of *eight hundred*. The Cardinal, who had expected as well as myself, that I should have met with a less parsimonious treatment, took the first favourable opportunity to speak to the Minister in my behalf, who, to exculpate himself, and also prevent further solicitations, answered, that "*he had done all that he was able with the King and Queen, who, themselves, had fixed the augmentation, so that there was no such thing as bringing forward that subject again.*" It is upon the Cardinal's reporting this impudent falsehood to the Queen, that her Majesty denies the fact, but though sensible of the Minister's rapacity, yet she thought proper to excuse him, by allowing that his situation, as a Minister, must often force him to deviate from the truth.

We

We come now to the Letter No. XVII. which requires explanation. It muſt not be forgotten, that the word "*Miniſter*" means the *King*. I have hitherto but ſlightly hinted at thoſe " OBJECTS," which are treated of in this letter. Thoſe " OBJECTS," ſo diſpleaſing to the Queen, " who take advantage of her imprudencies, " to maintain their power of vexing and thwarting her," are the Polignacs, " 'tis they," according to her Majeſty, " who have abuſed her confidence, her condeſcenſion, and have contrived, by their knowledge of certain circumſtances, to controul her at their diſcretion."

In what does the abuſe, here complained of by the Queen, conſiſt? In having intercepted and obſtinately kept in their poſſeſſion letters and papers, written proofs of thoſe *imprudencies,* of which her Majeſty accuſes herſelf. The Queen, then, had palpably committed what ſhe terms " imprudencies," antecedent to thoſe in which ſhe made me an accomplice? Is it then ſo improbable as my ſlanderers would have it believed, that ſhe committed or authorized the " imprudence" of the arbour, the " imprudence" of the falſe ſignature, the " imprudence" of taking the necklace to pieces, and that ſeries of other " imprudencies" which form the principal tranſactions of her life. In what do the " imprudencies confiſt, of which the Polignacs had, and ſtill carefully preſerve the written evidences? " In notes, in letters written with her Majeſty's own hand, in appointments and rendez-vous, " imprudently addreſſed, as well to the *Count d'Artois,* as " to other perſons at Court, and ſtill more imprudently " entruſted to faithleſs hands." In what more do theſe " imprudencies" conſiſt? " In memorials, with poſt-
" ſcripts

" scripts to them, in her Majesty's writing, containing
" the proofs of unheard of exactions, in conveyances of
" money, loans, good-wills, favors sold for money, &c.
" &c. &c. all passing through the hands of the female
" Treasurer, POLIGNAC!"----What has resulted from those first mentioned " imprudencies?" That the Queen, fearing the Polignacs, has been obliged to keep on good terms with them---that if she withdrew from them her secret favour, she continued to them the appearances of it in public while I, who have not been so daring as to intercept and detain *originals*, and have only taken exact copies to produce, am repulsed with harshness and disdain, and the same hand that feeds the avarice, the boundless luxury of those who have abused trusts infinitely more than I have done, refuses me the restitution of property, which was taken from me for having rejected the proposal of betraying the secrets of my Sovereign, nor is it considered that such refusal, as barbarous as it is iniquitous, deprives me of all means of subsistence!---Whatever be the effervescent heat into which these reflexions throw me, whenever they occur, I wish I could suppress the letter, and the S which will be taken for the initial of the word SOPHA, and that licentious passage which settles the place of rendez-vous: it may particularly be supposed, that I should have a great propensity to retrench from those scenes of gaiety, the part which I am made to act in them, but were I to leave out a single word, I should then leave an opening for my opponents, who would not fail to deny me all credit whatever. I shall therefore submit every syllable to the public eye.

The

The subsequent letter, No. XVIII. needs no comment. As I had long since lost sight of this correspondence, in reading over this number, I can scarce believe my own eyes. I recollect, that about the time of its date, the Queen was enraged against Madame de Polignac, and that seeing her Majesty determined to urge matters to the utmost extremity, I took the liberty to offer some observations tending to dissuade her from it. At that period, indeed, she was harrassed to an inconceivable degree, and the " leeches" she speaks of had formed a kind of party, which was growing extremely formidable. Another circumstance, I recollect struck me at the time, is, that for all the seeming heat that runs through the letters I am now come to, the Queen greatly exaggerated her restraint, and made a pretence of it to baffle, as far as possible, the Cardinal's importunities. He, who in the main was not much more sincere in his demonstrations of eagerness, commonly had recourse to the pen, whence that multiplicity of idle notes, of which I have already said, that at least *two hundred* had passed through my hands. I shall turn from the unaccountable things in this letter relating to the King, more *shocking ones* will be seen in the sequel of the correspondence. Upon the whole, it is an abomination which I shudder at, while I am bringing it to light, but mankind will be sensible, at least in *England*, that the production of it was indispensable for my own justification, for in all cases of impeachment and recrimination, the *prudent* English regulate their judgment by the character the first accuser bears. With respect to the first lines of No. XVIII there will be found in a

note

note of some length (page 65) particulars concerning the President d'Aigre, who is the person here alluded to. In the same note I will explain who "those per-"sons are that are supposed to be ignorant of nothing."

The letter No XIX is nearly an appendix to the foregoing. Rage against Madame Polignac breaks out in it with redoubled vehemence, but the spirit of diffi-mulation appears with less restraint. Mention is made again of the King, who through the whole correspon-dence acts a part which he doubtless would not have done, had he been consulted. This circumstance seems to introduce, rather naturally, an observation which, as it was my intention to make, may be as aptly fixed to this place as any other.

It must have been observed in No XVIII. that the Queen "knows how to chain up the lion," that she is accustomed to make him see and believe what she "pleases." She says in this, that " she knows how to " wind him up to what pitch she has a mind." It is in this confidence that she has long since " wound up" the King's mind on my account, and has made it her business to prepare him for the publication of my Me-moirs, which were so long ago reported to be preparing for publication.——But, deluded Princess!——what will that precaution avail you? When you formed it, you knew not then the nature of the attack you dreaded. Your sycophants have blinded you by a misinformation, by telling you that all the papers were seized and burnt that there existed no trace, no vestige of your corres-pondence with the Cardinal. Bezenval himself has de-ceived, or still voluntarily deceives you——for he is

well

well acquainted with all that I have in my possession, he is not ignorant how I preserved that treasure from the shattered remains of all that once belonged to me: but I suppose, he has his reasons for permitting you to remain in ignorance: at this moment I remove the cloud, which obscured it from your sight, yes, it is from this moment that you will at length know, with certainty, that whatever is contained in that correspondence destructive to you, exists in the most connected, most complete, most authentic state. You may, perhaps, assert that they are fictions? I question even your courage to do it, for you are surrounded with people who know your style, your manner. Many there are who have had a knowledge, more or less exact, of the greater part of those facts I here relate (*) By placing them again in a conspicuous point of view, those persons will recall

---

* With concern I see myself obliged to use frequent repetitions, but I have not the presumption to rely so far on the public attention, as to think that all I have written remains impressed on the mind. I therefore beg leave to remind the reader, of what I have set forth in various parts of these Memoirs, concerning the inviolable secrefy enjoined upon me by the Queen, from the first moment I had the honour to approach her, which I have more particularly said in another note, and which being a very short one, I shall here transcribe.

' The reader will please to recollect, what I observed in the beginning of these Memoirs, of the absolute

" secrefy

recall every thing to mind, as if they had perfonally beheld them The bare indifcretions of the Cardinal, have

---

" fecrefy the Queen had recommended to me. It is
" inconceivable how far the faithful obfervance of that
" command has been fatal to me; and how great the
" advantage which has been taken of it, to do me the
" injuftice of denying my ever having intimately con-
" verfed with the Queen. Her Majefty has carried the
" matter ftill farther, by telling the King " *She knew*
" *nothing at all of me!*" To that daring affertion, I am
going to anfwer by this fecond note.

I fhall not mention thofe of the Queen's immediate attendants, who have been acquainted, almoft as well as her Majefty and myfelf, with the nature of our intimacy. I fhall name no one among the croud of inferior tools of intrigue, who, to make fomething of the fmalleft difcoveries, are always on the watch, carry their audacity fo far as to peep through key-holes, and are unfufpectedly privy to the moft fecret acts of intimacy Many of them I could name, but Heaven forbid ! They are perfons defitute of fupport, and would lofe their places, a circumftance which I fhould much regret, but I will point out fome, who being independant of the world, are more enabled to bear the effects of the Queen's petty vengeance I pleaded guilty of faults at my firft fetting out, what follows will conftitute part of my confeffion.

The Firft Prefident d'Aligre, had rendered me fervices long before my connexion with the Queen When
Madame,

have infinitely multiplied the number of persons initiated in the fatal mysteries, to which I was but a too frequent

---

Madame, and Madame d'Artois took me under their protection, and gave themselves some trouble in soliciting for me, that Magistrate was the first to apprise me, that the Queen could not endure those two Princesses, that the very circumstance of their interesting themselves for me, was sufficient to make her Majesty create difficulties and multiply obstacles. " Of this " daily instances are seen. The Queen has engrossed " all favours, and whenever she finds an opportunity to " mortify her sisters-in-law by a refusal, ill-fortune fol- " lows those whom they patronize, for she seizes it with " amazing avidity."----In general, the counsels which Monsieur d'Aligre gave me, were afterwards highly useful to me. I was at that period compelled, from various circumstances, to launch into expences, which were by no means compatible with the contracted state of my finances. Monsieur d'Aligre had lent me sundry sums of money, at different periods, to the amount of two thousand crowns. This debt, I for some time past regretted, I had not the power to have discharged at the instant I had the fatal, though then flattering fortune to interest the Queen in my behalf. Her Majesty's generosity having rapidly supplied me with the means, I pleased myself with the thoughts of surprizing Monsieur d'Aligre, and went to him, possessed of twenty thousand livres, in bills on the Caisse d'Escompte, which I had

[68]

frequent witness. Consider, besides, Madame, that if calumny, and distress are at present doomed to be my lot,

---

just received (as I have before said). With much difficulty I prevailed on him to accept of his two thousand crowns, nor did I succeed, until seeing I had fourteen thousand livres left in hand, he yielded to my pressing entreaties.

By a few words which he let fall, on seeing me mistress of so large a sum, considering my means, he seemed to suspect my having received it from the Cardinal, with whom he knew I was on terms of friendship. My delicacy was hurt, and seeing no other alternative, but that I must submit to the suspicion of a personal stain, or an indiscretion, I entrusted him with the whole affair, except what regarded the Cardinal's *political* intrigue, not caring to proceed so far, knowing the mortal hatred the President entertained against him. He therefore had no farther knowledge, than that the Queen had viewed me with a favourable eye, had taken upon herself the care of my fortune, and in the mean time gave proofs of her attention by her munificence. He was delighted with my being communicative, gave me excellent counsels, and encouraged me to benefit by them, whenever I should think I had further occasion.

Monsieur d'Aligre did not come at the knowledge of what passed between the Queen and the Cardinal, until toward the period pointed at in the Queen's letter, No. XVIII.

lot, public hatred and contempt must follow you. Flatter not yourself with the idea of security, because

from

XVIII to which I promised to advert in this note, in order to explain, what is meant in its commencement.

That letter here powerfully assists me in proving that the Queen, who pretended, and who told the King that *" she had not the least knowledge of me,"* yet suspected, as early as the 18th of August, 1784, that the President d'Aligre had sought to dive into the motive that actuated her Majesty in the affair of the *Quinze-Vingts Hospital*, and supposed that the Magistrate, unable to make any discovery, had spoken of it to certain people, who are deemed ignorant of nothing. Those *certain people* were not in the plural, the Queen meant to speak only of the Baron de Breteuil, as I shall presently explain.

The Queen, as appears by her letter, had commissioned me to see the President d'Aligre, in her name; to prevail on him to put a stop to the law-suit carried on by the Administrators of the Quinze-Vingts against the Cardinal. It was on that occasion that the Magistrate expressed *the astonishment* referred to in the letter: he put many questions to me, as may well be imagined, on the very surprizing nature of her Majesty's concern for the Cardinal, but the Queen was mistaken, when she said, that " he could make no discovery," for I revealed every thing to him, and far from his having sought to get the secret out of the Baron de Breteuil, it was, on

the

from the exalted height of a throne, you look down upon your supposed victim struggling in the dust; from that

---

the contrary, the Baron de Breteuil who persuaded him to a disclosure, as I was shortly after informed.

A few days after my interview with Monsieur d'Aligre, by order of the Queen, I had occasion to write to the Baron de Breteuil, to desire a meeting, I had a favour to solicit for a person whom I valued. He made answer, that at the receipt of my letter, he was getting into his carriage to go to Versailles, where he should stay three or four days, that he was persuaded, *affairs more agreeable than his were*, would summon me thither, and that he should be at my command. I did not wait till he explained himself, to understand that he was acquainted with the nature of my *agreeable affairs*. I every day found out some apparent confidant, I knew not whence or how they could be so well informed. The Baron did not keep me on the rack for want of letting me know, from what source he had derived his information. The first thing he did, on sight of me, was to compliment me *on my intimacy with a person who would do every thing for me* ---As I seemed not to understand his exordium, he told me, that my discretion surprised him, the more as I had granted my confidence to one, who did not deserve it as well as he did, that his intent was not to wrest my secret from me to make advantage of it, and do me a prejudice, but rather to direct me, and shew me the road I should pursue.----

The

that dust I shall probably raise such a cloud of damning facts, as may overwhelm you, and perhaps reduce you to a level with myself.

The different parties were at strife who should be my adviser: I had then as many counsellors as the King.

The Baron seeing that I persisted in my reserve, descended into particulars, that convinced me Mr. d'Aligre had told him all I had entrusted him with. Without naming the Cardinal, to whom he is the most deadly enemy, he said to me, " You have connexions with " a man who will be your ruin. He is an ambitious, " vain, empty man, indiscreet above all, and will break " his neck in the end. Be you as discreet with others " as you are with me, and beware that a wrong step, " an inconsiderate speech, does not lose you the Queen's " good graces ----I have searched to the bottom of " every circumstance, and shall keep the knowledge I " have gained within my own breast. I have nothing " more to say on that head."

We afterwards conversed on the subject that brought me to him, having perused my petition, he told me, there was nothing he could refuse me, and that he would go and give orders that my client should have a place. He added, as he left me, that I should always find him disposed to do me what service rested in his power, and to give me such counsels as I might stand in need of.

Much

The letter No XX merits to be read with the greatest attention. Here, for the first time, we are presented

---

Much about the same time I heard, that I was the occasion of great uneasiness to the Ladies de Polignac Those haughty women, who had been so rude to me, that I might almost call their behaviour outrageous, had heard some secret whispers of the business I took so much pains to conceal Their favour was already much on the decline, they had but few means left of watching, as they used to do, the Queen's conduct, and they were resolved, cost what it would, to satisfy themselves concerning the reports buzzed about with regard to me

In the first pages of these Memoirs I mentioned the Marquis d'Autichamp, and observed that his behaviour forced M de la Motte, my husband, to resign his commission in the Gens d'Armes, since that event, which occasioned much conversation, I had not seen the Marquis He it that time lived in the strictest intimacy with the Countess Diana de Polignac She hearing that he had formerly known me, spoke of it to the Duchess de Polignac, and these Counts took a resolution to depute him to me, to endeavour at finding out what was going on

The Marquis d'Autichamp was connected with the Baroness D. daughter-in-law to Mr de Cromot, He made that a pretence to coming to me at Versailles and tell me, that he had long wished an opportunity of meeting with me, that
the

presented with that *political intrigue,* which had as it were from necessity induced the intrigue of gallantry.

I have

---

the moment Madame Dubourg had told him I sometimes visited at her house, he had multiplied his visits to her, but had never been so happy as to see me there he spoke of my husband, saying he should take the greatest pleasure in being serviceable to him, and convincing him he had never sought to do him an injury, as my husband had imagined He concluded by requesting my permission, which I granted him, of paying his respects to me. His first visit was short, he mentioned nothing particular to me, but this might be occasioned by the presence of Mr. Rouillé d'Orfeuil, Intendant of Champaign, who stayed with me the whole time. In taking his leave, he said he had something to impart to me, I answered, he might call on the morrow, that he ould find me alone.

Accordingly the next morning he came. What he d to say to me so particular, required some introduct on , who could be more conversant in those prefatory speeches than a courtier He began by entertaining me with his intrigue with the Countess Diana, gave me to understand, what I knew full well, that it was a mere matter of policy As he was sensible that I had reason to complain of both the sisters, he endeavoured to persuade me it was the Countess d'Ossun, Lady of the Bedchamber to the Queen, who was the contriver of the mischief, and the person who had prevented

I have spoken of a kind of midway established at Sa-
verre, to serve as a central point to the emissaries of
the

———

*****de Duchess of Polignac from receiving me, by
t*****, the Queen was tired to death with my solicitations, and resolved not to grant me any thing. The
Marquis added, that "this Madame d'Ossun notwithstanding her blandishments, was a bad woman, very
dangerous, very jealous, and wanton to a degree."
Then passed on to the Countess Diana, whose *penchant*
for*****he had just been relating, He told me, "she
'was an intriguing woman, but full of wit, and taking
'the lead in every thing," that "it was for that
'***** he paid her a painful attention.' "As to
the Duchess of Polignac," continued he, "she is a
'charming woman, I have the greatest value for her,
'the Queen has a strong attachment to her, but, no
'lo*****, any love. This Queen of ours," added the
Marquis, "is somewhat fickle and inconstant in her
'*****. It requires a great deal of address and
'***** to ***** her fleeting favour It is the Coun-
'tess Diana that informs me, you are the *raging fa-
'*****. I was not at all surprised at it. As she asked
'me several questions about you, I told her you was
'***** amorous nor malevolent, still less revenge-
'ful, in general very obliging, and indeed too gene-
'rous, that the only thing was an excess of viva-
'city ***** ***** ***** She answered me,
'***** ***** ***** to the Queen.

the Emperor and of the Queen; I have already observed that the Cardinal was extremely incommunicative in that particular.

He next entered into long details on the Queen's disposition and partialities, and summed up all in an offer of *counsels*, assuring me, that " he would direct " me in such a manner as to get me many friends, and " preserve the Queen's kindness towards me, &c. &c.

I was not seduced, the first time, by so fair an outside, but his visits growing frequent, and the counsels he gave me appearing to be the result of good will, I insensibly threw off my reserve, and in the unguarded frankness of my heart, bestowed upon him an unlimited confidence. Here is then one confident more, who has known all that I recollect, all that the Queen must no doubt have forgotten, since so frail is her retentive faculties, that she does not so much as remember that such a being as the Countess de la Motte ever was known to her, much less possessed her confidence but I must have recourse to those who may refresh her memory as need requires. I shall therefore name also the Bailli de Crussol, admitted to all her Majesty's parties of pleasure, who, unable to doubt of my intimacy with her, for a long time exerted his utmost endeavours to wrest from me the avowal of it, but finding he could not succeed, he concluded, like the Baron de Breteuil, by telling me " he knew it all." I shall also name the Abbé le Kel, Almoner, Confessor to the Bastile, and spy in chief to the Government, who, being urged to make me speak,

particular. I could only, from our conversation, form conjectures, grounded on a variety of circumstances, which,

---

to direct me, to make me declare whatever served the views of those whose interest it was to destroy me, at length forced from me the secret of the whole intrigue. I shall say the same of the Commissary Chénon, who knew every thing, when he examined me in the Bastile, of Monsieur Tillet, Administrator of the horrid house I was confined in, of Sister Martha, under whose immediate inspection I had been placed, of my lawyer, Mr. Doillot, to whom I had given in writing all the facts I this day relate. I shall further name the Sieur Bazin, confidant of the secret pleasures of her Majesty, and Governor of Trianon. I shall take the liberty to ask him, whether he knew *me?*---whether he knew the *Cardinal?* whether he did not convey letters from the Queen to the Cardinal, and from the Cardinal to the Queen?---whether he did not entrust the most secret particulars he knew to a mistress he had in common with a certain German Baron, who made that a plea to solicit my protection with the Queen. Lastly, I name Mr Puissant, a Farmer-General, to whom I had infinite obligations, who having long assured me he knew, from a multitude of persons, my connexions with the Queen, after long denying it, I was compelled to a confession. The same befel me with a number of persons of the first distinction; and I can say that spite of all the caution I observed, the

which, without giving me any precise idea of the nature of this secret communication, yet afforded the strongest presumptive evidence of the existence of a clandestine and settled correspondence between the Emperor on one hand, and the Queen and the Cardinal on the other.

First, I often saw German officers arriving, and holding long and mysterious conferences with the Cardinal. Secondly, My husband was frequently charged by the Prince with the delivery, at particular places, especially at the Port St Antoine, of packets to couriers, who appeared to him to be Germans Thirdly, The Queen's sentiments respecting the Cardinal were established, in my opinion, from having often heard her say, she had reasons to keep on terms with him. I could, therefore, attribute to nothing but political reasons of the most delicate nature, not only so extraordinary a coalescence, which I had looked upon as impossible, until the Emperor's influence had wrought the miracle, but also the consequent familiarities and deviations from decorum Fourthly, The futility of the Cardinal's affected mystery and reserve, whilst he often unguardedly betrayed circumstances,

the nature of my intimacy was very much like the secret in a play

I have even recently discovered, in London, tracks of a like confidence, made with still less reserve than to any other person, having had occasion to see the French Ambassador, he reminded me of my having at the time completely initiated his brother, the Bishop of Langres, into all the particulars of the farcical secret.

cumstances, which could not but confirm my suspicions. He more than hinted to me, that very soon I should be amazed,---that he should be Prime-Minister,---that he should not be directly obliged to the Queen for his elevation ---that, on the contrary, he should have compelled her to promote it, and that, of course, he should not consider himself to be under the necessity of giving extraordinary demonstrations of gratitude. Fifthly, and lastly, I was privy to all their correspondence. That part of it which I am about to communicate, made me consider the Emperor as the primeval source of the transactions I was witness to, and of the revolution they were intended to produce. What the might object was that precipitated the Cardinal's departure for Saverne, I will not take upon me to say, I will only relate what I heard relative to it about that time, and since, from persons who were imagined to be well informed. It was pretended by some, that the occasion was the idea of recovering Lorrain, but I protest I am ignorant of any such intention, though not equally so of a pecuniary negociation that was at the same time upon the tapis. The Emperor was in want of six or seven millions of livres, which he could not hope to obtain from the Comptroller General, a man too closely connected with the Count de Vergennes to be entrusted. The Queen and the Cardinal were to procure that sum for him by some other mode, for the latter, thinking he was secure in the fruition of his wishes, had actually made a promise to the Emperor, to obtain for him what he desired. He accordingly made numberless applications to the Jews Cerfbere, but Cerfbere, to whom the Cardinal was

already

already deeply indebted, refused granting him any farther loan. The Cardinal, by this refusal, was under the mortifying necessity of declaring to the Queen his inability to comply with the wishes of the Emperor.

I intreat the reader's particular attention to this circumstance, that the motives which prevailed on the Queen to pardon the Cardinal, to take him into favour again, and probably something more, by reviving what she calls *the stories of Vienna*, may be investigated, and traced to their source, by the clue which I have given in the above relation. Lastly, let him not lose sight of the necessity which the Emperor considered himself under of having the Cardinal's concurrence to, and assistance in, the promotion of his designs.---We see the pecuniary negociation terminating in air. If the Cardinal does not prove more successful in Lorrain, will the rapidity of his downfall be a matter of wonder?

The Queen, stung to the quick, but skilled, as she herself acknowledges, in the arts of dissimulation, pretended to be satisfied with the Cardinal's apologies for his incapacity to fulfill his promise to her brother, and pressed his departure for Saverne, with a view artfully to put him to the second ordeal, and in hopes to determine the Emperor to withdraw his protection, in case he should a second time miscarry in transacting the affair concerning Lorrain, which I can aver she secretly wished him to do. She therefore undertook, solely, to raise the before-mentioned sum of six or seven millions of livres.---Pope St. James was obliged, I believe, to furnish part, but it was Labo de who advanced the principal sum,

and

and this circumstance proved the origin of his favour with the Queen.

I recollect, if I am not mistaken, that Mr de Calonne, to whom her Majesty often had recourse, frequently advanced sums, till the revenues were paid into the Royal Exchequer.

But let us return to No. XX and XXI. The poor Cardinal is obliged to set off to Saverne, charged as he imagined, with the confidence of the Queen. He is in readiness to sacrifice *all, all*, except his love, we perceive him *jealous*, he leaves the career open to the handsome *Fersen*, Colonel of the Royal Swedois, and leaves the Court with the most dismal apprehensions——However, he must in preference to all other considerations, busy himself with *the grand object*, he will be preceded at Saverne by a courier *bearer of a packet* he has taken his measures to avoid all surprise, and *in case of a mishap*, to destroy every evidence. Does not this wear the appearance of some secret machination? Yet, it is in the mysterious chaos of this letter, we must look for a solution of every thing that relates to this unhappy affair——I again say, the Cardinal, myself, and in some respects the Queen herself, became victims to the unenlightened policy of Joseph II but what an enormous disparity in the sacrifices!

It is needless for me to point out the passage in No. XX that regards the Polignacs, as it cannot escape observation, but I cannot omit mentioning what I recollect hearing the Cardinal say on this occasion, because it will explain what he meant, by speaking of 'œconomy.' The meaning was, that her Majesty had

no

no other course to take, but *speedily* to make him Prime Minister, that then " the Polignacs shall have work enough upon their hands." These, or words to the same effect, was the language he made use of. "ERE LONG," said he, "I WILL AVENGE THE QUEEN, YOU, AND MYSELF, UPON OUR COMMON ENEMIES."

It will not appear extraordinary, that in the letter No. XXI the Cardinal should mention the reliance he placed on me, to give her Majesty information of the pains he had taken, to have the packet which is mentioned in the foregoing letter safely delivered, for on this occasion, as on many more of a similar nature, he had recourse to the Count, my husband. Had I not previously explained the nature of this letter, and given an intimate knowledge of the strange intrigue to which it relates, it must naturally have been conjectured, from the contents of it, that the Cardinal had taken leave of his senses, and had written it in a fit of delirium. The Cardinal was doubtless uneasy, but was not "jealous." my uneasiness, however, was far greater, because it was better founded! I foresaw that the period was not far distant, in which the Queen would exert herself to get him out of the way, and unable to judge with precision either of the urgency or importance of his mission to Saverne, I dreaded its being only an artifice which the Queen had recourse to, for saving appearances, and handsomely divesting herself of his importunities.

It appears, that there were two reasons assigned for his journey. In the first place, the Queen made him believe, that his absence from Versailles was necessary; and, in the next, that his presence at Saverne was indispensible.

[82]

people. I could not much credit the existence of the latter necessity, it appeared to me suspicious, because I knew the former to be little more than ideal. Her Majesty exaggerated the alarms relative to the interviews which had taken place, the fact was, the observations that had been made upon them, were by no means of that magnitude which the Queen pretended, and wished the Cardinal to conceive.

When I came to the knowledge of the letter No. XXIII. immediately after the Cardinal's departure, it confirmed the first idea I had conceived. The Queen, on delivering to me this letter, appeared more than commonly uneasy. I apprehended that papers of extreme consequence were in question; my ideas began to unravel, and I was not without some apprehensions, that the Cardinal had embarked in some act of treason.

This idea affected me so violently, that for some time my disposition was such as to create uneasiness, for that was a period of my life in which there were many who interested themselves in what concerned me; amongst those I thought I might reckon the Queen, but her Majesty has since given me reason to conclude, that *her friendship was of a description too gross, to admit of any other approach than that which was derived from the most formal communication*.

But to return to the letter, what her Majesty then wrote to the Cardinal, relative to the abuse of her confidence by the Polignacs, appeared inflicate to me at the very time when she had told me, *she was certain of the contrary*. Why then acknowledge no more than the strict truth to the man, whom she employs in the

rest

most delicate and the most perilous transactions, whom she calls by the *very familiar* appellations of "*thou*" and "*thee,*" and is so treated by him, is what no one can conceive that is not conversant with courts.

The conclusion of this letter has something more remarkable in it, than the Reader would probably be aware of, were I to omit explaining what is meant by "*the piece of well placed œconomy!*" That phrase, before it was committed to writing, had been repeated to me at least twenty times, on the occasion of the unfortunate necklace. The Queen could never relish that *piece of œconomy*, which she often termed *sordidness*. In the Gazettes, where every thing is represented in a manner, best adapted to the interest of the occasion, credit has been given to the Queen for the following saying, "*I had rather have one ship more of the line, than a necklace.*" It is a piracy committed on the King, the expression was his Majesty's ----The Queen would have given (to me a latitude of speech) an hundred men of war, for that necklace. She has surely purchased it at a dear rate, since that costly bauble robs her of her peace of mind for the remainder of her days, for callous she must be in the extreme, if she possesses a moment's quiet, from the sting of self conviction and reproach, for the turpitude of her conduct respecting the Cardinal, and the barbarous and ungrateful tenor of her behaviour to me, who have certainly, with all my foibles, merited of her a far different return.

The Letters No XXIII and XXIV relate entirely and solely to that *political* intrigue, with the particulars of which I was not permitted to be acquainted. The acknowledgement of my ignorance in that business, will I hope, assist in establishing my credit with the candid reader, for fidelity and veracity in the relation of those circumstances, wherein I was personally active, and with the nature of which I was thoroughly acquainted, by precluding the charge of a false affectation of knowledge, I do not possess. These letters are however necessary links of the great chain. Although I cannot give the reader a proper clue, to lead him through the secret paths of this political labyrinth, and point out the *political* views, which were the objects of the parties, yet I shall so far turn these letters to my advantage by fair conclusions, drawn from concurrent circumstances, as to use them for foils, by placing my *accomplices* and myself in a comparative point of view, and leaving my readers to judge of the proportional demerits of our internal conduct.

While I appear degraded by an ambition, that seems to stoop to the character of a sycophant, in what light must the guilty confederates be viewed, who were concerned in that intrigue in which I had no share? I repeat it again, do not all those significant notes, written to each other at the period of the journey to *Saverne*, wear on the face of them, the seal, the stamp, the character, the operation of *a censurable machination*? That *language* as enigmas as prudent! was the fittest medium to communicate a deed of iniquitous mystery.

Had I committed all the crimes attributed to me, had I acted however the reverse, what could my culpability be, compared with that of a Queen, sacrificing to a taste that knows no measure, to the unpardonable ambition

ton of her brother, in pretended amity with the King her husband, or with a *Lord High Almoner* of the same kingdom, who, indebted for every thing he possesses, to the bounty and indulgence of his Sovereign, basely and treasonably plots with a foreign power to injure his benefactor, and deprive him, if he can, of a part of his dominions?

The letter No XXV by giving an idea of the importance, and almost of the nature of the Cardinal's mission, confirms what I have said of the Emperor's dispositions towards him. The reader may there discover that he expects *a revolution*, that he anticipates some events, the completion of which is, as he says, *&, near at hand*, so far as to *offer* to the Queen the "*support,*" which himself expects from the Emperor. It is evident, that the words "*in order to enjoy doubly the advantages and the resources against contingencies,*" can advert to nothing but *money*, which the Queen, who was ever under some dilemma, was incessantly in want of, and the rapacious cravings of the Cardinal were such, as wou'd have swallowed up three kingdoms.

The letter No XXVI will naturally recall to the reader's mind, that from the Queen, wherein her Majesty recommends to the Cardinal to be "*perplexed and obscure.*" We have seen it acknowledged that "*the place yields obedience.*" I do not recollect to what purpose the wish the Cardinal expresses, of "*being serviceable*" to me, at the period in question, could possibly answer, nor what mutual benefits could arise from his *public reception*, but I perfectly recollect, that the *time* for the approximation of that event, was by no means

means mutual between the Queen and the Cardinal; and that expression concurs with a thousand more that were familiar to him, in proving how much, in that intrigue, the unhappy Prince laboured to impose upon himself.

The Queen's answer, No. XXVII relates to two objects made known already. The accident that befel the letter, was occasioned by the inflammable nature of the *secret* ink used by the Cardinal, of which we have seen that he sent a bottle to the Queen. As to the Abbé, his name is found in the preceding letter, which clears up what her Majesty says of her agreement with the Archduchess her sister. The most remarkable thing in that letter is the concluding sentence, as it evinces how much the Queen took to heart the business which was committed to the Cardinal's management. Her Majesty pretends that the duration of his exile, which in reality she had no desire to abridge, would be dependant on the expedition he should use in executing the commission he was entrusted with; but it is inconceivable how greatly her removal had relieved her, never had I seen her in such spirits before.

I am come at length to that part of the correspondence, wherein, for the first time, mention is made of the famous necklace. The reader, from the perusal of No. XXVIII will immediately perceive, with me, that the Queen has been long coveting that piece of female ornament, but prevented by the King's œconomic disposition, had manifested, by some means or other, to the Cardinal the most anxious desire *to become possessed of it*.

The

The note in question contains a positive avowal of her having *employed* him for that purpose.

What is it her Majesty complains of in this billet, evidently written under the influence of ill humour? That the Cardinal has not used, in the negociation she had entrusted him with, all the " mysteriousness" which she had charged him to observe. When I have developed all the circumstances necessary for an exposition of this affair, it will then be apparent, why " the slave" had deviated from the spirit of the injunctions he had received from " the Master."

It is certain that the Queen, when she commissioned him to make that purchase for her, had told him, that she would enter into " *private arrangements*" with him, but as neither his means nor his credit were extensive enough to enable him to treat so very considerable an object in his own name, he had found himself under the necessity of declaring, that he purchased on the Queen's account. And indeed it appears clearly, by the second letter, which her Majesty immediately writes to him, (No XXIX.) that, in the intervening space of time, he had owned to her the motive of his conduct, and it appears also, that on my part, I had faithfully reported every thing to the Queen. But all those circumstances will unfold themselves better, as they successively arise in their proper places, in the account which I have promised. Before I enter upon it, however, I beg the reader will form to himself a competent idea of the respective situations we then individually stood in, the Queen, the Cardinal and myself. Each in a proportionate expensive file of life, each daily reduced to extremities,

tremities, every where finding the harvest so engrossed by the Polignacs, that they had not even left for us the gleanings.

The Queen, as much from obstinacy, as through a taste for shew and splendor, passionately desirous to purchase the necklace, which, as she could not obtain, by surmounting the King's parsimony, the Cardinal undertook to accomplish for her, incessantly buoying himself up with the idea of being, the next day, Prime Minister, and, in consequence, enabled to repair his shattered fortune, and therefore thinking no sacrifice too great to gratify the inclinations or wishes of her, from whom he looked for his elevation and aggrandizement, though I was continually preaching up œconomy, and reading lectures to the Prince on that head. It is material to comprehend this last point rightly, because it accounts for the Cardinal's concealing from me, the engagement he had entered into, of procuring the necklace for the Queen. I was therefore unacquainted with this fresh piece of extravagant folly, when *chance*, not to say fatality, rendered me, in spite of myself, the chief instrument in that negociation, of which, it was intended, that I should remain in perfect ignorance.

One Monsieur Laporte, a lawyer, had, some time before, introduced himself to me, with presenting that famous scheme I have already had occasion to mention. Although that was the first time he had ever conversed with me, after explaining the object of his visit, he gave me to understand, that he was certain there was no person who had more powerful means to ensure the success of that affair, than I did,
though

through my interest with the Queen ------ I have mentioned how those papers delivered to me by Mr Laporte had been disposed of by the Cardinal, and only mention them a second time to point out the manner in which I became acquainted with that gentleman, for as every effect has its primeval cause, so it appears necessary that I should trace the origin from whence my misfortunes have proceeded.

Laporte being a very active man, and having thus gained an introduction, he attended morning, noon, and night at my house, and it seemed as if the success of the affair depended solely on my will. He frequently made a pretence of bringing me news of one of his children, to whom I happened to be a sponsor, with the Count du Creft. He had not failed to impart this confidential business to one Achette, his father-in-law, an intimate friend of Boemer the jeweller. The two last-mentioned persons happening to be at Versailles together, the former took it into his head to enquire of the latter, Whether he still had his necklace upon his hands? "Unfortunately I have," answered the jeweller, "it is a great burthen upon me, I would willingly "give a thousand louis d'ors to any one that could "procure me a purchaser for it." It is more than probable, that in this very first conversation on the subject, my name was brought in question, and that Achette made known to Boemer on what account his son-in-law had access to me, and to the Cardinal, nay, the one must, in this interview, have promised the other to procure him an introduction, for it was not long afterwards when he was mentioned to me.

I had

I had known neither of them, and I was ignorant that Boemer was jeweler to the Crown, and I was equally so that he was in possession of a very costly ornament, which he had endeavoured to sell to the Queen.

One day that Laporte had dined at my house, being left alone with me, he, for the first time, made mention of several particulars relative to the *fatal necklace*, and as he, no doubt, had concerted with Achette and Boemer, plainly told me, that Boemer grounded all his hopes on me, that if I would but "*say a word to the Queen*," he was persuaded that her Majesty would so much the less hesitate at making a purchase, she had already been desirous of, and the jewellers were inclined to assent to any arrangement that might be agreeable to her Majesty. He added, it would be doing an essential service to the jewellers, and to him (Laporte) in particular, as, in case of success, he had been promised a considerable douceur, which would enable him to purchase an office he had in view. I answered, that I had never known any thing of the circumstance of the Queen's having kept the necklace during a whole year; that, in general, I was unacquainted with what passed in her Majesty's houshold, and did not intermeddle in her affairs. To speak the truth, I should have dreaded having any concern with this business, because the Queen would not have failed to conjecture, that I had a particular interest in the sale of it. Having much more important objects to solicit, I did not chuse to afford opportunity for a suspicion to be formed, of my being one of those with which her Majesty upbraided some of those about her, saying, "*they wished to*
"*grati-*

" *grasp at every thing, and turn all to their own advan-*
" *tage.*" Here dropped the conversation the first day that Boemer was brought into question. But about a week after Laporte appeared again, renewed the subject, and met with a second repulse, I declaring to him *positively*, that I would not so much as hear it mentioned again.

Nothing can conquer the assiduities and importunity of persons of intrigue. I was, on a subsequent day, at my toilet---Mr. Achette's name was announced, whom I had never seen before. Recollecting the name, and judging he came to trouble me with the same proposals with which his son-in-law had teazed me, I directed the servant to say I was gone out, and, that he might not have a sight of me, as he crossed through the apartment, I attempted to slip out at a door that opened on the landing place, where I actually met Mr. Achette, attended by two other persons. Thus compelled to give audience, I went back into my apartment, desired them to be seated, and asked the person who introduced them, what had brought them to my house?

This Achette is a man of insinuation and adroitness, and very loquacious, after having highly extolled my generosity, my good nature, my inclination to oblige all who had the happiness of gaining admission to me, with many such introductory compliments, he presented Mr. Boemer, who, he told me, was the proprietor of that necklace, of which his son-in-law had spoken to me, that he was not come to persist in the entreaty which I had rejected, but merely with an intent to shew me that piece of ornamental workmanship, before he sent it into

Portugal,

Portugal, whither he intended to have it immediately conveyed "*It could cost nothing to see,*" as those gentlemen expressed it. I permitted them to open the casket, and after surveying the necklace, I sent a request to the Count, my husband, to come down and view it, as a curiosity

Hearing something said about jewellers, he imagined they had brought me some articles to tempt me with, and sent me in answer, that he had no money to lay out in jewels. On being acquainted, however, that his attendance was requested, not to purchase, but merely to inspect the jewel, as a matter of curiosity, he came down, cast a transient eye on the splendid bauble, and walked back, without asking a single question. I was therefore left alone with my three visitors, who looked at each other with an air of perplexity, till their orator, Monsieur Achette, renewed the conversation "Is it not a
" pity Madame," says he, " that so magnificent a jewel
' should go out of the kingdom, while we have a Queen
" whom it would so well befit, and who has so great an
" inclination for it?"----" Of that I am ignorant,"
answered I, " nor do I comprehend why you apply to
" me to convey your proposals to her Majesty ---I pro-
" test to you I have no opportunity of making them
" known to her, as *I have not the honor to approach her*
" *person*" --- " Madam," says Achette, with a sly and
significant look, " we are not come here to explore your
" secrets, still less to suggest any doubt concerning what
" you are pleased to tell us, but believe me, I am well
" acquainted with Versailles, and with what is done
" there, and when I took the liberty to bring my friend
" to

" to you, it was with a perfuasion, that if you would
" honor him with your intereft, no perfon at Court is
" better able than yourfelf to do him the fervice we pre-
" fume to folicit." Boemer's mouth was already open;
I forefaw that he was preparing to add fomething about
acknowledgement, and prefents, I therefore made hafte
to interrupt the difcourfe, and in order to extricate myfelf from the difficulty, I told them that I would fee,
whether *through my connexions*, I might not be able to do
them fome fervice *indirectly*.

Three weeks had elapfed, during which time I had
heard nothing of the difaftrous necklace, the remembrance of which had fo foon been done away, that I had
not even thought of mentioning a word of it to the Cardinal, when one day he paid me a vifit. He had on
his finger a very handfome ring, which I did not take
notice of. After talking to me on fome fubjects relating
to the Queen, of whom he made complaints, affecting
at the fame time, by his actions, to difplay his hand in
every poffible direction,---" but you pay me no com-
" pliment," fays he, " on my new ring! it is an ex-
" change I have made for odd diamonds, and other
" ftones, of which I was tired "---" 'Tis a handfome,
" a very handfome ring', faid I," " but I faw fome-
" thing finer a few weeks ago," and then told him
nearly all that I have been relating of the proceedings of
Laporte, Achette, and Boemer. I was ftruck with the air
of eagernefs and furprife that was evident in his countenance.---" It is a very ftrange thing!" fays he to me,
" Have you fpoken of it to the Queen?"----" No,"
replied I, " I would not take it upon me."---" It is very
ftrange,"

strange," added the Cardinal, " that those people should " have made application to you!"---And did they tell " you, they knew that the Queen had a great desire to " have that necklace?"---" They assured me so," continued I,---" I have some reasons to believe it,"---Here the Cardinal seemed to muse, considering I suppose, whether he should explain himself to me, and having determined in the negative, he turned off the conversation. Two or three days afterwards, I received a note from him, desiring me to send him the jeweller's address; which being unacquainted with, sent to Laporte for it. He gave my servant a written one, which he immediately carried to the Cardinal.

The well known derangement of that Prince's affairs, ----his reservedness with me, on that head,---his interrogations relative to the jeweller,----the sudden demand for his address, altogether made me immediately suspect, that his intention was, to make what they call a jobb of it, that is, to purchase the necklace, in order to convert it into money. I knew him to be extremely adroit in such *negociations* I moreover knew that he, at that instant, had much at heart the silencing his most clamorous creditors, ever since the Queen had told him, that the way to render himself acceptable to the King, was to satisfy the demands of those to whom he stood indebted, and settle his houshold on a more orderly footing He had repeatedly said to me, that since her Majesty had graciously given him that piece of advice, he was become the greatest œconomist in the kingdom, that by means of considerable reductions he had introduced into his expences, he hoped, in a few years to

be

be entirely unembarraſſed.----It was true, he added, that ſome of his debts became payable at ſo early a period, that the diſcharge of them could not wait for the rather tedious produce of his œconomic ſavings. Hence I could not queſtion but the necklace was an object which he had in view, as likely to be productive of the means for diſcharging debts of that deſcription. He came to ſee me the next morning. He ſpoke neither of the jeweller or of the necklace, but much about his own " prudence and reforms." " The Queen is in the
" right of it," ſaid he, " I was ruining myſelf. The
" King loves order and œconomy.---I was informed,
" that whenever I had been propoſed to him, for the
" adminiſtration of his kingdom, he would have had
" no other objection, than the miſmanagement of my
" own affairs; which the Queen aſſured me his Majeſty
" was well acquainted with.---In reality, ought I not to
" ſacrifice ſomething to weighty conſiderations? By re-
" trenching from my preſent enjoyments, I ſhall have
" them tenfold hereafter.---The moment in which the
" Queen is to fulfill her engagements with me, is nearer
" at hand than you imagine, ſhe is ready prepared for
" the King's anſwer,---ſhe knows he will not fail to
" exclaim againſt my extravagancies, my debts, &c.
" Then, if it be demonſtrated to him, that my mode
" of living is changed, that I have introduced order
" into my houſhold, made great reforms, cleared off
" debts with the bare ſurplus ariſing from my retrench-
" ments, then the King will have nothing to object, and
" the malicious inſinuations of my enemies will be
" ſilenced. I am meditating ſtill farther reforms, and I

" mean

" mean to practife, within my own walls, the fyftem of
" œconomy I propofe to adopt in the adminiftration of
" the ftate "----*Sully* could not argue better, faid I,
laughing; Heaven keep you in thefe good difpofitions.
I did not think fit to tell him my opinion of the matter,
fince he did not difclofe to me any thing relative to the
plan which I fuppofed him to be meditating. When
he had left me, I gave way to a few reflexions, and it
appeared to me fomewhat extraordinary, that with all
this difplay of œconomy, the Cardinal fhould, from the
ftrange idea of clearing off his exifting debts, by con-
tracting a future enormous one for an article, by which
it appeared probable he would be a confiderable lofer.

These reflexions, which had at firft originated in a
wifh for the Cardinal's welfare, recurring to me, I con-
fidered whether the purchafe of the necklace, for the pur-
pofes I fuppofed, would not bring *me* into difficulties. I
had been at firft applied to for facilitating the fale of
that ornament, *I* had given the jeweller's addrefs to
the Cardinal, there was a poffibility of his mentioning
me in his dealing with them, and a ftill greater of the
odium reflecting upon me, if the negociation, which I
might appear to be a firft promoter of, fhould be attended with any difagreeable confequences My alarm
feemed to be well grounded, from my knowledge of
the Cardinal's fituation, for little could I comprehend
how he would be able, upon reafonable terms, to make
good a fum of " fixteen hundred thoufand livres "

Maturely confidering the matter, I concluded that I
ought, at all events, to conduct myfelf in fuch a manner,
that it fhould be impoffible to fay that I had been any
ways

ways concerned in it. I therefore repaired to the jewellers, and told them, that the Cardinal, to whom I had spoken of their necklace, having sent to me for their address, I conjectured he was meditating the purchase of it, though he had not given me any verbal reason to think so: that in case my conjecture was well founded, I begged of them to remember, that I had not been in the smallest degree instrumental in promoting the sale of it to the Cardinal, that I had absolutely no concern in it, but notwithstanding this, it was by no means my intention to create apprehensions in them, but that I exhorted them, when they concluded an agreement for such sale, to take all customary precautions to insure an exactitude in the payments.

By pursuing this measure, which I thought prudence dictated, I did not foresee the difficulties I was preparing for the Cardinal. I own I had considered myself only, that I dreaded the sarcasms so liberally circulated at Court, where no transaction can take place, without a general curiosity being excited, to know what kind of interest actuates the party concerned. I must therefore acknowledge, that from my not considering the consequent embarrassment resulting to the Cardinal, from the cautionary steps I had taken respecting myself, I was the cause of that misunderstanding which ensued between the Queen and him, and occasioned him to receive the disagreeable letter alluded to. The fact was, that the jewellers, to whom I had recommended such precaution, actually followed my advice so minutely, that they compelled the Cardinal, not only to declare, that he was treating for the Queen, but even to produce a

Q proc

proof of it. This last circumstance was what gave place to the pretended bargain, which I shall presently speak of.

Before I proceed, may I be allowed to ask the severest, the most prejudiced of my readers, whether, if it be allowed, that even at that period (as it has been impudently asserted), I had cast an eye of appropriation on the necklace, I should have debarred myself from the only practicable method of getting it into my possession, by depriving the Cardinal of the means of procuring it. I ask, at the same time, whether, on the same supposition of my having, even at that period, premeditated the theft of the necklace, it was not my interest to let the Cardinal be the purchaser in his own name, instead of exciting in the Jewellers a distrust, which by necessitating the Queen's interposition, produced the *forgery*, which is attempted to be affixed upon me? The Jewellers held themselves to me, in such a manner, as to convince me, that as the necklace was a heavy charge upon their hands, they would have parted with it on the most easy conditions, to any one that had offered them a security, such as requisite they should demand. No doubt the Cardinal, involved as he was, could have named persons upon which he could have given securities that could not have been rejected. Had I not excited in the Jewellers apprehensions of being involved in the business, had I not impeded their treating with the Cardinal on his own account, he certainly would have got possession of the necklace without any difficulty, and then I could, at my perfect convenience and ease, have possessed it, without recurring to the expedient of a *forgery*.

forgery Thus there was not even a probability, whereon to ground a charge of *forgery* against me, any more than the *theft*, which was only imputed to me, because the *Queen* must be exculpated, the Cardinal exonerated, and the whole of the ignominy, of necessity, heaped on my devoted head, a severe instance of party and cabal, as I shall hereafter prove. Even now I must repeat, it is apparent as the day at noon, that had I meditated the imputed peculation, I should not have acted as I did, and have prevented the object of my desire from passing into those hands, out of which alone I could purloin it. A few particulars concerning the *pretended* forgery, will reflect an additional light on the dark transaction I am now exposing to the unprejudiced eye of public candor.

I must now make a retrospective reference to a period of time, antecedent to the date of the letter I have been adverting to (No. XXVIII.)

I have explained the motives which induced me to act as I did, respecting the jewellers, and which arose from the reflections that occurred to me on the subject, and led me to conduct myself in that manner, in consequence of the intention I imagined the Cardinal had of procuring the necklace, and in that to find a resource to extricate himself from his immediate difficulties.

Several days had elapsed, without my having heard from the Prince, a circumstance rather unusual. The Queen, whom I had the honour to see during that interval, said nothing in her conversation with me that had any reference to the necklace. All I learnt was, that she had seen the Cardinal two days before, and her

Majesty expressed her surprize that I had brought her no account of "a commission her Majesty had charged "him with." I could answer only by the truth, which was that I had not seen him since a particular day, which I mentioned. Until I received further information I had not entertained any idea that the commission her Majesty had mentioned related to the necklace. Having paid my respects to the Queen, I returned home to dinner, when my porter delivered a note from the Cardinal, wherein he acquainted me, that he should be at my house at six o'clock that evening, and requesting my being at home, because he had something of consequence to deliver to me. I sent him word I should be ready to receive him, and accordingly he came. As his absence had been longer than usual I reproached and interrogated him.---"So, so, says the Prince, you
" are curious, you want to know every thing'---Well
" then, let your curiosity be satisfied-- The business is
" done---the bargain is struck---I have purchased the
" necklace for the Queen. Don't you exclaim against
" the extravagance---I know what I am about---Besides
" it is agreed upon---In a word, I have private ar-
" rangements with her Majesty---Here is the packet,
" you must have it to-day--set off immediately."

Great was the satisfaction I felt when I found I had been mistaken in my conjectures, that instead of a bad business the Queen had adopted a very good one, in settling the Queen's inclination. I made therefore no difficulty, but said that I could wish I had wings, but contented me I took a phaeton to convey me more _____ and set out about six o'clock, whence
I repaired

I repaired to the palace. The Queen was with the *Polignacs* the persons who had access to her Majesty on such occasions, were not in her apartments: it was growing late, and I was extremely fatigued; I resolved, for these reasons, to take my repose, and defer the execution of my commission until the next day. Previous to my going to bed, according to the habit, I have said, I had contracted, I took a copy of the letter from the Cardinal, and read the whole of the conditions of the bargain with the jewellers, which he had taken upon him " to have sanctioned by the Queen's approbation." The obligations were written " in his own hand "---I entreat it may be observed, that they were " in the Cardinal's own " hand writing," and that I was ignorant of the nature of them, as of the bargain itself, till the moment the Cardinal had given me the information, and I had, at the time I am speaking of, perused the papers.

It appeared to me so much the more natural that the Queen should be disposed to sign this paper, from the circumstance of the Cardinal having said to me, as I have mentioned, that he had " private arrangements with " her Majesty." I found myself, therefore, perfectly easy concerning an affair, which, as it has been seen, had given me sufficient grounds for disquietude.

Next morning I dispatched a servant to Mademoiselle Dorvat, to know if I could see the Queen: she sent me word that the whole morning was engaged, and that she could not answer for any other moment in the course of the day. I was sensible that such an uncertainty, ill-suited with the Cardinal's impatience, and not thinking there was an absolute necessity that I should
personally

deliver the packet, provided it was delivered, I sent it to Mademoiselle Dorvat, with a note, to desire she would with all speed convey it according to its address; adding, that I only waited for her answer, to set off on my return to Paris

Two hours after, Mr. L'Esclot, Groom of the Chambers, brought me a parcel, sealed up, with a short note, in which the Queen commanded me to use the utmost dispatch, and return that same evening to Versailles. I hastened my departure in order to accelerate my return: By the way I opened the packet I was charged with for the Cardinal, and therein found the articles of the bargain, just as I had read them the day before, *unapproved*, *unsigned*, and accompanied with that letter from the Queen (No. XXVIII) which I have already twice referred to, and which is perfectly explained by circumstances since related. It is manifest, that her Majesty had agreed with the Cardinal, to negotiate *private arrangements*, but not to put her name to any bargain with the jewellers The Cardinal, who had been compelled to accede to this last condition, had written to the Queen, that it must be a matter of indifference to her Majesty to sign or not sign, since the articles and the approbation would remain in his hands. But the Queen, it seems, not having the same conception of the business, sent him back the paper, with the rebuke in the note that accompanied it

No sooner was I got back to Paris than I sent to the Cardinal, who being absent from home, a note was left with his Swiss servant, requesting he would come to me on the receipt of it. He did not come till ten at night, pretending

pretending he had been detained by bufinefs of the higheft confequence. I anfwered, I was forry for it, for he made me mifs an appointment the Queen had given me for that very evening, and at the fame time delivered the packet from her Majefty. His firft concern was to fee whether the bargain had met with the Queen's approbation. When he found it juft as he had fent it, he changed colour, and his confternation was ftill more ftrongly marked, when he read the letter with which it was accompanied (No. XXVIII) He communicated the contents to me, and talked for fome time like a man whofe mind was deranged, when on my putting a few queftions, with a view to bring him to himfelf, he faid to me----" I am forry I made a myf-
" tery to you of this bufinefs, whilft I was tranfacting
" it, you, perhaps, would have advifed me better. I
" have told you that I had bought the necklace for the
" Queen, and that the bargain was concluded.----Here
" it is, this very paper, written with my own hand,
" that you have carried to the Queen, and which her
" Majefty fends back to me, with as much ill-humour,
" as if I had departed from the tenor of the articles
" ftipulated between her and me----You fhall pre-
" fently judge whether I am in the wrong or not."

" You muft recollect, that when on account of my
" ring, you told me of the application the jewellers had
" made to you, I thought it was a ftrange circumftance.
" I did not then explain to you, why it was fo. It was,
" becaufe but a few days before, the Queen having
" told me that the necklace was deftined for Portugal,
" (how that information reached her I can not tell) and
" feeming

"seeming still to regret it, I had told her, there were
" means to possess it, without being obnoxious to the
" King, by making some slight alterations, as well in
" the pattern, as in the form of the most remarkable
" stones. These first overtures having led us into a
" more connected conversation, and the Queen's de-
" sire seeming to grow more keen, in proportion as
" she conceived it more easy to disguise the jewel, I
" had no difficulty left but about the payment, the
" means of which were far from being in her Majesty's
" power at a moment's command. I proffered the ex-
" ertion of all my abilities and credit——Her Majesty
" thanked me obligingly, and said to me, that in case
" she should accept of my offers, she should engage
" with me by *private arrangements*, with which I was
" to make those correspond that I should personally
" enter into with the jewellers. The matter seeming
" to me rightly understood, I came back to Paris, de-
" lighted with my being empowered to do any thing
" that was pleasing to her Majesty.

" The next day I sent for the jewellers address, and
" went to them immediately, under pretence of getting
" some jewels set, which I had purposely taken with
" me. The conversation once begun, I made it turn
" upon the necklace, which was immediately exhibited
" to me, and while I was surveying it, Boemer related
" to me all that had passed. I then said, I had in charge
" to enquire the price of it, and that in case the person
" for whom I should purchase, did not chuse to appear,
" I would enter into a private agreement with him

This

"This first advance, that did not wear the appear-
"ance of difficulty, being concluded, I set out for
"Versailles. That very evening I saw the Queen, I
"informed her, that the necklace was in my power,
"consequently at her Majesty's command, which I was
"come to receive. She answered (observe her own
"expressions) " I shall approve of every arrangement
"whatever that you shall take, provided my name does
"not appear in it." Thus authorized, I returned to
"Paris, sent for the jewellers, talked of bringing the bu-
"siness to a conclusion, and of settling the ultimate
"price; but to my surprise no longer found the same
"dispositions, the same eagerness in them (*) They
"raised difficulties, put questions to me, suggested
"doubts and fears ----To remove all obstacles with a
"single word, I declared that I was purchasing for the
"Queen, that particular reasons made her Majesty de-
"sirous of keeping the transaction a secret for some
"time,

---

* It is here my readers will be so good, as to recollect, what I mentioned (page 97) concerning the step
I took, with the jewellers. As I hope they will be
pleased to re-peruse that passage, I shall make no farther
observations. But is it not evident from the Cardinal's
narrative, that, had I not charged the jewellers to act
cautiously, they would have transacted with him personally on his own account, and would not have insisted
on the Queen's approbation; that consequently the *pretended forgery* had not taken place, and the *theft of the
necklace* would have been easier and less dangerous.

" time; but that I, fully satisfied with the arrangement
" she vouchsafed to make with me, was charged
" to make with them any that should be suitable to
" them, and appear reasonable to me. I then called
" for pen, ink and paper, personally drew up the arti-
" cles of the bargain, such as I knew would meet with
" her Majesty's approbation, and imparted them to the
" jewellers. They were satisfied with the conditions,
" but one of them (Basanges) observed to me, that
" being indebted a very considerable sum to Monsieur
" de St. James, they could not conclude with me,
" previously to their making him acquainted with the
" arrangement To put an end to all difficulties I then
" said to them, " Hear me, I have a means of ex-
" citing in Mr. de St James himself all the confidence
" requisite: I will bring you the agreement just as it
" now is, *approved and signed* by the Queen; but, *as she*
" *will not absolutely have her name to appear in it*, it will
" be seen by none but Mr. de St. James and your-
" selves, and shall afterwards remain in trust with me,
" till final payment, for which I must necessarily be-
" come security.-----Will you repose that confidence
" in me? Will you be satisfied?" They unanimously
" answered *Yes*-----protested to me, that setting aside
" the circumstance of the sum due to Mr. de St. James,
" they would be satisfied with my bare word.-----I left
" them, and immediately wrote to the Queen, giving
" her an account of the particulars of my agreement,
" and requesting her Majesty's approbation in the mar-
" gin to the writing which I sent to her. I observed
" to her, that seeing it is expressly stipulated, it should
" remain

"remain in my hands, her Majesty's intentions would
"be complied with, *her name would not appear*-----Be-
"hold the answer I have received:----Such is my re-
"ward for the pains I have taken, for the zeal I have
"evinced-----of the sacrifices it will perhaps cost me,
"for, in short, I am bound as security, and God knows
"whether she will pay, whether her *blood suckers* will
"leave her the means of payment.---O women---women!
"---and especially Princesses!----but worse than all of
"them, Queens!---She writes to me as to a valet,---*If
"she had not required mysteriousness, she would not have
"employed me* ----What name then does she give to all
"that I have done, if not that of *mysteriousness?*"

He was in a perfect rage, appearing every moment ready to tear the agreement to pieces, and, as he expressed it, " TO SEND THE VIZIERSHIP, WITH THE SUL-
"TANA, TO THE DEVIL." I let him, for a while, give vent to his spleen, and when I saw he was become more calm, I observed to him, that " I saw nothing so very
"offensive in the Queen's letter, as he imagined to
"himself, that to me it appeared a mere misunder-
"standing, owing to the vague expression, " *that her
"name should not be seen in it*," that though she sent
"back the agreement, she did not say she would not
"have it concluded, but seemed to intimate, it should
"be drawn up in some other manner so that the first
"thing I conceived to be done, was to consult her Ma-
"jesty, a measure so much the more indispensible, as
"on sending me back with the agreement, she had en-
"joined my return to her the same evening ---that
'seeing the impossibility of my getting back to Ver-
"sailles

[108]

" fales time enough that day, I would set off early the
" next, in order to seize the first moment her Majesty
" would be visible. I added, that I hoped to bring
" him better news, and to make the Queen understand
" what had probably escaped her in his letter, that pro-
" vided the approbation remained in his hands, her
" Majesty's name would not in reality be seen." The
Cardinal was appeased, seemed to approve of my observations, and allowed that it was at any rate necessary I
should repair the next day to Versailles, since I was commanded.---In consequence of this he gave me the agreement, and took his leave, in order, as he said, to my
setting business to rest, and being ready to depart early
in the morning.

On my arrival at Versailles, I heard from Mademoiselle Dorvat, that the Queen had expected me the night
before till after twelve o'clock, that she had been much
out of temper, and employed the whole time in writing.
A few hours after I received two lines, to this purport:
" PEOPLE CANNOT RECEIVE YOU TO-DAY, REMAIN AT
" VERSAILLES, YOU SHALL BE APPRIZED OF THE HOUR
" WHEN I CAN BE VISIBLE." This was a very formal message, which displayed very little earnestness in
the business, which I viewed as an unfavourable
omen for the success of my embassy. The next day I
went out on a visit, at my return I found a note
telling me thus: " TO-NIGHT, AT HALF PAST NINE."
I attended, almost trembling, at the appointed hour,
and had the satisfaction to find that my forebodings had
deceived me. The Queen received me with her usual
roundness, and, after having uttered a few obliging speeches,

which

addressed personally to me-----"Apropos," says she, "do you bring me nothing from the Cardinal?"----- "I have a paper," answered I, "to deliver to your "Majesty, on condition it should be demanded of me, "and to receive your commands concerning the con- "tents." Then drawing the agreement out of my pocket, I took the liberty to set before her the situation the Prince was in, the difficulties he had to conquer, the address with which he had succeeded, in bringing the Jewellers over to his terms, by giving them, in fact, no other security but his own, since he retained, in his own hands, the writing, to assure himself that her Majesty's name should never appear "I comprehend all that," said the Queen, "but I had positively told him, that I "would enter upon no arrangement but with himself, "and here he proposes to me a direct one with the "Jewellers Now (as I wrote him word) had I been "inclined to treat with them, I stood in no need of his "assistance----Now my name is actually mentioned, "it is an unpardonable indiscretion----he had better "have given me notice, than to take upon him a busi- 'ness he was unable to execute"----Might I presume 'to represent to your Majesty, that he had not foreseen 'that difficulty,----that zeal alone had made him pro- 'ceed into this negociation----that upon the first over- 'tures he had made, the jewellers seemed disposed to 'take his own personal security, but when it came to the point, they spoke to him in a manner that made him too clearly understand, they suspected him of a design to purchase the diamonds in order to convert them into money----Thinking then that he should
'equally

"equally fulfill your Majesty's views, by securing every "writing, wherein your name must of necessity be seen, "he mentioned your Majesty's name, in order to in- "duce their confidence; nor do I think that they, ap- "prized as they are, that it is your Majesty's absolute "will the transactions should be kept a secret, will dare "to mention it to any one whatever." "From all that "you tell me," returned her Majesty, "I am sorry "that I wrote to him as I did -----I will give you a "letter to him.----But is there not some degree of un- "faithfulness in his conduct?----If no more was requi- "site than to inspire confidence, was there no other "way?----HE IS PERHAPS IGNORANT OF IT, BUT I "TELL IT TO YOU, THAT I HAVE CONTRACTED WITH "THE KING A FORMAL ENGAGEMENT, NOT TO SET "MY NAME TO ANY THING WITHOUT FIRST COMMU- "NICATING IT TO HIM, the thing is therefore imprac- "ticable. See between you, what can be done, or let "us give up the idea of a purchase----IT APPEARS TO "ME, THAT THE WRITING BEING ONLY A MATTER OF "FORM, THAT THOSE PEOPLE BEING UNACQUAINTED "WITH MY HAND-WRITING-----YOU WILL CONSIDER "OF IT ELT, ONCE MORE, I CANNOT SET MY NAME "TO IT However, let the matter end which way it "will, tell the Cardinal, that the first time I see him, "I will communicate the nature of those arrangements "I mean to make with him"

To draw as an inference, from this conversation, that the Queen should have advised me to commit a forgery, might seem a kind of sacrilege Possibly, she did not form a more exact idea of what the nature of a forgery

was,

was, than I myself did, before I was made sensible of the consequences, it is likewise possible, that the observation she made of the jewellers being unacquainted with her hand-writing, did not mean that another might be substituted in its stead, for, upon farther reflection, I found it might have quite another meaning; though the fact is, that I then affixed that meaning to those expressions.

I did not dissemble, when I took up my pen to commence these Memoirs. I confessed I had committed many imprudencies---this was one of the most grievous. I can scarce plead ignorance to assist me in my justification, though it was in fact the real principle of my fault. Unaccustomed to reflect, hurried away in the vortex of courtly compliance, plunged into that kind of delirium which the spirit of intrigue diffused in every thing about me, corrupted, in short, by the bad example incessantly before my eyes, and habituated to treat too lightly all that is connected with moral duties, I saw nothing more in such a transaction, than one of those ordinary impositions which people allow themselves in the world, when they are conscious within themselves, that in reality they mean no injurious deception. "In reality what " matters it," said I to myself, " whether the jewellers " see the *Queen's* writing, or that of *any other hand*, since " they are to see it but for an instant, that it will not " remain in their hands, that it is immaterial to their " security, since they have they Cardinal's bond, and " that in case the Cardinal should not be able exactly to " make good his payments, at the different instalments, ' the Queen, who means to keep the affair a secret,
" would

" would, of neceffity, fulfil the private engagements
" which fhe affures me fhe will enter into with him."
Secretly arguing thus, and not arguing long, not being
accuftomed to very deep reflection. I determined, that
for form's fake, fomething muft be fhewn to the jewellers, which they might take for the Queen's approbation, that the Cardinal muft not be confulted about this
meafure, which he would perhaps think himfelf bound
to reject, but which he would be pleafed with me for
putting in practice, after it had produced its effect;
befides, (continuing my reverie) I am fo much
the lefs in danger of expofing myfelf as, in fact, if the
Queen did not precifely fuggeft the idea of my figning
her name, fhe left to my option the choice of the
means. She told me " *thofe people knew nothing of her
" hand writing,*" and that was what gave rife to the
idea which I fix upon, revolving all thefe things in my
mind, I drew near to Paris---my refolution was taken---
I was going on my arrival to put down in the margin,
approved by me, the Queen but upon reflection I afked
myfelf, whether or not, in cafe the Queen had not been
reftrained by her agreement with the King, fhe would
thus have fubfcribed herfelf, but could not folve my
doubt. A blunder muft however be avoided, for that
would have deftroyed the whole plan. I propofed to
myfelf to confult my hufband, who knew better
what fignature the Queen made ufe of. I dwelt fome-
time on this latter idea, but gave it up, upon recollecting all the difficulties he had ftarted, concerning the
affair of reprefenting the Queen by Madame de Cruffol.
Being returned home in this ftate of perplexity, I con-
fidered

considered whether I knew any one to whom I could unbosom myself, when Mr. Retaux de Villet's name was brought in; I was particularly acquainted with him, he was on the point of obtaining, through my solicitation, a military employment. he could hardly refuse me a service to which I affixed little consequence. I kept him to dinner, after which, I took him aside to have a private conversation with him. He was in the secret of my connections with the Queen and the Cardinal: I believe, I had even hinted to him, the political effort the latter attempted to make, by procuring, on his own credit, for the Queen, a piece of ornamental dress, which she had for a considerable time been desirous of obtaining. I told him what turn that business had lately taken, the Cardinal's embarrassment, the Queen's discontent, the explanation I had with her Majesty, and the constructions I had put upon what she said to me, when she observed that the jewellers did not know her hand writing.

I was just communicating to him the course I had taken, in consequence of that conversation, when a letter from the Cardinal was brought me, he said he was extremely uneasy, and being unable to come himself, begged to see me at his own hotel. I sent for answer I would be with him in less than an hour: that in the mean while I might assure him every thing went on extremely well.

The porter being gone, Villet and myself resumed our conversation. He told me, that "not doubting "but the Queen had made use of the expressions I had "been reporting to him, it appeared to him as it did to "me,

" me, that she meant to insinuate that it was of little
" consequence, what hand the approbation was written
" by, since the jewellers were unacquainted with her
" Majesty's writing but" added he " neither the Queen
" nor you surmise what hazard is encountered in coun-
" terfeiting the hand writing of any person. It is an act
" which the law deems criminal, under the denomina-
" tion of forgery. Doubtless" continued he " you
" would not advise me to the commission of a crime,
" but this we may do Setting off upon the principle
" laid down by the Queen, that those people do not
" know her hand writing, it is an equal wager they do
" not know what her signature is. Your idea of sign-
" ing only *Antoinette* is a downright forgery, but the me-
" tamorphose of an Austrian Princess into a French one,
" (to say for instance *Antoinette of France*) has absolute-
" ly no meaning at all Were the business indeed, to
" swindle away the necklace, whenever the villainy was
" discovered, such a signature would stand as a proof of
" it, but there being no doubt of the jewellers receiving
" their payments, since they will be possessed of the Car-
" dinal's security, secretly backed by the Queen's, I
" think one may, without great fear of detection, yield
" compliance to circumstances, which I shall do in the
" manner I am going to explain First, I shall not
" counterfeit my hand Secondly, I shall bestow on the
" Queen the inaccurate title of *Antoinette of France*, the
" writing being presented by the Cardinal, they will not
" scrutinize it and you shall promise me to own it in
" my presence when the jewellers are paid, and the bu-
" siness over. I give you my word of honour it
should

should be so, and he signed the approbation conformably to our agreement. I immediately left him and hurried away to the Cardinal's. I have said, that for an instant I entertained the thought of giving up to him the agreement approved, without telling him, just then, how I had managed the business; but when I entered his house, as he made me wait a little, I reflected that Villette and myself were not very competent judges, that the cause might be more serious than we were sensible of, and that on such a supposition, the Cardinal might eventually be drawn into a disagreeable premunire, I determined to give him a full account of the whole transaction, but first I wished to ascertain, whether, in case I had chosen not to tell him till he had made use of it, he would have discovered the imposition. My first word to him on his appearing was, therefore, "*Here it* "*is at last.*" He examined the approbation, observed nothing particular, and said to me "*Here it is at last.*" I burst into a fit of laughter, and then related all that had passed, nearly in the same terms I have been repeating it. He then looked the paper over with more attention than before---"You are right," said he "An-
"toinette of France, and Queen of the Moon are the
"same thing: but I have been taken in with it, and I
"don't think those people have a sharper eye, or a rea-
"der understanding than myself. I call to mind near-
"ly what you tell me of the Queen, I think I have
"heard her Majesty, or somebody belonging to her,
"say, that since her purchase of St. Cloud, she had pro-
"mised the King not to set her name to any thing, with-
"out first imparting it to him. But why did she not
"re-

" remind me of it when she talked of a private agree-
" ment to be entered into with me? Was I not to un-
" derstand its being written?---However you assure me
" she is appeased, that's the most essential point, the
" necklace, I hope will compleat the rest. I will go
" immediately and conclude the business, perhaps I
" shall not even shew them this paper. I have seen
" them since your last journey, their confidence is re-
" stored, I shall tell them the bargain which I hold in
" my hand is acceded to and signed, and at the same
" time shall present them with my personal engage-
" ment.'

After discoursing a moment on other topics, I quitted the Cardinal, from whom I heard nothing the next day, although he had concluded, on that very day, (30th of January) with the jewellers. The ensuing day I received from him two letters, one for the Queen, the other for myself, in which he urged my departure to Versailles, in order to deliver the former as soon as possible, and to likewise give notice, that the necklace would, in the course of the day, be at his house, that on the subsequent day he should have the happiness to deliver it himself into the Queen's hands. I therefore acted as his precursor. The Queen was somewhat indisposed, and I could not see her Majesty, who sent me a note for him, which I have lost the copy of, but nearly of the following tenor.

' Take care to be to-night at nine o'clock in the
" Countess's apartment with the box in question, and in
" your full dress, and do not go out of it till you have
" heard from me.

On

On the Cardinal's arrival I sent him this note; at half past eight he came to me disguised, and carrying under his arm the box containing the necklace. He laid it down on a beureau, and remained in expectation of hearing from the Queen, as expressed in the note. He conversed with me on various subjects, which it is needless to repeat, relative to his amours, and the sacrifices he made to politics. At half past nine, Lesclaux, that same groom of the chamber, who is said (page 102) to have delivered me a note from the Queen, her Majesty's trusty messenger, and by her employed on sundry delicate occasions, as I shall more amply unfold, Lesclaux, I say, a man perfectly known to the Cardinal, the necessary confidant of all the little irregularities, mentioned in the correspondence, came with a note from the Queen in these terms:

" The Minister, (the King) is actually in my apartment, I know not how long his stay will be: you know the person whom I send, deliver the box to him, and stay where you are. I do not despair of seeing thee to day."

The Cardinal, after perusal of the note, (written, as well as the foregoing one, by the Queen's own hand, which he but too well knew,) himself delivered to the faithful Lesclaux, the box and necklace, as he had himself laid them down on my escrutore. Lesclaux went away, saying he had orders to be in waiting at M. de Misery's till twelve o'clock. Accordingly, at half past eleven he returned with another note, of which I do not exactly recollect the terms, but was in substance, that "she was very much crossed," that "the Minister was

[118]

"to sleep with her," she acknowledged the receipt of the box, and concluded by telling him, "she would see him the following day."

All these facts being incontestible, how could the Cardinal afterwards be prevailed upon to say, in order to get himself out of difficulty, that "he did not know what was become of the necklace?" and what is still more unaccountable, what proves the absolute design of destroying me to extremes, that he should have laid to my charge the disappearance of the necklace, whereas he never entrusted me with it, but he himself delivered it into the hands of a trusty servant of the Queen's. Was it not more natural, more just, he should call Lesclaux to account for it? Yes, undoubtedly, but by bringing Lesclaux forward, the Queen would have been exposed, and he was obliged, as well as myself, to utter a word, tending to expose the Queen. There lies the mystery of this iniquity. There the fatal necklace has passed, almost in an instant, from the hands of the jeweller into those of the Cardinal, and from his into those of a well known emissary of the Queen. I hear a thousand voices crying out, *What became of it afterwards?* to which I could answer *I do not know*. and I was candid, whether it was given me to keep?—and indeed it would be impossible for me to have known what became of it, if a number of circumstances, which I am about to relate, allowed me to doubt of its being almost immediately taken to pieces; and if, from the time that I cannot declare the use it was absolutely put to, at least I should be able to shew what it was intended for. But before I enter upon a complete elucid-

da

dition of those points, the most important of all, I must resume the thread of the occurrences, following, as I have hitherto done, the order of time, and concatenation of things.

I have to run through a period of above six months, that is to say, from the 1st of February, 1785, the day on which the necklace was delivered, till the 15th of August, the date of the catastrophe.

On the 2d of February the Cardinal received a letter from the Queen, which he communicated to me, and which I could not possibly take a copy of, which is a great disappointment to the public. That letter outdid in licentiousness all that I have antecedently laid before the reader's eye. The Minister, (the King) was treated in it with an indecency, perhaps never equalled, between obscure individuals, plagued with domestic squabbles. Her Majesty set out with bitter complaints on the fatiguing and tedious ceremonies of that day, which had deprived her of the pleasure of receiving her dear slave, in the next place she spoke of the disagreeable night she had passed with the King; all her expressions were those of contempt and loathing, she particularly alluded to the vice of drinking, and the condition it reduces those to who give themselves up to it. She called upon the Cardinal to lament her hard fate, which condemned her to yield her person to the transient brutality of such a man, as she had no other way to make him do what she required of him, &c. &c. It was a very long and curious letter: it appointed no meeting, and but very slight mention was made in it of the jewel, which had been (by her) admired. But those words, few as they were,

were, proved sufficient for the Cardinal at the time, who in reading them said to me, *the vessel has sailed safe into harbour*, a proof that he understood the Queen acknowledged to him the receipt of the necklace. This he has since been pleased to forget.

Three or four days after, that is to say, on the 5th or 6th, I went to the Queen's apartments with the Cardinal, but was witness neither to their conversation, nor to what passed between them; all I know is, that they were alone, that I overheard more sighs than words, and that I concluded they perfectly understood each other's meaning.

Three or four weeks then elapsed without any thing remarkable occurring. Letters without number and without end, appointments baulked, renewed, thwarted, successful, above all, parties of going for me from Paris to Versailles, from Versailles to Paris, to Trianon, &c. &c.

It was about that time the Queen wrote to the Cardinal, that (on oath), had assured her, the necklace was at least two hundred thousand livres too dear, and that if the Jeweller would not accede to such an abatement, she was determined to return them their ornament. The Cardinal, as usual, flew into a rage, made use of abusive language, and cursed the whole set; yet what could he do? He must needs be Prime Minister. He had not laid himself under so many restraints, given himself so much pains, so easily to give up the game.——He sent for Boemer and Bassange, and communicated her Majesty's letter, which to them appeared very extraordinary. Indeed they had thought it was a bargain

is concluded, and figned, and the property delivered, the purchafer fhould demand an abatement in the price agreed upon. Such extraordinary and irregular proceedings can only be adopted by extraordinary perfonages, but that was exactly the prefent cafe. On the part of the jewellers, the fear of difpleafing on the one hand, and on the other, that of being obliged to take back a burthen which had long laid heavy on their hands, perplexed them, but the former confideration preponderated, and after much remonftrating, they acquiefced in the propofal, and confented to make the abatement.

This is a circumftance, amongft others, which my adverfaries have had the cruelty and folly to lay to my charge, and reported that it was a manœuvre of mine. In the name of common fenfe, where lay the fineffe of it?---What could it lead to?----What benefit could accrue from it to me?

It has already been feen, that when, for the firft time, the purchafe of the necklace was brought into queftion, fufpecting the Cardinal of an intent to turn it into money, and apprehenfive left I fhould be drawn into a fcrape, in the more than poffible contingency of non payment; devoted as I was to the Cardinal, I thought myfelf obliged to fee Boemer, to forewarn him, and prevail on him to act cautioufly. It has alfo been feen, what confequences had nearly refulted from my conduct in that bufinefs;---in fhort it cannot have efcaped the reader's recollection, that the negociation had, by that means, been almoft broken off. If it could be fuppofed as fome people have had the auda-

R city

city to declare, that from the very first moment in which I saw the necklace, I had formed the idea of obtaining it by fraud, it is manifest that, on the first opportunity, my conduct was such respecting it, as entirely counteracted any intention of the kind, and prevented even the possibility of ever its coming into my possession; since I was stopping the only channel through which it could reach my hands, namely, through those of the Cardinal. I flatter myself, I have sufficiently demonstrated the absurdity of the first piece of calumny my enemies have laboured to load me with.

The second is yet more absurd, if possible. What offence could they lay to my charge, what private advantage could I derive from the delivery of a letter to the Cardinal from the Queen, the purport of which was to demand an abatement in a sum which, even according to the hypothesis of my infamous detractors, was never to be paid? Without recurring to the observations already made on the subject of letters, fictitious and false, (*) such as that which it was said I had manufactured,

to

(*) What a strange extremity was the Cardinal's family reduced to, when Solicitor Target declared to them, *in full assembly*, that they had no other way of saving the Prince, than by denying every thing, even to the smallest knowledge of the Queen's hand-writing; but, as all sensible persons, who have examined the matter with an impartial eye, have uniformly observed---how can be persuaded that a courtier, who has known
the

to play off that great trick of finesse I have alluded to, I will confine myself to a very plain argument. The necklace was gone out of the Cardinal's hands. Either Lesclaux was a knave, set on by me to purloin it, or he was a faithful servant who had delivered it to the Queen that very evening. If the latter, how dare they ask me to account for it?---if the former, *Lesclaux* had returned me the necklace, thus purloined, it was in my possession---my views were accomplished---my avarice gratified. The Cardinal was security, he had entered into private arrangements---he had one with the Queen. What was it to me, whether the Queen or the Cardinal should pay sixteen, or fourteen hundred thousand livres? Nay, what was it to me, whether they paid either or neither of those sums? for if I acted a villainous part, my thoughts would have corresponded in every particular, and I had cared little, whether the Jewellers were ruined or not. Besides---I hope I may flatter myself that the reader shares the indignation I experience---Besides, I say---supposing me capable of having conceived, of

having

---

the Queen from her youth, who saw her frequently and familiarly when she was yet Archduchess, even though he had not seen her still more familiarly since her being Queen of France, and must, in his capacity of Lord High Almoner, have received orders from her hand, and an hundred times seen her writing, in the hands of twenty other persons at Court, whom he had visited, and who were likely to have received it frequently? who, but must be confidently persuaded, that her writing was as familiar to him as his own?

having executed the project of that daring theft, the moment the stroke was struck, that I rolled in diamonds, taken to pieces, is it consonant to sense, that I should have been such a fool, as to have exposed myself to a compulsive restitution? for the letter, which I am said to have had the incomparable *address* to forge, intimated that, unless the Jewellers would consent to the abatement, their ornament should be returned to them (*).

A blind fate only seems decreed, by Providence, to govern the actions of those whose wicked deeds have made them forfeit its protection, and leads them on insensibly in errors which must eventually destroy them! The slanderous

―――――――――

(*) I am so much afraid of some of my readers not attending minutely to circumstances, that I must ask pardon of the rest for the impatience I occasion in them, by suggesting reflexions which would not escape them. Here is one of a very decisive nature, and which relates also to the senseless allegation which I have already, I trust, victoriously combated. If it be wholly improbable that I should be so stupid as to forge a letter, that might have compelled me to restore my supposed plunder, that letter was however written, since mention is made of it in the trial, by the Cardinal's own council. If it could not be written by me, it must assuredly be so by the Queen, whom, alone, the price of the necklace concerned. If it was written by the Queen's hand, the Cardinal has then, on this occasion at least, seen her Majesty's writing, he could then compare it with a hundred other letters that had passed through my hands.

ous imputations which I have been already animadverting upon, are so characteristic of folly, they so manifestly discover the blind precipitancy of malice, driven to its last efforts, that had I no further proofs to adduce, of the absurdity and impotence of my opponents, I might think myself at liberty to dispense with any other arguments in favour of my innocence; but I have a superabundance; and however powerful those may be, which I can deduce from reason, I still have a greater reliance upon those which may be inferred from facts. Let us therefore proceed to facts, and to those I intreat a double portion of attention.

The second arrangement was, as I have stated, concluded upon, the Jewellers had consented to a reduction of two hundred thousand livres, as demanded by the Queen, from the price of the jewels as originally agreed for, the necklace was in her Majesty's possession, she might do with it what she pleased. It was not long before I saw my conjecture verified, that her Majesty would vary its appearance in some manner or other, so as to deceive the King; an idea, which it has been seen, was suggested to her by the Cardinal.

From that period, to the time when the charge was made against me, of having purloined that unfortunate jewel, there gradually arose clouds, which could not fail sensibly to alarm me. The appointments between the Queen and the Cardinal became less frequent---her Majesty appeared gloomy---her temper was visibly soured, and I had much to suffer personally from that change of disposition, I saw clearly that she sought, without wishing to appear active, to *punish* me

for

for the share I had in bringing her and the Cardinal on a more intimate footing, he seeming, daily, to grow more insupportable to her: I have said, *to punish*----it is no exaggeration. She, no longer, spoke to me of the the Cardinal. It was, no doubt, to practice those petty cruelties, till she could get rid of me, for I cannot question but she had already formed that idea, when she resumed that of undoing the Cardinal. It was probably, I say, with both those views, that, one day, after bestowing on me some of her *sweet* looks, she said, presenting me with a box, " Here, its a long while
" since I have given you any thing, but don't tell the
" Cardinal that I have made you this present, nor even
" that you have seen me,----*Do you hear? Do not talk*
" *to him of me.*"

My conduct towards the Queen had been certainly wrong----I avow it----I have already confessed, that in the affair of Mademoiselle Oliva, I had revealed the secret her Majesty had imparted to me, to the Cardinal, the same incitements made me, on this second occasion, repeat the same trivial breach of confidence. After I had examined the contents of the box, without being able, in any degree, to estimate the value, my first concern was, to fly to the Prince, and acquaint him with the Queen's bounty, telling him, all that had passed at Versailles, and conjuring him to be secret. After he had, in a cursory manner, looked over the diamonds, which he poured out upon his table, he said to me, " This appears to me something considerable!
" What do you intend to do with them?"----I answered, that my intention was to sell the greatest part, and have the rest set for my own use. He surveyed

them

them once more, and eventually proposed my leaving them with him, till the next day, which I did without hesitation. It was highly fortunate for me that I did so, since, by compelling the Cardinal to own, that he had sent them back to me again, I produced an indisputable proof, that I had shewn them to him, at the moment of my receiving them, and that, consequently, I had not stolen them. I withdrew, therefore, leaving my diamonds loose upon the table, and the Cardinal, as he saw me out, told me, he would weigh them, and let me know within a trifle, what was their real value. Accordingly, the next day, his Swifs servant brought them back to me in a parcel, carefully tied up and sealed, with the addition of a note, to the following purport, " I will see you to-morrow before I depart for " Versailles, and will speak to you, more confidentially, " concerning the object, I send you back: let me pre- " vail on you to part with it, as soon as possible."

My husband hitherto uninformed of, what, I then called my good fortune.------Oh Heavens!------How much I was deceived!----Before I communicated any thing of the circumstances to him, I set apart the stones which encircled the button, and those that part'y formed the drops, which I purposed selling *privately*, in order to purchase with the money they should produce, various articles I wished to be possessed of. The remainder I then gave to my husband, who immediately said, those stones appeared to him to belong to the necklace, and that therefore before we tried to dispose of them, we must disclose the matter to, and consult with the Cardinal, that probably, it would be necessary to use

prudential

prudential measures in order that the diamonds, through the quickness of circulation in trade, might not fall into the hands of Boemer and Bafanges.

While we were talking about it, the Cardinal came in, but he was then in haste, and only just had time to tell me, he would see me at his return from Versailles, and that in the interim he advised me not to shew my diamonds to any person whatsoever.

At his return he called upon me, and told me he had seen the Queen, who had not made the least mention of the necklace to him, that he could not account for her silence---that having examined the diamonds he had sent me back, he had discovered the most remarkable stones of that piece of ornament,---that he did not think it extraordinary, that the Queen should chuse to make some alteration, in its form, but that it was very much so, she had not mentioned a word to him respecting it. That it would vex him extremely, if the Jewellers should happen to hear that their piece of workmanship had thus been taken to pieces. "This would not fail,
" presently, to be the case," added he, " if you were
" to seek to dispose of those irregular shaped stones in
" Paris I therefore advise you to get them sold at
" Amsterdam Believe me, the Queen has not the
" smallest notion of the value of the present she has
" made you Those flat oval stones, not corresponding
" with the design of her Majesty's intended suit of dia-
" monds, she has looked upon them as trifles, but I
" assure you, that you are possessed of more than the
" amount of *three hundred thousand livres*, and that you
" cannot too soon, nor too privately, dispose of them."

Having

Having communicated this conversation to my husband, he approved of the Cardinal's advice, as it was conformable to the sentiments he had held of the business. In consequence thereof he, that same day, called upon a jew named Franks, who upon certain stipulated conditions, undertook a journey to Amsterdam, for the purpose of disposing of the jewels, but the troubles that had arisen in Holland, rendering the transaction impracticable at that time, the Jew returned without effecting the business. Then, it was, that my husband determined to visit England. Chevalier O'Neil, a captain of grenadiers, and a knight of St. Louis, having proposed accompanying him, they began their journey on the 12th of April.

I propose to give the most accurate and circumstantial account, of Mr. de la Motte's operations in London during that, his first visit, but as more important matters claim an immediate preference, I beg leave to postpone that account, and to give it a place at the conclusion of my Memoirs.

From the first of February to the 12th of April, to which period I have now advanced, it has been seen, that the Queen's coolness and reserve towards the Cardinal had made a rapid progress, the frequency of their meetings constantly diminished, the interviews were passed in altercations, the Cardinal had almost lost sight of the necklace; only sometimes would say to me " It is very particular
' she makes no use of her diamonds,---there's no ap-
" pearance of any of them---have you seen any thing
' new about her dress?" to all which, I answered, as the fact was, in the negative, but he now seldom spoke

S

to me on the subject. Grievances of a much more serious nature, lay at his heart. First, he began to suspect the Queen (and I believe not without foundation) of having prejudiced him in the opinion of the Emperor, from whom he now ceased to receive any communications. In the next place he reproached her with having trifled with him, in suffering *positive agreements* .... *by her*, to be tediously protracted in the execution. He did not explain the nature of them, but I .... conceived, that he meant the *promised ministry*. He besides took umbrage that the Queen did not as he expected, receive him publicly. As she was ...... less disposed than ever so to do, some people having at that time awakened all her former prepossessions ...... does this unfortunate, madly do, but determine ...... *compelling* her Majesty speedily to keep her word with him? It is impossible for my reader to surmise the method, he had formed the resolution to adopt. It will never be conjectured that it was——by making her experience *the state twos of chsice*.

He once ... imparted to me ... dream, telling me very .... "The .... stood in need of him——she could not do without him—that the only way, to compel her to give him consequence, and to get himself .... *favorite*, was to retire, and pretend ....——He amazed me and made me tremble ...

I .... not fail to make a merit of my remonstrances to him on the subject—alas! he never, at any time, gave the least regard to them, such blindness, such .... I told him positively, that it

the

the moment he was speaking to me, I could not but think him delirious, on the brink of a precipice, putting a fillet over his eyes before he took the leap. I even shed tears. ---He made no account of any thing I could either say or do.

Ten or twelve days after my husband's departure, the Cardinal set out for Saverne, fully persuaded, it would not be long before he was recalled. I was so much the more deeply affected, as he had entrusted me with a conversation, which a few days back had passed between him and Queen, and which, as I conceived must have been infinitely displeasing to her Majesty. The subject had again been about a sum of money, he was at that time unable to procure for her. In answer to something her harsh, which the Queen had said to him, he replied, (according to the account he gave me) "Madam, 'you are acquainted with the state of my affairs, ever 'since the bankruptcy of Madame de Guémenée, I "find it hard to obtain credit. Were I in a different "situation, a matter which depends on you, I should "find means and resources, which I do not now pos-'sess, and all should be at your command. Without 'elevation I can do nothing, as a proof of which, with "all the efforts of my zeal, I have not been able to get the sum you required."

He had not seen the Queen from the time of that interview, until he retired to Saverne, towards the end of April. Between that period and the 22d of May, when the Queen dispatched me to Saverne, to deliver a packet to him, of which I shall make mention, I continued to my court to her Majesty, who never spoke of him to me, but in a disagreeable strain. I plainly saw that a great deal of jealousy, was blended with a thousand other causes, to sour her temper; that the continual reports made to her Majesty of the Cardinal's intrigues, of his indiscretions, of the unpardonable imprudencies he had been guilty of, in speaking of her Majesty, to noblemen, whom he thought his friends, had exasperated her to a degree that left no hopes for the recovery of her good graces.

Matters were in this state, when on the 22d of May, as I have already observed, the Queen ordered me to set off for Saverne, and to deliver into the Cardinal's own hands, a packet which she entrusted me with, charging me to take the greatest care of it. I departed that very day. It may easily be imagined, I would have given the world, to know the contents of the packet, but it was wrapped up with a silk twist sealed every way, so that there was no such thing as gratifying my curiosity, unless I would resolve to make a confession of it, which was too delicate a point. I hoped that the Cardinal would let me into the secret, but he did not, so that I never precisely knew what the mysterious packet contained; though, by the Cardinal's dejection, I but too well apprehended, that the purport of my commission was distressing to him; and that the packet was the precursor of a confirmed disgrace. He muttered some vague complaints, informed me that he should go off to Paris the next day, without letting me know whither he was sent for, or whether it was a resolution he had himself formed, to ward off the blow that threatened him. However that was, he returned to Paris,
an

and wrote to Versailles---but was not sent for thither. The Queen's resolution was irrevocably fixed. His last piece of folly had extremely irritated her, and the Cardinal's enemies, as I had foretold, had availed themselves of his absence, to demonstrate to her Majesty, the danger of having any connection *whatever* with a man, who was *morally and physically* ruined. I particularly mark those last expressions, because, they are those, which Mademoiselle Dorvat made use of at the time, in speaking to me of the Cardinal. She, no doubt, had learnt them in the right quarter. Meantime, he unremittingly continued writing to the Queen, who did not yet chuse to discover her resentment, or who, more probably, was not yet wound up to that pitch, to which the Baron de Breteuil strove to exasperate her, and which at last he effected to the highest extreme. The Queen, indeed, sometimes condescended to write a few lines in answer to him, from which I had but two opportunities of taking copies, those copies are two notes, of the 6th and 9th of July. Although the former, does not actually coincide with the period of time, which at this moment fixes my attention, as it contains nothing circumstantial relative to a particular event, and can only point out, indeterminately, the disposition and reserve of the Queen, at an epocha so clearly connected with that of the catastrophe. I shall place it here. There is a little dissimulation, not to say falshood, discernible in it, but the reader cannot have lost sight of those letters wherein her Majesty accuses herself of that failing, which will still more sensibly be perceived in No XXXI. the last of the correspondence, when by

com-

comparing the dates, it will be apparent, how nearly that of July 19th, approaches to that of the 15th of August.

I have just now spoken of the Baron de Breteuil: it is him at present, who is going to play the principal character in the horrid drama.

I shall not repeat what I have already observed, that *retailer* of *lettres de cachet*, that thunder-bearer of despotism was the Cardinal's mortal enemy. I think I have pointed out the source of that implacable enmity. As the supreme head of the higher police, one may conceive, that with the help of fifty thousand spies in his pay, few things are hidden from him. He had, long since, been informed of the necklace negociation, and had conceived hopes of fabricating, on that foundation, the utter ruin of the Cardinal. With this view he paid strict attention to every transaction. He had several times sent for the Jewellers, who, each time, had given intimation of it to the Cardinal. The Cardinal had in consequence enjoined them to secrecy, and even advised them to say, " *that the necklace was sent abroad* " The Minister impatiently waited for the term, on which the first payment became due, in hopes of making the Jewellers publicly vent their complaints, in consequence of a failure therein, which he flattered himself would be the case. The Cardinal on his side, destitute of the means within himself, looked forward with the most anxious expectation, that the Queen would filfil, with regard to him, what he called *her private engagements*. On the 19th of July he received from her the letter, (No XXXI.) which I have announced as being the last

last of the correspondence. The very first paragraph is sufficient to give one an idea of the Cardinal's embarrassment; but I will render it yet more apparent, and adduce an additional circumstance to the many, that concur in my justification, by transcribing a *memorandum* of the Cardinal's, brought forward at the trial; and which his eminence acknowledged to have been written by his valet de chambre, by his direction, and indited by himself in these terms:

July 22 or 25, sent a second time for B. (*Boëmer or Basanges*) think it is to speak to him again, of what was said to him the first time, concerning the secrecy in question.---If sent for by the Minister (Bréteuil) let him say, "*that the matter in debate has been sent abroad.*"

These perplexed expressions, which the Cardinal caused to be committed to paper, in order to help his memory, in case of need, evidently prove that he, well informed of the Baron de Breteuil's measures, was wholly intent on securing the Queen's secret from discovery. He was persuaded, therefore, that the Queen had the necklace?---That, in whatever mode she was pleased to dispose of it, she was bound to pay for it?---Besides, the payment of thirty thousand livres on account of the interest, bespoke her intention of doing honour to her private engagements; so that, all rightly considered, the Cardinal made himself easy, and still imagined, for one moment, that he pursued the road, to what he called *elevation*. The Jewellers, after some representations, refused the 30,000 livres, in part of the interest, but accepted of them on account of the capital, and

and

gave their receipt, acknowledging to have received that sum from her Majesty, &c (*)

The Baron de Breteuil, informed of this last transaction, left no means untried to raise disquietude in the Jewellers, and before he knew from the Queen, whether or not, she had authorised the Cardinal to treat with them, he boldly took upon himself to declare, that the assertion was false, that the Cardinal had imposed upon them, adding, that they had no other course to take, but to present a memorial, preferring their complaint to her Majesty.

The Jewellers being alarmed, gave the Minister an exact account of the whole transaction. Amongst the number of circumstances which excited his attention, that of the signature, "*Antoinette de France*" was singularly striking, and that circumstance Mr de Breteuil seized with the utmost avidity. Affecting the indignation of a zealous subject, he immediately requested a private audience of the Queen, in which he set forth to her Majesty, with particular energy, the whole of the discovery he had made.

It requires no great degree of penetration, to conceive, that the Queen, thus taken unawares, did not think proper

---

* This is a third *fusse*, of the nature of those I have already had occasion to speak of. It has been said, on my trial, that I myself furnished 30,000 livres. I have not yet been able to conceive, what I could get by parting with 30,000 livres. My slanderers were never able to make it appear, so I leave it still to be furnished by them.

er to make a confidential declaration to the Minister; there was less danger in affecting surprise and indignation. The possession, or any knowlege of the necklace being once denied, could not but be denied for ever. There was no possibility of retracting, there was no alternative between exposing herself, and making a sacrifice to her own credit, of two unhappy persons. Mr. de Breteuil, transported with joy at the prospect of having his views gratified, again sent for the Jewellers, and, without telling them that the Queen had explained herself to him, urged them still closer to present a memorial to her Majesty. The Jewellers followed his instructions, and on the perusal of the first line, her Majesty cries out, with affected surprize: "*What do these people* "*mean?* I believe they are parting with their senses!"

I must observe, that the presentation of the memorial did not follow the Minister's conversation with the Queen, so closely, as those two facts seem connected, by my manner of relating them. A space of time had elapsed, between the two periods, the latter of which was the 2d of August, and of that time I must give an account.

My husband was returned from London. I have promised I would relate the particulars of his journey at the end of my Memoirs. Towards the close of July, probably the day after the step taken by the Baron de Breteuil with the Queen, I was told that my house was beset with spies. The Cardinal, to whom I spoke of it, answered "he was persuaded *his own* was, in the same "manner---that he could not conceive the meaning of "it." "If that is the case," said I, "I'll speak of it to

T

" the

"the Queen." For that purpose, I immediately departed for Versailles. I imparted, what had passed, to her Majesty, who answered me in very vague terms, and affected to turn the discourse to other subjects. In the course of conversation, she asked me, whether, in the present season, I was not generally accustomed to go into the country? Though somewhat surprised with the question, I answered, that my sole desire was to pass near her Majesty all the moments she deigned to bestow upon me, that I would never absent myself any farther than I received her express command so to do. I then withdrew in a violent state of agitation. I was sensible that my fate was linked to that of the Cardinal, and that was a reflexion which produced very melancholy ideas. I went immediately to his hotel, considering him already as the author and partner of my calamity: I informed him of every occurrence, he spoke little, appeared thoughtful, and more deeply affected than usual.

The next day, after having seen the Jewellers, who were evidently in league with the Baron de Breteuil, he returned in a rage, bitterly inveighing against the Queen. Never had I heard him, before, vent such coarse, such unguarded expressions. He was, it is true, in no danger, from giving a loose to his rage before me, but I reflected, with the utmost apprehension, that he had been as little upon his guard in the presence of the Jewellers, that he had even proceeded to discoveries of the most secret nature, and which conveyed the most indelicate ideas, that, in a word, judging from his language to me, I feared he had spoken of the Queen, in such terms, as were scarcely applicable to those beings, with whom her

Majesty

Majesty was pleased to make me take up my abode, as a reward for my fidelity. All was in an undescribable ferment, I concluded the Cardinal's ruin was absolutely inevitable, and in that ruin expected to find myself involved, when, I received from the Queen a little box, containing three bills on the Caisse d'Escompte, of a thousand livres each, and one hundred louis d'ors in cash, together with a note in her Majesty's hand writing (which note was burnt at Bar-sur-Aube, with a hundred more) purporting, that for particular reasons, which she would communicate at a fit time, and in a proper place, she desired I would set out for the country, promising that I should hear from her, and assuring me of her kindness

The Cardinal, to whom, unfortunately, I had contracted a propensity for disclosing every thing, read, in that note, the prediction of his immediate disgrace. He hurried to consult Cagliostro, and received from that *empiric*, the fatal counsels that produced his and my misfortunes These fatal counsels were to the following purport· First to prevent the Cardinal from entering into any personal negociation, for the satisfaction of the Jewellers, who would have thus been pacified Next, he instilled into the Cardinal a notion, that the Queen would never dare to open her mouth upon the business, but would be obliged secretly to compromise it. In the next place he suggested to him the monstrous idea of terrifying me, and inducing me, by that means, to remove myself to a place of security, to the end that, in case the Queen should deny her having received the necklace, he might then advance

[140]

the circumstance of my flight to a foreign country, as a most incontestible evidence, and a tacit avowal of my being guilty of committing a fraud upon the Jewellers, and being possessed of the diamonds. Such were the dark, the base, the treacherous counsels of that malignant monster---such was the unpardonable weakness of the unsteady and timid Prince, that he listened to the subtle and cruel deluder, and determined to follow his advice.

Accordingly, the Cardinal called upon me at ten o'clock on the evening of that day, and pretended he had made important discoveries. He endeavoured to persuade me, that the Queen had formed the blackest schemes against himself and me. The note and the present I had just received from her Majesty, certainly could not, by any means, appear to correspond with such a determination; nevertheless, taken thus by surprise, and being off my guard, not taking time for reflexion, and accustomed as I had been, to pay an implicit deference to the will and advice of the Cardinal, I was at this instant confounded. He seized the moment, to bear me away, by telling me, I was ruined if I did not, with my husband, take refuge in his hotel. Taking with me my waiting woman, a trusty servant, who had often been witness at Versailles, to the meetings that the Cardinal and myself had with the Queen, I blindly suffered myself to be led by this perfidious counsel, derived from the wretch Cagliostro, and leaving instructions for my husband, upon his return home, went with the Cardinal, attended by my woman, through the streets, to his hotel.

When

When Mr. de la Motte came home, the porter delivered the note I had left for him, by which, I barely let him know, that on the receipt of it he must attend at the Boulevard, where he would meet Mr. de Carbonniere, who would conduct him to me. Unable to conjecture what could possibly have happened, for he was yet ignorant of the present scene of confusion, he implicitly complied with my instructions. He found Mr. de Carbonniere attended by two Heydukes, completely armed. He was mysteriously conducted to the hotel. To the enquiries he made upon the road, he could procure no other answer, than that the Cardinal would give him an explanation. Being arrived in the Court, the Cardinal cried out: "Ah Heaven be praised! there is nothing more to fear." Mr. de la Motte came up stairs, and as he was rushing towards me, to enquire what had happened, the Cardinal accosted him with these words. "All this surprises you, because you are 'ignorant of every thing, but be under no uneasiness, 'you are now safe, I now defy the Queen, whom I "laugh at, and her whole gang. we shall see what " turn matters will take—it is late, go to your rest— ' I will see you to-morrow early, and we will talk to- ' gether on the subject."—He withdrew, shut all the doors, and carried away the keys.

My husband appeared like a man just awaked from a distressing dream. When I had explained to him the nature of the circumstances, he reproached me, in the sharpest terms, for complying with such absurd advice.

"On

"On the supposition," said he, "that it is, at best, but an absurd and unnecessary precaution, which you are advised to, but by the air of satisfaction I discovered in the Cardinal, at having us in his possession. I cannot but suspect some worse intention; and that a man of his disposition may, under such circumstances have some artifice in view, we must, at all events, as soon as it is day, get out of this voluntary imprisonment." After passing the night in forming various conjectures on the singularity of the circumstances, we had the satisfaction to see the Cardinal enter, at seven o'clock in the morning ---"It was highly necessary," said he to us as he came in "that you were removed last night, and have taken refuge with me ---I believe there is a suspicion of your being here, we shall see to night, and take the necessary precautions for sending you off to *Couvrai*, your house and mine have been surrounded all night, but there is nothing to be feared here."

Mr. de la Motte still suspecting the Cardinal of having some ill design, suggested by Cagliostro, determined not to stay till night, and said to him resolutely, "My Lord, I can make nothing of what you say, having no manner of share in your intrigues with the Queen, not likely to be called in question for them, and having nothing to reproach myself with, I have nothing to fear. You will therefore give me leave to return to my own house this very instant, where, being near my departure for the country, I have people employed packing up my things, and servants, who must be uneasy at my absence."---And indeed we

had

had, at that time, furniture packed up for Bar-fur-Aube, and the waggons were to go off the next day, a circumstance which did not bespeak much uneasiness about our situation, since we were to follow our furniture so much the earlier, as I meant to comply with the Queen's commands, and absent myself, as I thought, for some time.

The Cardinal, disappointed by the resolute air with which this answer was accompanied, exerted himself to the utmost, to bring my husband to his lure, but finding it impracticable, he said to him, " Since you " will run to your ruin, I clear my hands of it, but " wait, at least, the return of my courier, who will " bring me news from Versailles." He insisted so strongly on this point, that Mr. de la Motte acquiesced, on condition he should write a few words to his porter, to make his people easy, respecting his absence.

The courier arrived, and this was the account the Cardinal gave us, addressing his speech to my husband, of the intelligence he had brought: " Well, your " schemes are baffled, I am now certain search is made " after you, and that you will be arrested if you go " out.---The following is the course you must abso-" lutely take ---I will cause you to be conveyed to " *Couvrai*, there you shall find a carriage that shall take " you to *Meaux* The Post-master, with whom you ' must make yourselves pass as being of my retinue, will " furnish you with horses, you will then cross over " the Rhine, and come to a village in Germany, where " you will settle yourselves with a person to whom I shall recommend you There you may remain, un-
" known

"known to every body, till affairs have taken a more "favourable turn. I will provide you, however, with "a passport and all necessary letters"——"I have the "honour to tell you again," answered my husband "that I do not conceive what *I* can *personally* have to "fear; yet, as I am ignorant how far the Countess "may have carried her imprudence, in the unhappy "intrigue you have engaged her in; and as, when a "person has powerful enemies, there is no knowing "what may happen, I shall certainly not forsake her, "but share with her in her exile, if you judge it ab- "solutely necessary, but I have the honour to fore "warn you, that before I think of a journey into Ger- "many, I am determined to spend some time at Bar- "sur-Aube, to settle my affairs, and prevent the asto- "nishment and noise which would naturally take place "from so sudden and extraordinary an absence."

Here the conversation growing somewhat warm, and my husband threatening to jump out of the window into the garden, the Cardinal yielded. "You are "perverse," said he to him, "and that perverseness "will be your ruin; you are suspicious of nothing, "you do not know the people you have to deal with, "they are capable of every thing. Till to-morrow take "time for reflection——this day I will not permit you "to go out of my Lodge—this is just the hour that "spies prowl about. I shall see you to-morrow morn- "ing, if you are still in the same mind, the doors shall "then be opened to you."

The Cardinal was as good as his word, next morn- ing, and permitted the accused to depart, after taking

his

his word of honour that, let what would happen, he would not discover my place of retreat, he promised also to return that night, and to consider on the proposed journey to Germany.

He found every thing quiet at home, the porter telling him he had seen no strange face. In the course of that day, he went about his business, appeared in public, at the Palace Royal, in a word, he made himself conspicuous every where, without discovering in any place the least sign of spies being abroad. Having, the next day, some packages to send off, he endeavoured to disengage himself from his appointment with us; for which purpose, going to the Boulevard, at the stated hour, he told Mr. de Carbonniere, that he could not absolutely attend him that evening, but the next day would come and fetch me away. He then went home to bed, a circumstance extremely lucky, by producing to him on the morrow, circumstances of such a nature, as set forth, in the clearest light, the manœuvres of the Baron de Breteuil.

Early in the morning, as he was in the court-yard, viewing the people who were busily engaged in loading the waggons, Basanges, whom he had not seen for a long time, presented himself at the gate, and seeing the Count, went up to him and asked him, Whether I was in Paris?——

As what I am now relating, and what is immediately subsequent to it, is only known to me by report from my husband, I here request him to take my pen, and continue the particulars to the public, with the same simplicity,

U

simplicity, the same veracity, he used in his accounts to me, and to express himself as nearly as possible in the same terms. While he proceeds with that part of the narrative, I will collect every necessary circumstance for concluding my Memoirs.

It must be remembered, says she, COUNT DE LA MOTTE closes.

Bassenges accosting me, asked whether he could see the Countess, to whom he had something important to communicate. I told him she was at Versailles, that if he would go into the house, we could converse more conveniently, which proposal he accepted.

"What I had," said he, "to impart to your lady, "is, that I saw the Cardinal yesterday, who was greatly "agitated. I am extremely concerned for his disgrace, "and *shall be sorry if Mr. Boemer should contribute to* "*bring him into greater distress* (*). His eminence makes "complaints to us, exclaims in our presence, against "the indignity with which he is treated. However he "may in this respect be affected, the circumstance has "no analogy to the business which now requires a set- "tlement between us. Whether it was for the Queen "or for any other person that he procured the neck- "lace,

―――――――――――――――――――

* It is by Boemer that the Baron de Breteuil is plotting to turn this temperate conduct from the Cardinal. It appears to me very signi- ficant.

" lace, it matters not to us, we were not even desirous
" of knowing it One day he told us, that we ought to
" make ourselves easy, that he had concluded all the
" necessary arrangements about the payments, that it
" was just we should be paid, and that he would pay
" us. Then walked hastily about the room, writhed
" himself about, made speeches which I cannot repeat,
" and concluded by telling us, " that *since the receipt of*
" *the necklace was denied to him, he might as well deny it*
" *too*." That was certainly done, to create a great deal
" of uneasiness in us, for we have no deed, we are en-
" tirely dependant upon his integrity, and were he to
" *deny* the receipt of it, as he threatened to do, *we*
" *could have no recourse but to authority* (A lesson
" this from the Baron de Breteuil) In this state of
" anxiety, I came to consult the Countess, and endea-
" vour to know from her, what is the Cardinal's final
" resolution we wish him no harm, and should be
" vastly sorry for *the consequences that might ensue from*
' *this affair* -----BUT"-----He paused on the word
but, which to me appeared expressive It was manifest
they were pressed to render the matter public, but were
still withheld, by the fear of losing the price of the
necklace, as they were possessed of no written security
from the Cardinal to prove the purchase. The case in
reality was alarming to them, Cagliostro incessantly
urged the Cardinal to *deny* even the negociation for the
necklace In the steps taken with them, by the Queen,
at the instigation of Breteuil, she gave them no hopes
of payment, and certainly the Baron de Breteuil was
not inclined to take it upon himself. All things therefore
considered

considered, though they were no strangers to the derangement of the Cardinal's affairs, yet they knew he had so many resources, such immense revenues, if unincumbered, that they preferred any settlement whatever with him, to all the promises made by Breteuil. They were moreover so much the more inclined to close with every proposal that might proceed from him, as they were sensible, and had the candour to confess, pretty openly, that they saw they were intended to be made the instruments of the Cardinal's ruin; but the burthen of the song still was, "*in the end of all this, who is to pay us for our necklace?*" Basanges repeated this to me at least ten times. At length after a very tedious conversation, in which I had but a small share, sensible that I had no influence over the Cardinal, and being well acquainted that Cagliostro possessed it, in the highest extent, he left me, begging I would send him notice when the Countess returned. "It is to be hoped," said he, as he went out, "that she will bring "us good news."

Towards the close of the same day, I returned to the Cardinal's, who came home a moment after my arrival. I related to him the conversation I had that morning held with Basanges, in consequence of that which had previously passed between him and the two parties. He did not interrupt till I had concluded, and I observed, that in the progress of my relation, he grew warmer and warmer. He began to inveigh against the Queen, in terms of severe reproach, scarcely applicable to the most dissolute, and at the same time most disgustful of common creatures. It would be offensive to all who have

the

the least sense of delicacy to present to their view, the shocking images which his momentary rage and distempered imagination at that time delineated. I shall confine myself to saying, that more than once, not only before me, but in presence of other persons, the incensed Cardinal allowed himself to express in the coarsest terms, and with the most indecent particulars, circumstances which created loathing and disgust even amongst those scenes of fancied enjoyment, which his ambition had made him so eager to obtain. The declarations, of this kind, repeatedly made, during the impetuosity of the Cardinal's passion, before several witnesses were, no doubt, deemed too atrocious to be forgiven, and certainly are a sufficient explanation, and if I may be allowed to say so, some excuse for the cruel proscription which an implacable female resentment occasioned to be pronounced against him (*)

I thought

---

* Unhappy Prince! no doubt but he knew it to be so, and to whom was he indebted for that knowledge? To the Countess, who seeing him under the influence of the most ungoverned passion, said to him, nay repeated to him on ten different occasions, that he had but one means left to save himself, which was, to throw himself at the King's feet, and disclose the whole business, except what ought to be concealed from him as a husband. That was, to represent his intercourse with the Queen, as a mere matter of policy, in which he had been led by his ambitious views, and in the course of

which

[150]

I thought he never would have ceased, however he found himself weary, and after an inconsiderable rest, he again introduced the subject of the journey to Germany, which was what Cagliostro had most earnestly recommended. I was really deafened with the violence of these errors during the ebullition of his rage. I confessed however, that the Countess must, of necessity, assent herself, and that I should disoblige her if I did not accompany her: in a word, as it was necessary some resolution should be taken in that end, I told the Cardinal that I consented to go into Germany, but that it was an indispensible proviso, that I should previously pass a few days at Bar-sur-Aube, and that during my stay there, I would spread a report that I was going to Spa. The Cardinal again talked of danger, perverseness, and obstinacy, but I would not recede the least from my intention. He then took up a card on which he marked down the day of my departure from Paris, the

————————————————

which he had, in order to gratify the wishes of her Majesty, extended his credit beyond his abilities, and through other circumstances in the purchase of the necklace. Ten times had he promised her, that he would ask her advice, and as often did the infamous Cagliostro assure him now it. It was that vile empiric, who was really the ruin of the Cardinal, my wife and myself. His insatiable covetousness, by opposing the Prince's entering into terms with the Jewellers, as he had promised, was what especially brought on the catastrophe.

the time of our progress to Bar-fur-Aube, that of our stay there, and lastly that which it would require to convey us to Germany. The whole time necessary for these purposes was estimated at 14 or 15 days. He gave me directions what route we were to pursue, and an account of the place at which it was purposed we were to settle; but as to the passport and letters he had promised me, Cagliostro had observed to him, not without a degree of reason, that, if after accusing us with having defrauded the Jewellers of the necklace, (*) it were discovered that he had been assistant to, or winked at our flight, the circumstance would inevitably fix him as a partner in the guilt. He therefore told me, with respect to those documents, that I no occasion for them. We then left him, without urging him further on that head, as in truth, I was far from being resolved on taking the journey to Germany, which in fact I saw no necessity for, and indeed at this time the Cardinal's conduct

---

* This mean evasive manner, was not in the Cardinal's disposition, but Cagliostro so well prepared him, that at the moment when the King had occasioned him to be arrested, he repeated like a parrot the words taught him by that wretch, " I have been deceived by a wo-
" man named Valois de la Motte, who I am told is
" gone abroad "---He believed we absolutely were, and hoped that by means of the instructions he had given us, we should not be discovered. In the mean time, as it will be seen, we were quietly seated at Bar-fur-Aube, knowing him to be in the Bastile.

duct appeared to me extremely suspicious. The event has manifested that the doubts and distrust I then entertained, were but too well grounded.

That candidous declaration which he made to the King, at the moment of his arrest (a declaration, so ridiculous, when all the circumstances previous to it are considered) produced, without the least advantage to himself, the most fatal effect to us, who were far from conceiving, how we could be involved in his disgrace.

We were at B⸺-sur-Aube, where we had already passed a fortnight in perfect quiet. On the 17th of August we visited at the Duke de Penthièvre's seat, at Château-Vilain, it was the eve of that Prince's departure. Thence, we had taken the road to Clervaux, where we arrived at the close of the day. We had just received information, that the Cardinal was in the Bastille, and on that bare information, if we had been conscious to ourselves of any criminality, we were at liberty to have embraced so favourable a moment to evade all pursuit. We had with us at the time all our diamonds, a good carriage, four fresh horses, and four more that had brought us from Château-Vilain, we might that very night have escaped out of the kingdom——but what did we do? We returned home to B⸺-sur-Aube.

In consequence of the intelligence we had just received, the first care, I ought to say, the first duty of the Countess was, to burn all the letters, or notes, she recollected to have in her possession, either of the Queen's or the Cardinal's which employed her two full hours, before she went to bed. The next day, 18th, when I rose, I perceived her office was ashes, which I took up
to

to throw into the fire-place. I had scarce done, when my valet acquainted me, that two gentlemen desired to speak with me. Being introduced, one of them told me to make no disturbance, that they had orders from the King to seize on all my papers. Without the least opposition, I delivered up all the keys of my escrutores, chests of drawers, &c.

While they were employed in securing all the papers, which they put into a box, and which I sealed with my own seal, the Countess was rising. One of them took me aside, and told me, they had orders to take the Countess into custody, who was to be present at the breaking open of the seals. That she need not be terrified, as they should take her to the Baron de Breteuil's, where matters would presently be settled.

I imparted this circumstance to her, which she heard with great composure, asking only for time to prepare for the journey. I asked those men, whether I was free to accompany my wife? They answered, that they saw no impropriety in it, pursuant to which, I went into my apartment to dress, and ordered the carriage to be prepared. When I returned to them, they observed to me, that if I went off with them, it would be believed they had orders to arrest me, with the Countess, that it would be more eligible for me to stay a few hours in town, to appear publicly, and then to follow them. " Besides, said they, you have better horses
' than we have, we go no farther than Nogent to-night,
' it will be easy for you to overtake us." In consequence of this advice, which to me seemed rational, I determined to stay, intending to follow them in about two hours.

hours---Would to Heaven I had done so, it will shortly be seen, of what consequence that would have been to the Countess and myself.

I had hardly lost sight of the carriage, when I shut myself up in my apartment, situated in a wing, opposite to that which contains the apartment of the Countess. I had in it an escrutore, made at Paris, by my direction, with a secret place to conceal money or papers. The exempts had searched it, but had not discovered this security, which was very ingeniously contrived. At the time of our last removal from Paris, the Countess had put some papers into it, which she chose to conceal from me; and luckily, when she laid her hands on all she thought she had been possessed of, in order to burn them, she had not recollected those she had placed in this repository.

When the exempts had searched that escrutore, they had found a small pocket book containing 35 thousand livres worth of bills on the Caisse des Formes, and had made seizure of them, though I had strongly remonstrated that those papers were bills, and not any papers they could be in search of (*) Their answer was that their

———————————————

(*) It is almost superfluous, no doubt, to point out a second time to the observation of the reader, that, if we had thought it possible, we should be brought into question in the smallest degree, by the Cardinal's disaster, it was easy for us to secure those effects, our ready money and bills, from the search of the Police, but their orders were to seize *all written papers*, without regarding what they were.

The Baron de Breteuil personally informed of the whole correspondence, as we have seen that he gave broad hints of it to the Countess, was persuaded, that among her papers would be found letters from the Queen and the Cardinal, and had forbid his emissaries to cast a profane eye upon them, to the end that, himself being sole master of the Queen's secret, he might make a merit with her of his discretion and activity; but

---

but our attention had been solely confined to papers which might be liable to expose the Queen and the Cardinal, and indeed papers were the only thing sought after. This circumstance, gave room for a remark made by the Countess on the morning of her entrance into the Bastile. Mr de Crosne, the Lieutenant of the Police, coming to interrogate her, told her, that the Cardinal accused her of having defrauded him of a necklace, under pretence of the Queen's having a desire for it. After signifying to him her surprise, she said, she could not imagine how the Cardinal could have accused her of a thing, he knew to be false, that however, even admitting the fact, she wondered, that instead of seizing on all her *jewels*, in order to ascertain the crime, and convict her, they should have confined themselves to a strict inquisition after all *papers* in her possession, a very needless proceeding in such a case. It was on that occasion, that she insisted on producing all the *jewels* the Exempts had left in her escrutore

but chance had otherwise directed. Casting my eyes upon the escrutore, which I had just seen so scandalously plundered, a thought came into my head to open the private recess, when, I was not a little surprised, to find in it a parcel of papers, wrapped up, tied round with packthread, in a bag that had held money. I locked my door, examined those papers, and judging them to be of serious consequence, I was at first tempted to burn them. Providence held back my arm.

The Duke de Penthievre passed through Bar-sur-Aube, that morning; an officer in his retinue, whom I met, as I was returning from handing the Countess to her carriage, acquainted with what had just happened, told me, that in a business like the present, I should be to blame to remain as unconcerned as I seemed to be, and that the most prudent course I could pursue was to secure myself, till I heard what turn things were likely to take; my relations and friends whom I saw in the course of the day, gave me the same advice. I, in consequence, resolved to pass over into England, where I had formed connections during my first journey, and had left some diamonds, which it was natural I should procure.

The Countess set out at eleven o'clock in the morning, I took my departure at ten at night, with a hundred louis d'ors in my purse, and two parcels of pearls, *** shall be spoken of hereafter, leaving with my brother in law, all my jewels, those of the Countess, *** the keys of all that belonged to us. I saw my *** as far as Meux where we parted. I gave her my address in London, persuaded that the first letter I received from her, would give me intelligence that the Countess was at liberty, and waiting for me at Paris.

I arrived at Boulogne on Saturday evening the 20th of August, on Monday the 22d, about twelve o'clock, I embarked, and being arrived in London, alighted at the same hotel I had lodged at when I previously came over to England. My first visit was to Mr. Gray the Jeweller, with whom, as I before observed, I had left some diamonds to be set in a necklace and ear-rings, intended, when I delivered them to him, for the use of the Countess. I found them completed, and had it not been for that resource, I should have been reduced to the last extremities of want, having supported myself a considerable time on the produce of them.

Three days after my arrival, I found out Mr. Linguet the counsellor, to whom I gave a faithful account of the whole affair, as I have now related it. He advised me not to make myself uneasy about the fate of the Countess, as, by what he had learnt from persons well informed, the Queen's intention, apparently, was merely to ruin the Cardinal, and that the necklace had served as a medium and pretence. He further advised me to send my servant to my sister, at Paris, in order to gain intelligence of what passed, as nothing could be done, he said, till certain information was obtained, in consequence of which a plan of future conduct might be laid down.

The next day I sent my valet de chambre, who the
moment

moment he got to Paris was taken up, nor have I ever seen him since.

Two days after this, an Irish priest paid me a visit, he was a friend of M'Dermot's (*) and told me the latter was at Lancaster, that if I had any thing to impart to him, he would write to him that day, and would take charge of any commission. I returned him thanks, but declined his offer.

All my acquaintance were out of town, and I was greatly at a loss how to pass my time, on parting with the Irish priest, who, no doubt kept his eye upon me, I repaired to the Hay-market theatre. As it rained when the entertainments were over, I took a hackney coach home. Scarce had the coach reached Picadilly, when I received so violent a blow upon my head, that I was stunned for some moments. Luckily I had a round hat on, which had partly warded off the stroke, and prevented my receiving further injury. At first I thought the coach had overturned, but recovering, and finding it was going on, I endeavoured to find out what had given me so rude a shock. Turning myself round I perceived a hole in the back glass, and rising to examine it, I saw a man with both hands on the straps by which the servants hold. In one of his hands he held, what I took for a cane, I then conjectured that the man, attempting to get up behind, as is frequently the case, and missing his aim, the point of his cane had struck

---

(*) It will presently be seen who this M'Dermot was, and the part he acted in this affair.

struck against the glass, broken it, and with the force given me a blow. I therefore replaced myself on the back seat, and inadvertently threw myself into the right hand corner, in doing which, chance befriended me, more than prudence, for in the instant the coach turned down Duke-street, to pass into Jermyn-street, where I lived, there came through the same hole, the blade of a sword, which passing on a level with my eyes, broke the glass of the window on that side whereon I sat. Had I been seated towards the middle, in a less recumbent posture, the weapon would certainly have pierced my throat. Apprised at length of the danger I was in, and having no arms, I pulled the check-string, upon which the coachman got down, I made him observe the two glasses broken, and a man running away full speed, but not knowing a word of English, and only able to express myself in dumb show, the coachman again got upon his box, without being able to understand any thing more, than that I had broken his glasses, the payment for which he demanded, as soon as he had set me down at the hotel, where I at last found some one who could understand me. I related what had just happened to me, and received in answer, barely, an advice to take care of myself. On the morrow I saw Mr Linguet, who said to me that my life was not safe in London, that the stroke was levelled at me, either by the Queen, or the Cardinal, that I had as much to fear from the one as the other, that he comprehended why my existence disturbed them equally; but in short I must absolutely conceal myself in the most sequestered place, taking care to remit my address

to

to her as soon as I had fixed upon a residence, that he might be able to convey to me whatever news my valet de chambre might bring back, and direct me what course to take, as circumstances should point out.

I departed the same day, with a servant for my interpreter, who never left me from that moment until my return to London. After having wandered through various places, thinking that M'Dermot might be serviceable to me in such a critical juncture, I determined to go to him at Lancaster, where arriving, I was told he was at a place twenty miles distant. I went thither. He was greatly surprised to see me: he knew of the melancholy adventure of the Cardinal and the Countess, and imagined that I was also in the Bastile. During this interview and the succeeding ones, I entrusted him with the particulars relative to the intrigue between the Queen and the Cardinal, and revealed the affair of the necklace, with all its circumstances. I shewed him that which I had just taken out of the hands of M. Gray, as likewise the ear-rings. Generally speaking, I laid myself open infinitely too much, and what followed, evinced, that as fast as I supplied him with information, I did but stimulate in him a desire of making his advantage of it. Accordingly, after two days communication on my part, and consideration on his, he advised me to cross over into Ireland, and assume another name. He furnished me with various letters of recommendation, and we agreed upon his setting off next day for London, where he should see Mr Linguet, and send over to me my valet de chambre's dispatches: in short, that in all occurrences whatever, he
should

should so act as to prevent or rectify any circumstance that might militate against me. Thus we parted at Lancaster, nor did I hear any thing of him afterwards, till I was given to understand, that the Cardinal had sent for him, at a great expence, to put his name to a deposition, prepared by Target the lawyer. He had already began his impostures and treacheries at London, where depositions had been dictated to him, which are a collection of ill-contrived *falsities*, so demonstrated to be, by *facts* (*). And yet upon such a basis of falshood,

---

(*) The Capuchin, M'Dermot, having given in a deposition at London, at the instigation of Carbonnieres, afterwards repaired to Paris, at a vast expence, to bear evidence to a heap of falshoods that proved nothing. I am going, on this occasion, to relate the behaviour of the Solicitor and Recorder, in endeavouring to intimidate the Countess, when she entered the Council Chamber. She perceived in the countenances of those two gentlemen a certain gloomy aspect, a dejected air, which she had not before perceived. The Solicitor, Dupuis de Marcé, addressed her in these terms, and with a ghastly tone of voice. " Madam, I " am sorry to tell you, that you are going to be con-" fronted with a person that comes a great way off, " and whom you undoubtedly do not expect." The Countess, imagining, at first, that it was me, repeated what she had said a hundred times before, that my presence could not but be advantageous to her, persuaded that I should speak truth and convict the Cardinal.

" Madam,

hood, does the shameless Target, raise the ridiculous superstructure of that bombastic memorial, which forced tears

---

' Madam, I am afraid of throwing you into fits.
' Be not afraid of any such thing," answered she, " the
" presence of that person cannot but give me plea-
" sure." Seeing at last, that he could not succeed in
intimidating her, he said to Fremyn, fetching a deep
sigh, " go then, Fremyn, and bring that person here."
Fremyn got up, went and opened a door, through which
the Countess saw a hypocritic looking figure come close
up to her, with his eyes cast upon the ground, at whose
first sight she exclaimed " What! another wretch
to the purpose of subornation! let us see how well
this being is instructed." They first read over to
him his own deposition which had certainly been drawn
up to the lawyer Target. Accustomed as she was to
hear this language daily, she perfectly knew again the
stile and phraseology of a man, versed in chicanery. At
the conclusion of the reading, which she often interrupted,
by observations tending to humble the villain, and express
the contempt and abhorrence she was inspired with,
against those who had any share in such iniquitous prac-
tices. She said, that deposition was a heap of falshoods, abominable lies, and that he who was so infamous as to utter them, deserved exemplary punishment
As he was upon proceeding on the secrets, he said I
had imparted to him, concerning the connections of
the Countess with the Queen and the Cardinal, she re-
p

tears from the Cardinal, when he saw that every thing in it was false.

Every

---

presented to him, that since I reposed so great a confidence in him, I must have told him the place of my concealment. She insisted on obtaining from him a declaration of it, that I might be brought face to face with him, to which he answered, that he knew nothing about it. Dupuis de Marcé and Fremyn, who had their views in finding her guilty, often said to her (especially when she pressed her arguments home upon the Capuchin, and used expressions suited to his villainy,) " But, Madam, you cannot tell what your husband may " have told the Abbé M'Dermot in their conversations " together. he is a man of integrity, incapable of com- " ing hither to deceive." " We shall see that presently," " said she, " since Mr de la Motte is not here to con- ' vict him in those points that concern himself, I am go- " ing to do it, from the observations I have made upon " his deposition." He had told a long-winded story about the jewels, which he said, he had seen me have, at my first journey to London. The Countess had taken notice of a number of absurdities, among others, of the mention he made of a superb pair of shoe buckles set with brilliants. Luckily I had left them at Bar-sur Aube, and they were deposited in one of her boxes, at the Bastile. She had them brought, not without great difficulty, and the knavish Friar was humbled at the sight of the *superb jewel*---worth about *two guineas*, so it

fared

Every body knows that he rejected it, forbad its appearing, solemnly denied the whole contents, and cried out in his indignation, that he would not be made to appear a fool.—To which Target replied, " My Lord, your family, will have it so, there's no other way for you to save yourself."

Being arrived at Dublin, I, in person, delivered the letters I had received from M'Dermot to their respective addresses, was perfectly well received, and in a few days introduced into the genteelest companies. I had even an opportunity of seeing the Lord Lieutenant, who made a number of enquiries concerning the Cardinal's situation, and said some polite things to me, among the rest, that when he was in town (for he then resided chiefly in the country) he should be glad to see me. In the course of the conversation he affected to admire a steel chain which I wore to my watch. To this hung my seal, which he examined, a circumstance that left me no doubt but he knew who I was. It will be shortly seen, by the secrets Court d'Adhemar afterwards disclosed to me, that I was not mistaken.

I had been about three weeks at Dublin, without hearing from M'Dermot, which made me very uneasy,

---

*** *** of no evidence. After she had used him as *** ***, she told the Collector, that she supposed *** *** would send for the cobler at the corner of *** *** to give evidence against her, having made this *** *** to the place concealed and enraged at *** *** of the conduct

easy; but if he did not write to me, he did to others; and appeared inactive with regard to me.

I was often invited to parties of pleasure in the neighbourhood of Dublin, to which I used to resort without the attendance of my servant. I one day returned from one of them much indisposed, I lost my appetite, but attributed my condition to the uneasiness and vexation which preyed upon me. Dragging every where a listless existence, suspecting that I was known in Dublin, in a word, tormented by unpleasing presentiments, though very lucky ones for me, I resolved to quit that island, and pass over to Scotland. I told my acquaintance I was going to see the famous Lake of Killarney, that I should then take Cork in my way back, having an inclination to view it. Pursuing a direct contrary road, I got to a small sea-port town opposite the coast of Scotland. My disorder grew every moment worse, I was not to be known again. I had been eighteen days without performing the most natural and indispensible functions of nature, when I arrived at Glasgow. I sent for a physician, who after much examination and questioning, told me there was something very extraordinary in my malady, which he could make nothing of, and that he advised me to repair without loss of time to Edinburgh, where I should meet with more assistance from the faculty, than in any place in the world. In the mean while he gave me some cooling draughts, that proved ineffectual. Arriving early next day at Edinburgh, I sent for a physician and a surgeon, of the highest repute, who having consulted together for a considerable time, left me, saying they would come again next day,

to

... judge of the effect produced by the medicines they would feed me. The next day I found myself much worse, and a few days after I was not able to leave my bed. It was at this utmost extremity, I discovered, by their questions, and the medicines they administered to me, that poison had succeeded a disappointed assassination, they telling me, that eight days later, it had been impossible to save me------Whose hand had directed the murderer's steel? whose hand had filled the poisoned cup?------What follows will but too clearly point it out. The French Ambassador left me no doubt----I shall not explain myself more clearly, as presently it will be seen, he himself did it,---but ...

The consequence of this second attempt upon my life was putting three months to my bed, and between four and five, without leaving my apartment, during all this time I heard not one word of the Cardinal's ... When I was in a condition to bear reading, my servant proposed bringing to me a master of languages, whom he met with every day, at the tavern, whence my table was provided, and to prevail with me to receive him, he told me, the man taught Italian at the Dukes of Gordon and Buccleugh, that he daily heard me talked over, and that I might without affectation draw form him interesting particulars. Had I been sure of getting intelligence, I could have penetrated to the centre, I therefore relished the proposal, and sent for the man that same evening, to whom I said, that by way of recreation, I had an inclination to learn Italian. He was very loquacious, and without

my

my, leading him to the topic I wished, he blended, with his medley of news, the names of the Cardinal, of the Countess de la Motte, of Cagliostro, told me, there had appeared Memoirs under those three names, but that was the extent of his knowlege. As I had noticed at Glasgow, that a certain coffee-house took in the Leyden Gazette, I took coach and went thither, when calling for the whole file of papers, I turned them over hastily, and with a surprise equal to my indignation, saw, by fragments from those memoirs, the insidious turn that had been given to the defence of the Countess. I cursed, without knowing him, the senseless or knavish lawyer, who had so absurdly or basely perplexed a business, of itself so plain. I spent two days and two nights, in writing out all that seemed to bear on the most essential points, and then returned to Edinburgh, firmly resolved to dispatch an express to Master Doillot, whom I was not acquainted with, and whom I still less knew to have been chosen and directed by the Baron de Breteuil. The circle of my acquaintance in Edinburgh being rather contracted, *I unfortunately* (*) cast my eyes on the Master of Languages, who being in almost a

starving

---

* Very unfortunately indeed. This was still worse than M'Dermot. The man I am speaking of, and who is to act so atrocious a part, in what I have left to relate of my personal concerns, was an arrant adventurer, who went by the name of *Benevent*, but known in England by that of *Costa*, for which he had exchanged his real name of *Mus..*

[163]

starving condition, seemed likely to be disposed for undertaking a journey, that would bring him some pecuniary advantage.

As he, immediately on my return, took it into his head to tell me a long story of his misfortunes, a tale he had already repeated over and over again, I embraced the opportunity to hint to him, that I had it in my power to render him a service. I disclosed myself to him, and proposed his taking a trip to Paris, in order to deliver to a lawyer, some papers I would entrust him with. His answer was an offer of doing any thing that might be pleasing to me. Next morning he came to tell me, that he had considered of my proposal, that since the delivery of a parcel, was all that was requisite, I say he could perform the business as well as himself, nay better, as she would be less liable to suspicion, and her journey would be attended with less expence. I was satisfied with his desire, wrote a letter to Master Dolet, in form of a memorial, in which I informed him of all that had happened, asked counsel of him, relative to the conduct it was necessary for me to adopt, and positively assured him, I was determined to return to Paris, in order to show myself, to defend her, and to speak the truth, if forced to it. Those were my expressions (*) I added that I only waited for his answer to enable my departure.

I sent

---

* The doting old Dolet, in his Memorial, which he drew up in consequence of here, but still under

I sent this Costa to take a place for me in the coach for Edinburgh, gave his wife the money necessary for her journey, delivering the packet destined for Doillot, and added necessary instructions to prevent her meeting with disagreeable incidents. She set out the following day, the second or third of April, 1788.

On her arrival at Paris she procured a conveyance to the Sieur Doillot's, to whom she signified her being possessed of papers of consequence, intended for him. The old, squint-eyed, clownish fellow, whimsically fancied, that he discovered this woman to be a man,—— a spy in petticoats, and refused to speak to her, until she had undergone an examination by his wife: an inquisition, which Madame Doillot very gravely made, and on that lady's report to her spouse, of the *regular conformation* of the said messenger, the limb of the law vouchsafed to examine the writings, which he

the murderous influence of the Baron de Breteuil, who had forbid him to mention the Queen's name, and charged him to criminate the Cardinal without restraint; that venal idiot, I say, quotes, in his wretched rhapsody, intituled " A Summary, &c " the identical paragraphs in my letter. He there says in italics, that I am " *determinately disposed to attempt every thing practicable, to unite my fate with that of my wife.*" But that is swallowed up in a flood of lies, the more criminal, as he knew the truth, and the Countess had given him, in writing, all the particulars, exactly as we now relate them.

he also found in proper order. He then advised Mrs Costa to remain at the hotel where she had alighted, till she heard from him. What does this faithful counsel of the Countess next do?---instead of immediately sending back the messenger with the answer, which his employment by the Countess required he should send me, instead of affording her time to get out of the kingdom, before he communicated my letter, in case he thought himself obliged so to do; he, that instant, flew to the Baron de Breteuil's, pitifully, to know his orders. He called, in his way thither, at the Lieutenant de Police's, to prepare him for the reception of such orders, and fearing that the police, accustomed to secrecy, would not ring an alarm, he officiated himself, by proclaiming, wherever he passed, that he had received letters from Count de la Motte, who was coming over to surrender himself a prisoner! What was the consequence? the Countess far and wide informed that I was preparing to quit France, in order to *speak the truth*,---the truth was to meet family a thunder-bolt. How could the blow be warded off? by applying *secretly*, yes, very secretly, to the Count de Vergennes, who while affecting desirous to have me in his custody, employed all the petty resources of his obliging politics, in reality to prevent my appearance. I readers will certainly express signs of the utmost contempt when they presently understand the methods used by this then great statesman, though now so *little*. The truth is, that notwithstanding what the romancing Countess has freely told me, he (de Vergennes) heartily hated the Queen, and, if I am not mistaken in the conjectures I have formed, and which are not wholly
con-

confined to myself, he had reason to rue it on his death bed. Hating the Queen, he was consequently the secret supporter of her enemies. The Cardinal was become one of them, he must therefore be supported; but that could not be done, if Vergennes had openly declared himself, he therefore found it consistent with prudence and his own refined policy, ostensibly to blame him, at the same time that he privily took means for his safety, in proportion so he exaggerated his crimes.

Let us revert to Doillot and Breteuil: all those honest people ought to be coupled together. The *ministerial Baron*, after taking a few days consideration, sent for the lawyer Doillot, and told him, he might write me word, that the best course I could take, was to repair to Paris, without a moment's loss of time, and to assure me, in his name, that I had nothing to fear. Doillot accordingly wrote the same day, and personally delivered the letter to Mrs Costa, charging her to set out, and to use all possible speed. Pursuant to his directions, this female courier began her journey back on Easter Sunday, 1786 --- but she proceeds not far.

Whilst the Doillots and the Breteuils were concerting measures, without properly understanding each other, the crafty Vergennes had dispatched a messenger to Count d'Adhemar. The scheme was, then, to secure me at Edinburgh, and a *Secretary* of the *Ambassador* was charged with the honorable commission. The business was to secure me, *dead* or *alive*, but the former was infinitely preferable, so that, had the Secretary (whose name was d'Aragon), proved successful, I certainly never

should

should have seen Paris, an assertion I shall shortly render more than probable.

This resolution once formed, it became necessary to avoid putting me on my guard, and consequently Costa's wife was to be prevented from delivering to me Doublot's letter. Mr. de Vergennes provided against all those obstacles; he let her depart, and when at a certain distance from Paris, he caused her to be arrested, and carried to the Bastile, where she was detained two days.

During these transactions in France, I perceived in Scotland, that I was dogged about and watched. I imparted my observations to my *worthy* companion Costa, who was already in the Ambassador's confidence, and had been honoured by several interviews with d'Airagon. He answered me, there was no probability of such a circumstance; that my uneasiness might present to my imagination, objects which had no existence; that however, if I did not think myself safe at Edinburgh, I should do well to change my situation, and immediately proposed the town of Newcastle upon Tyne for my retreat. The truth was, he had met with too many obstacles to the execution of his orders at Edinburgh, the seizure of my person, which he was commissioned with. He flattered himself that by drawing me to a less considerable town, where I had no acquaintance, he should more easily effect his purpose. I fell into the snare, and set out for Newcastle. The kidnapping *d'Airagon* the same day took the road to London, to carry information to the Ambassador, of the fresh dispositions taken by Costa, and as the expence of cou-

... was an object of no consequence in so capital an affair; Count d'Adhemar dispatched one to the Count de Vergennes, to inform him of the new turn matters had taken. When this *Pacificator of Europe* heard, that the scheme had been obstructed at Edinburgh, judging the farther confinement of Mrs. Costa needless, he had her brought secretly out of the Bastile, escorted by two exempts of the police, who took her to the Baron de Breteuil's. That minister, whom the Countess so well pointed out, by the appellation of the *thunder-bearer of despotism*, caused a hundred louis d'ors to be given her for smart money, and a letter for me, signed Doullot; not written by Doullot, but in the office of the supreme head of the police, who, moreover, made her the fairest promises, if she prevailed on her husband to enter into their views: that is, to deliver me up, alive or *dead*.

When she left the minister's hotel, one of the exempts took her to his house, and never left her afterwards, till he conducted her to Calais, and saw her safe on board a vessel. Arriving at Dover, she found the neverfailing d'Arragon waiting for her on the shore — What honours lavished on a poor creature, who, at the moment of my writing this, receives her daily food at my servant's table! Scarce had she set one foot on land, when the ready d'Arragon respectfully gives her his hand, makes her his property, puts her into a chaise, and carries her to the indolent Adhemar, who, on so extraordinary an occasion, probably condescended to half raise himself from his easy chair. He ratified the promises she had received from the Baron de Breteuil, and refreshed

her

her memory, by repeating to her, with much amplification, the instructions given to her at Paris.

It is now necessary to inform the reader, that Costa had written to his wife to join them at Newcastle, where we then were, as soon as she arrived from France, and, in case that letter should not be received at London, he had left one to the same purport at Edinburgh, at the house wherein he had lodged; but those cautions were superfluous; Arragon, who had got our address, almost as soon as we had fixed our abode at Newcastle, gave it to Costa's wife, whom he sent off, telling her, he would follow her in two or three days. Upon her arrival, which was whilst I was at dinner, she delivered to me, at her first entrance, the pretended letter from Doublot, whose hand writing I was a stranger to, so that in that respect, it was an easy matter to impose upon me; but when, on perusal, I found it was not an answer to mine, in any article, I began to entertain suspicions, which gained strength, when questioning the woman, I received answers expressive of the utmost embarassment on her part; she blushed at every word, and although I affected to fix my eyes on the letter, she had delivered to me, they were not so much employed as to let the winks and signs of encouragement, from the husband, escape me.

I had already seen and heard enough not to doubt, that I was fallen into very bad hands; and the resolution of removing society from them, immediately succeeded the birth of my suspicions. But, in order not to give them any alarm, I avoided putting captious questions, affecting rather to believe all the woman told me, me, and dinner being over, I seized the moment of their withdrawing, to call my servant, to whom I disclosed my suspicions, so much the more confidentially, as, luckily, he detested equally both the husband and the wife. I therefore acquainted him with my intention of leaving them at Newcastle, charged him to pack up my things secretly, and to have a chaise in readiness at twelve or one o'clock in the morning. My orders being given, I went up gently to the door of the room, into which these *honest* couple had withdrawn. Unable to distinguish their discourse, which was in English, I bounced into the room and, as I made my appearance unexpectedly, I found spread up on the table, the chairs, and even the bed, all the articles purchased by Costa's wife, at Paris, with part of her hundred louis d'ors. I had need of no more than one glance of my eyes, and therefore immediately retired, saying, "you are busy, I'll "go and take a walk."

Costa, who knew me, surmised that what I had just seen, would fill me with conjectures, and, probably, would drive me to some resolution that would baffle all his hopes. To prevent, what he deemed, the greatest misfortune that could befal him, and inspire me with confidence, he determined to entrust me, with part of what was plotting against me. He told me, his wife had been in the Bastile, how she had got out of it, had been carried to the Baron de Breteuil's, her passage over sea, the meeting with d'Arragon at Dover, and the expectation of the speedy arrival of that little *man-catcher*, at Newcastle. After he had thus, as he termed it, *unloaded his heart*, he swore to me an inviolable fidelity;

...... I took for no more than it was worth. I ... him ... ever promise, at all events, that he would do nothing without consulting me, assuring him that I would furnish him with means of getting money from the Government of France, provided he acted in concert with me, and make no secret of any thing, this he promised to do, and I declined for the present leaving Newcastle.

Two days after this, at ten o'clock at night, while we were at supper, Costa received a letter from d'Arragon, to acquaint him with his arrival, and desired his company ......, to which the former repaired, and .... two hours. Upon my asking him .... he told me, that the French .... was coming, to have me carried .... by two exempts of the police, ... G...... and Qu...or, that they expected a .... from Dunkirk, with a swarm of myrmidons of the police, under the command of the exempt ......, that they had all assumed titles, and changed their names, that their pretence, in order to give no umbrage in Newcastle, was a trial of the trade of pit coal, and they were furnished with letters of recommendation for that purpose. I asked Costa, what he had ... to them? "Nothing, answered he, except requesting time to reflect till to-morrow. I am, pursued he, to set out at six in the morning with d'Arragon, to view the harbour, and settle the mode of .... on board a ship." I advised him to promise every thing, to give every possible assurance, to assure him that he had a thousand good guineas
paid

paid down to him, "which when you have secured,
"said I to him, you will tell them, that, all rightly
"considered, the forcibly carrying off a man, in so fre-
"quented a port, and at such a distance from the town,
"is a thing impracticable, that they may go back to
"London, and assure the Ambassador, that in four days
"you will be there with me, and that, in some way
"or other, you will engage to convey me to Paris,
"for the sum of ten thousand pounds sterling. You
"know that I sent your wife to Paris, to furnish me
"with means of repairing thither myself. I now de-
"clare to you, upon the word of an honest man, that
"I am going to take my departure for London, where
"I intend to see the Ambassador, then take myself to
"Paris, and be the means of your getting ten thousand
"pounds sterling."

The first demand of the thousand guineas, was granted at a word, with a trifling defalcation of sixty, which *honest* D'Arragon withheld for his fees. As to the ten thousand, they were promised, on condition, that the same D'Arragon should make a stoppage of one fifth on his own account. What a worthy man, is this Monsieur D'Arragon! How calculated for----how fitting to the trust----how creditable to the office he this day holds, of *Secretary to the French Ambassador*. If more is want-ing, let me give a more substantial proof, which only came to my knowledge, subsequently to the plan I had been forming with his counterpart, the no less worthy Mr Costa. The honest little myrmidon was provided with a phial, filled with a liquor, which he said, had the property of putting a man to sleep for only four

and

and twenty hours successively, and he had tried to make Costa administer that small dose to me, in some tea or wine, the vehicle was no doubt to be at my own choice, telling him, that when once that gentle soporific had taken effect, I might be put into a sack, like a bundle of foul linen, be carried down to the harbour under favour of darkness, conveyed on board, by way of a portmanteau, be thrown into the hold, and, I have no doubt, in the end, be cast into the sea. It is more, than demonstrated, that they had no occasion for me alive, which I shall presently put beyond all question. These agreeable particulars I have from Costa's wife, who let me into many other circumstances equally satisfactory.

Notwithstanding this apparent confidence, by which Costa had sought to ensure mine, he had absolutely entered into the plot, the ten thousand pounds were ready, and if he did not get them by making use of the phial, it was, because my man was an invincible obstacle in his way, who must have been made to swallow the like dose----in order also to turn him into a *porth cuteau*, and that was a thing somewhat more than difficult. I watched him narrowly, he knew how far he was grown obnoxious to my suspicion, the least motion that he had made, bearing marks of an attempt to force me, would have been his undoing, with so much the greater certainty, as from my knowledge of the number and even the names of the satellites, employed in this undertaking, I might have informed against them, and have produced proofs of their villainy. Where a halter is

suspended

suspended before a man's eyes, he will look twice before he leaps once.

These gentlemen retainers to the police, apprehensive that nothing could be done at Newcastle, set out for London, just as they had come from it, but fully persuaded, in consequence of Costa's promises, that their prey would not escape them.

I reached London a few days after them, and that very night D'Arragon found out Costa, and told him, the Ambassador wanted to speak to him the next morning. He came himself to fetch him, and took him to a street, where they met his Excellency, who condescended to get into a hackney coach with those two worthies! Such was the council-chamber where the noble Triumvirate deliberated on the methods of carrying me away. D'Arragon said he had thought upon a plan, and he would answer for the success, and that was, to procure some person to swear a debt against me of six thousand pounds sterling. He had bribed a sheriff's officer, who was to have arrested me, and had engaged to put me on board a ship, provided the Ambassador would be answerable for the events that might ensue, and defray the expence.

Costa who thought I could not be imposed upon by such designs, said, that it was a stale trick, and that I should not fall into the snare; that at the moment I was arrested, I would cause myself to be conveyed on foot to Newgate, followed by a mob of people, which would marr their intention. He concluded by telling the Ambassador, that he would weigh the matter more maturely,

turely, and that on the morrow his Excellency should hear from him.

Acquainted with the appointment, I formed a resolution to prevent the effect of it, by writing directly to the Ambassador, with a view to bring him to a compromise with me, and divest him of the confidence he had in his Costa, by letting him know that, through the means of the very agent he had employed, I had information of the whole transaction. I acquainted him that, after the steps I had taken towards my return to Paris, I was surprised at the attempts, the artifices used by him to ensnare me, that I wished to have an explanation with him, and ended by telling him, I would meet him wherever he should think proper to appoint, his own house excepted. He gave me the meeting the same day at Lady Spencer's, to whose house I repaired with Costa and my own servant, who staid at the door, pursuant to my orders. The company was not risen from table, but Count d——— appeared in the parlour. I had been prepared, at the very moment that my name was announced. He took me to the recess of a window, that Costa might not overhear our conversation. After I had given him a cursory account of the contents of these Memoirs, had laid before him the Cardinal's conduct respecting the Queen, his unguarded speeches, his senseless projects, his furious ambition, the necessary consequences of the shattered state of his affairs, the misfortune of the Count being attached to him through gratitude &c. &c. In short, almost all that the Countess has already written, I asked him, with what view some persons seemed so obstinately bent on entrapping me,

me, since I had offered to betake myself to Paris of my own accord, and that I was now ready so to do, if they would only give me the securities usual in similar cases, and that, under no pretence whatever, should any attempt be made upon my liberty——" *That is ex-*
" *actly,* said he *what those persons will not do* (*) But
" believe me, I have thought of another way, come to
" my house to-morrow, I will acquaint you with it,
" and we will have a thorough conversation on all mat-
" ters which concern you, I give you my word as a
" gentleman, that you have nothing to fear. You *know*

that

---

* Those few words dropped from the Ambassador's mouth are a solution to the whole affair. Why would not those persons have me appear? Because I *should have told the truth.* I had declared to many persons, that my intention was to demand of the Judges in open Parliament, whether, in case I uttered all that I knew, they would take me under their protection, save me from the Bastile, and appoint the Conciergerie for my prison, till the definitive sentence was pronounced. That was, what " *those persons would not do.*" Why therefore try to carry me off? It is evident as I have said, that it was not for the sake of having me *alive* and capable of *speaking the truth*, which they dreaded, but *dead* and silent as the tomb. It is consequently, equal presumptive evidence that the pretended *sleeping draught* was *downright poison.* But my interview with the Ambassador altered all those dispositions which my *worthy friends* had made, as I am going to set forth

"that I am of the Queen's party, intimately connected
"with Madame de Polignac, consequently a professed
"enemy of the Cardinal's, the Queen has sworn his
"ruin; you can, better than any one in the world,
"facilitate the accomplishment of her Majesty's wishes,
"since your Lady has such an ill-judged partiality for
"him, so dangerous to himself. I know that in even the
"commencement of the affair, she had very bad coun-
"sels given her, which she imprudently followed, and
"which would infallibly bring her to her ruin, if there
"were not means of prevention to be found---luckily
"there is one way left: your presence and depositions
"would entirely overthrow all that has hitherto been
"done, and the business would take quite a different
"turn." Here, asking me the particulars of certain
points which I had but slightly touched, I saw that my
answers afforded him infinite satisfaction, joy sparkled
in his eyes, he already saw the Cardinal brought to the
scaffold.

Before I departed, I told him I was determined, let
what would befal others, to reveal the whole matter,
having nothing in view but the safety of the Countess,
and the honour of us both, but that I feared the house
of Rohan would have interest enough to ward off the
blow and get judgment passed before my arrival. To
that he answered, that I had nothing to fear, that *"the*
"*Bourbons ought to prevail over the Rohans*, and that
"*policy required that the King should be right*" that his
"Majesty referring the cognizance of that affair to his
"Parliament, was prejudging him guilty, and that he
"must of necessity be so criminated. The Queen"

con-

[183]

continued he, " is concerned in it, in every relative
" view, from a thousand considerations, therefore, from
" the knowledge you must necessarily have, of every
" situation in the acting of that scene, you can have no-
" thing to fear from the influence of the Rohans, when
" in competition with the Bourbons, in the *fact*, or to
" speak more properly, in the *form*, the Cardinal pleads
" against your Lady and yourself, for you are merely
" the representatives, the real party is the Queen;
" think, therefore, of making advantage of what I tell
" you. At the commencement of the affair, I could
" have had you taken up at Dublin, the Duke of Rut-
" land (*) had written to me in consequence, pro-
" mising to facilitate the means I had transmitted to
" Versailles an account of his letter, but, as at that
" period, they thought they had enough to convict
" the Cardinal upon, your presence was not deemed
" necessary, and I received for answer, that I need not
" proceed any farther, but let you remain quiet.
" However, when some time after, the Rohans were seen
" to get the upper hand, then it was that no stone was
" left unturned, to get possession of your person the
" Queen would have sacrificed half the kingdom to that
" object So circumstanced are things at present, that
" is the principle of my activity nor shall I dissemble,
" that your letter having given me a sensible pleasure
" I immediately sent off a courier to Versailles, to ac-

---

* That same Lord Lieutenant who had examined my
seal, but, " *de mortuis nil, nisi bonum* "

" quaint

[14]

" quaint Mr de Vergennes I was to see you this day,
" and to concert with him about your departure I
" inclosed your letter in the packet, to the end that
" Mr de Vergennes, seeing with his own eyes, that
" you are ready to attend, may give immediate orders
" to suspend all proceedings till your arrival, so you
" see you have nothing to apprehend from a precipitate
" trial."

I quitted the Ambassador with a promise of returning to him the next day, and reflecting on all that he had communicated to me, I easily accounted for the different views, which had actuated the conduct of different people respecting me, according to the difference of circumstances, and saw how little the life of an individual is valued, when it serves the purposes of power, to put him to it.

The following day, punctual to my appointment, I repaired to the Ambassador's, who, in almost the first sentence that escaped his lips, elucidated with more accuracy than the preceding day, the cause that, after wishing to have me a *corpse* in their possession, they now wished to have me a *living evidence*. " IT HAD BEEN
" FEARED, said he to me, " LEST YOU SHOULD US-
" ED THE CARDINAL'S LETTERS, PREFERABLY TO
" THAT OF THE QUEEN. At present I am easy, and
" the contents of your letter, which I enclosed in mine,
" as I informed you yesterday, will give fresh spirits to
" the party, and I question not, but they will speedily
" transmit to me every necessary vouch t I have re-
" quested, for your security, but, sent to me. Since
" yesterday I have had leisure to reflect, and have to-
" tally

" tally altered the difpofitions we had agreed upon I
" am going to make you perceive, there would be an
" inconvenience in precipitating your departure. You
" are fenfible, that being abfent, you are in the wrong,
' that the Rohans accufe you of flying with the remain-
" der of the necklace, and, that they have in general fuc-
" ceeded in empoifoning the public mind with that idea.
" If under fuch circumftances you were feen, on a fud-
" den, to appear at full liberty, and under protection,
" every body would exclaim,----There he is! he fears
nothing! if he had any compunction for his guilt, he
" would not venture to fhew himfelf, or quit the afylum
" where he has fo long lived in fecurity. On the other
" hand, your depofitions being deftructive to the Car-
" dinal! his family would cry out. Yes, there he is,
" fhielded by the power and influence of the Queen!
' it is the Queen who fends for him, after having him
' properly inftructed at London! He brings his depofi-
' fitions in writing, or elfe they have been dictated to
" him, and he has imprinted them on his memory----
" he alone was wanting to confummate the Cardinal's
" ruin! and----all which would produce the effect of
" of public obloquy to you. But there is another way,
' in which you may appear before your judges, and
" which anfwering the fame purpofe with refpect to you,
" cannot render the Queen liable to fuch reproach Fa-
" vour me with your attention.

" The Cardinal, continues the Ambaffador, politi-
' cally affects to fay, in all places, that he ardently
" wifhes for your prefence.----The King, fuppofed to
" be informed of that circumftance, may fay, " I chofe

Bb   " to

" to give him that satisfaction, and accordingly ordered
" all necessary preparations for apprehending Count de
" la Motte, which have proved ineffectual, but he,
" apprised of the attempts made against him, applied
" of his own accord, to my Ambassador to his Britan-
" nic Majesty, and signified his design of returning to
" Paris, if I would grant him a safe conduct and se-
" curity. There being no other way of securing him,
" and it having been represented to me, that the Car-
" dinal looks upon his presence, as essential to his
" carrying on his suit at law, I have granted to the
" said Count de la Motte, the safe conduct petitioned
" for.

' On that foundation, the Cardinal and his family,
' can have nothing to alledge; and you will find your-
' self at liberty in Paris, in the midst of people of
' understanding, who will direct you in every point.
' I only tell you, before hand, you will be obliged to
' pass a day or two in the Conciergerie prison, in order
' to obtain a reprisal of the warrant for your arrest,
' a mere matter of form, that cannot be dispensed with.
' I will write again to Mr. de Vergennes, to give him
' a more circumstantial account of what you have re-
' lated to me yesterday, and in this second interview,
' and will press him to send to me, by the return of the
' Courier, the passport, which you will be supposed to
' have for the King himself.

' D'Angely, my Secretary, shall be bearer of the
" packet; in a word, hold yourself in readiness for your
' departure. I am sure the passport will be here in
' eight or ten days at farthest.'

I re-

I represented to Mr d'Adhemar, that my property having been seized upon, and having very little money, it would be impossible for me to get my business settled and appear as I had before done, and befitting my rank, to which he answered, " that ought to give you " no uneasiness, I have at my disposal, a considerable " sum remitted over to me to proceed against you, but " I shall be much more flattered with applying it to- " wards doing you a service, and, if you have need of " *five or six thousand louis d'ors*, I will supply you with " them."

Circumstances being thus arranged between us, he said, " *the only thing remaining to be known, was, what* " *I should say in my defence?*" I made answer. " that " as to the story of the necklace, I did not well know " what turn to give it, so as not to expose the Queen " more or less, that as to any thing else, I was not at " a loss." He recommended to me, never to say that the Countess had access to the Queen still less, that I knew of the Cardinal's having carried on a correspond- ence with her Majesty, and had appointments with her at Versailles and Trianon, " Only say," added he, " that the Cardinal shewed you a number of letters, " which he assured you were written to him by the " Queen, adding, that he has often said, that he used " to *have possession* of her. contrive, when you repeat " all that he has told you on that subject, to embellish " the story, be particular not to omit his indecent " speeches, take it for granted, *the Queen will not be* " *displeased with it* but beware of saying a word about

" the following gentlemen: de Polignac, Coigny,
" Vaudreuil, Dillon, Fersenne (*)

' As to the business of the necklace, I would advise
" you to say, that you are persuaded the Cardinal gave
" it partly, or wholly, to your Lady, your Lady
" should never allow that to be the case, but I am cer-
" tain in reality was so."

I felt the blow, but neither answered in the affirmative or negative. Having afterwards talked to him of
the Baron de Breteuil, he told me to be sure " not to
" pronounce his name, and above all, not to take any
' steps respecting him, because, THAT WOULD BE TOO
' POINTED. Follow my advice," pursued he, " Mr.
" de Vergennes has the reputation of being an upright
' man, 'incapable of caballing' (†) to gratify the
" Queen's desires, nevertheless, without its appearing,
" he is of her party (‡). He was highly incensed at
" the behaviour, the scandalous speeches, and senseless
" ambition of the Cardinal, and sided with the Queen
" in her resentment. It is at his house you must
' alight, though you have a passport---tell him you
' are come to surrender yourself his prisoner,---you
" will

---

* It must be confessed that the Ambassador of his
Most Christian Majesty, was very kind, to give me thus
gratis to say, a list of the *Pleyad* tribe, in case I had not
possessed one of my own---even somewhat more co-
pious.

† The truth of this assertion will presently be made
evident.

‡ The reader will shortly perceive what foundation
the Count had for this assertion also.

" will find that produce a good effect, and that your
" conduct therein, will meet with his approbation."

Upon my acquainting him that my intention was to deliver up to that Minister, the necklace which I have mentioned, Gray had set, Mr. D'Adhemar highly approved of my design, and told me, " that the King
" would be pleased with, and reward me for my disin-
" terestedness for," added he, " that necklace is your
" own, and you may dispose of it as you think proper."

After a very long conversation to the foregoing effect, I took my leave. At parting, he told me to remain easy, till I heard from him, that D'Arragon should go off in two or three days, as he had other dispatches to send by him. " There is no hurry at present," he repeated to me, " nor any thing to be feared, Count de
" Vergennes has previous intimation."

He desired I would change my name, to conceal my return to London, and avoid the tattling of the *Courier de l'Europe*."

Every thing appeared to proceed with the most perfect cordiality,---but his Excellency was drawing his conclusions from false premises. The Count de Vergennes was any thing, but attached to the Queen's party, as the Ambassador supposed (who from the nature of his connexions ought to have known better,) being, on the contrary, bound by the strongest ties to the Rohans. When, therefore, the crafty Minister, saw by the Ambassador's letter and mine, that there was no time to lose, to extricate the Cardinal, in lieu of granting a delay of fifteen days, which the Countess had requested, he hurried on the final sentence, which to the astonish-
" ment

ment and high indignation of the Ambassador, and of his party, was pronounced the day before, or, on the very day of D'Arragon's arrival'----It is true the Count de Vergennes has been punished for his perfidiousness, but it is no less true, that the unfortunate Countess de la Motte fell a victim to it, and that even the death of that Minister has but feebly avenged her.

As soon as Count d'Adhémar received that piece of intelligence which astonished him, he wrote to me, making an appointment in Hyde Park, (I am in possession of his letter) I attended, and found him gloomy, disappointed and vexed. He told me, he could not conceive, why they had, in such a manner, precipitated the judgment on that trial, (though for my part, I had foretold it, as has been seen,) that there was something unaccountable and mysterious in it, which he could not unravel; that upon the whole, "*there was nothing in it* "*disagreeable to me*," that I must not let it affect me, " that it need not hinder my departure for Paris, where " my presence was more than ever requisite." I asked him to what purpose? he answered, that " when the " King had referred the cognizance of the affair to the " Parliament, the necklace was the only circumstance " mentioned in the commission, the Queen's name had " not been brought into question, that, unfortunately, " the confess given to the Countess, having terminated " to her disadvantage, the Cardinal had gained a supe- " riority, and grounded on it his defence, but that " when his unbecoming speeches against the Queen " came to be discussed, and the papers which he had " shewn, he would be at a loss what answer to make--- " It is a fault committed in the drawing up of the pa-
" tent

" tent of commission," added he, " that suggested to
" the party, which the Rohans have in the Parliament,
" the idea of adhering to the literal meaning, and
" confining themselves solely to the business of the
" necklace, which has not furnished a sufficient ground
" whereon to convict the Cardinal, but now, that point
" is definitively settled, I give you previous notice of
" what will presently happen, in order to make you
" sensible, how necessary your presence will be at Paris.
" The *Attorney General is going to prefer a fresh complaint*
" *against the Cardinal* for CRIMINAL ATTEMPTS *upon the*
" *Queen,---for the language he has used---the letters he has*
" *exhibited---the meetings by night, &c &c* and forth-
" with a decree of arrest will be issued out against him.
" I can assure you he will not have the same good for-
" tune on this second trial, which he had on that, re-
' specting the necklace. When you are at Paris, that
" business will be renewed, for there are statutes ex-
' tant, by virtue whereof, the Parliament will be ob-
" liged to begin the whole process over again, be there-
" fore at ease, and communicate to no person whatever
" has passed between us."

I thought I discovered some appearance of probability and encouragement, in what the Ambassador now
suggested I withdrew in better spirits than I came,
but a few days afterwards D'Arragon came from him,
to inform me, that " particular reasons had determined
" the Queen to drop the prosecution, that no second
" complaint was to be preferred, that it would give
' room for the circulation of many malicious speeches,
" a circumstance her Majesty wished to avoid, and
" that she rather chose to revenge herself, by exerting
" the

[192]

" the whole weight of supreme power to deprive the Car-
" dinal of his blue ribband, and his humours as well as
" his places at Court, and banishing him, to exist amongst
" a herd of Monks in the savage parts of Auvergne."

While he communicated to me this piece of intelligence, which was like an electric shock, D'Arragon had without doubt, received his instructions, and with all that hypocrisy and insincerity, which Ambassadors are ever amply provided with from their respective courts, affected to pour the balm of comfort into the wounds, he concluded must be inflicted, by such a fatal stab to my hopes.

" You must be sensible,' said he, " that the course
" which the Queen has taken, by no means lessens the
" merit of your conduct, which his Excellency has not
" concealed from her, that, she will not abandon either
" you or your lady, and that she will gratefully reward
" the desire you have expressed to oblige her. The
" Ambassador is going to Versailles, and has charged
" me to tell you, that he will omit no opportunity to
" serve you, and during his absence you may dispose
" of me, on all occasions, where you shall think I can be
" any ways serviceable to your interest.

I wrote to the Ambassador before his departure, but received no answer. At his return from France I wrote two letters, (which at that time made their appearance in the public papers*) of which he took as little notice as of the former.

It

---

* Vide Morning Chronicle, for December 29, 1786, and January 1, 1787.---Morning Post of March 2, and 6, 1787.---The above two letters were inserted in the Exeter Flying Post, March 8, 1787.

It is a matter of no consequence---I do not mean to reproach him with it.---He had been in a capacity to know what passed; he was not ignorant that when the Queen expressed a desire of saving the Countess, from the iniquitous sentence passed against her, those people, whom she calls her "BLOOD SUCKERS," and notoriously the *Abbé de Vermont*, persuaded her Majesty, that if " she only appeared to know the Countess, she would ' certainly expose herself in a shocking manner," which would be infinitely exaggerated by avowing in her conduct, any concern for her.

From the plain statement of facts, which I have related, I should deem it an insult to the reader, were I to offer a single reflection upon the subject. It is plain that the Cardinal's life was suspended but by a thread, that, had the slightest breath broken that thread, the Countess must have been cleared from all impeachment. It remains therefore to determine, whether the victorious influence of the *Rohans*, had been able to establish a guilt, which the Queen's influence would have done away, if it had possessed sufficient power.

Before I conclude my task, and relinquish my pen to the Countess, whose substitute I am at present, I will endeavour to prevent an ungrateful office to her, which she had mentioned, but that relates to matters more familiar to me than to herself. I mean the account she promised to give of that portion of the diamonds, which the Queen had bestowed upon her,---probably without her Majesty's being aware, that their value amounted to one eighth part of what it really was. The following account will shew what they produced, and the use I

made

[194]

made of them. I should have sold them in Paris openly, had not the Cardinal observed to us, that they might possibly fall into the hands of the Jewellers, a circumstance which could not but have proved disagreeable to the Queen.

I arrived in London on the 17th of April, with Chevalier O'Neil, who was perfectly acquainted with the object of my journey. As he knew the Countess was admitted to the Queen, I made no mystery to him, of the present she had received from her Majesty, nor of my motive for parting with them in London. I had a letter of credit on Messrs. Molland and Co. to whom I sent the day after my arrival. On making enquiry for the most capital jewellers, I was directed to Jefferys and to Gray, I first saw Jefferys, told him I had some diamonds to dispose of, and left him my address. The next morning he came to my lodgings, where I shewed him the eighteen oval stones that belonged to the necklace, and acquainted him with the price which the Cardinal had fixed. He requested me to let him take them home, in order to examine them, and offered me his acknowledgement, which I accepted of. He promised to bring me an answer in four days, the next day I set out with Chevalier O'Neil for Newmarket. During five days that we remained there, I gained by betting, nine hundred and sixty guineas, fifty of which I expended in travelling expences, the purchase of cloaths, and numerous other articles, Chevalier O'Neil has made of the sorrowful circumstances.

On my return to London, I went to Jefferys, who told me, that a gentleman had offered four thousand
pounds

pounds sterling, that he could not pay ready money, but would give notes at six and twelve months date, and would find ample security. I told him I would confider of it, took back my diamonds, and returned him his acknowledgment. The same day I went to Gray's, left with him the largest oval stone, and directed him to come to me the next day, when I would let him see a greater quantity, the same day I purchased of him a self-winding watch. The next day he came, with a Jew named Eliason, I entrusted him with the same stones I had left in Jefferys' hands, he told me he had already examined them, and that a broker whom Jefferys employed, had brought them to him. I then let him know the offer that Jefferys had made me, and the terms of payment, adding, that not knowing Jefferys, nor the person he had recommended to me, I did not chuse to part with so considerable a property upon credit. That besides, I proposed staying but a few days in London, whither I might probably never again return, and that I did not think proper to leave any thing behind me that might create any anxiety. He answered, that I was in the right, and that if we agreed on the price, he would pay me ready money. I told him my price, he took away the diamonds, and promised to bring an answer the following day, which he did, but still accompanied by Gray. He made me an offer of three thousand guineas, which I would not accept. After pointing out stones that had flaws and other defects, they left me, with an assurance that the offer they made me, for ready money, was very adequate; and that I should not meet with a more eligible offer.

I let

I let them go away, telling them I would keep my diamonds, rather than part with them at that price. Next morning they returned, and afked to furvey the diamonds a fecond time. I permitted them. O'Neil was prefent, as well as my valet de chambre. Eliafon then drew out of his pocket, a pearl necklace, confifting of two very beautiful rows, a fnuff box fet with brilliants and pearls, with a medallion on the lid, and feveral parcels of pearl feed. He valued thofe different articles at about five hundred and fixty pounds fterling. I faid, that if he would give me four thoufand pounds, together with thofe articles, the bargain was ftruck. He exclaimed loudly, and then made a motion to go, offering three thoufand pounds, and the articles I had felected, a propofal which I rejected. In the interim Jefferys made a fecond application, I told him my refolution was, to fell them for ready money only. I then fhewed to him thirteen ftones of the firft quality I poffeffed; the two fineft, which belonged to the necklace, not having been given to the Countefs, and no doubt but the Queen made a prefent of them to Mademoifelle Dorvat, or fome other woman in her intimacy, for there were feveral which were fimilar. I had felected two, one intended to be fet in a ring for the Countefs, the other for myfelf. Regnier, my jeweller at Paris, fet them both before my departure for London. Both myfelf and the Countefs commonly wore them. The Cardinal has feen them both.

I called the next day at Gray's, to purchafe feveral articles in fteel, there I found Eliafon, who told me I was over tenacious, that his offer was a very fair one.

He

He shewed me some very fine pearls for a pair of bracelets, and a ring, forming a neck button, I went into a separate apartment, where we entered into a bargain. After two hours difficulty on both sides, we at length agreed for the eighteen oval stones, viz. three thousand pounds sterling ready money, the pearl necklace of two rows, valued at two hundred pounds, the snuff box one hundred and forty, the pearl seed one hundred and twenty, and a diamond star which I took in Gray's shop, valued at three hundred.

This was the first bargain. When I had received the money and jewels, he told me that Jefferys' broker had brought him other diamonds, which were no doubt my property, that if I chose to sell them, I had better do business with him than with another that I should gain by it the commission and some ready money. I went the same day, and took out of Jefferys' hands, the thirteen stones I had left in his possession. He had come to the knowledge of my dealing with Gray, and being vexed at having missed the opportunity of making the purchase himself, he, upon that account, pretended, as will be seen hereafter, that he had acted, respecting the diamonds, with more propriety than Gray, for that he, Jefferys, surmising the diamonds to have been stolen, had given notice at a public office, (which in fact was a falshood) and had refused to buy them. He afterwards the more readily made a declaration to this purpose, before a certain notary named Dubourg, as will hereafter appear, at the request of Mr. de Carbonniere, agent for the Cardinal, as he said he believed me to be in Turkey, and depended upon never

seeing

[198]

seeing me again in England. His behaviour to me, when I returned to London, will shew how *delicate* this Jeffer's was in his conduct: since he came to me, after judgment was passed, to ask me whether I had not diamonds to dispose of, telling me, he would be the purchaser, and allow me a greater advantage than Grey would. It will soon be seen what answer I made him, and the method I took, in order to make apparent what the satisfactory sayings, produced by the Cardinal, consisted in.

The thirteen stones taken from Jefferys, I carried to Grey, telling him I would come the next day to his shop myself, and that he might appoint Eliason to be there at the same hour. The departure of Chevalier O'Neil prevented my keeping the appointment. He had received a letter from his brother, and another from his Colonel, requiring his return with all possible speed, to join his regiment by the 15th of May. He had not been able to obtain a longer leave of absence as he hoped, the troops the Emperor was then marching towards Holland, were the occasion of the orders he had received, he was therefore forced to leave me in London. He took charge of several purchases I had made, and of the parcel of pearls I had got in exchange. As I went by the coach, he took his place the day before, at M. Guyton's office, where he found the Capuchin M'Dermot a professed spy, who for the things made known to me by his own confession, and those certainly are the least of his crimes, deserves to be made an example of (*) The Capuchin knew Chevalier O'Neil, with whom he renewed acquaintance, and finding in the course of conversation he had come over with me, he begged he would introduce him to me, which the Chevalier did. He told me, that as I did not understand English, he would be my interpreter, and do me all the little services in his power. I accepted of his obliging offers, and that day he dined with me. He had been procurator of his order, at Vassy, six leagues distant from Bar-sur-Aube, he knew my family, and had seen me, by his account a child. He said he had been employed by Mr. de Choiseul, and the succeeding ministers, that he had done great service to the state, that to reward him, he had only, a hundred louis d'ors pension settled on him from the Marine fund, that he feared lest some minister, in a fit of ill humour, should take off his pension; that in order to protect him from that disagreeable event, and at the same time lessen the burthen to government, he petitioned that his pension might be converted into, or changed for a church living, and then, that he might be secularised. He added that he had presented a memorial to Madame Louisa, who was his protectress, but that he feared the matter would be protracted, that he had sustained a great loss when Mr. de Choiseul resigned, as it was under his ministry he had rendered those services, he expected to

re

---

* This is the same M'Dermot I have already had occasion to distinguish in these Memoirs, at this period acquaintance commenced.

receive confiderable rewards from him, and fuch had actually been promifed him. Having by degrees gained my confidence, and got intelligence at his laft paffing through Bar-fur-Aube, that the Countefs had accefs to the Queen, was beloved by her, and that all our fortune came from her, his eagernefs to pleafe me may eafily be guefſed at. Infinuating and hypocritical, he made himfelf ufeful to me, and as he was a prieſt well known to many of the Catholic nobility and gentry, he introduced me into fome of the beſt families. I made a number of excurfions with him round London, and in thofe little trips it was, he told me what he had heard at Bar-fur-Aube, he talked of the Cardinal, and faid if I had a mind to ferve him, I had it in my power, that the Cardinal could get him fecularifed as he had obferved, by firſt giving him a finecure place under him, and then caufe his penfion to be changed for a living, by which a faving would be made to government. I advifed him to draw up a memorial, which I would willingly take charge of, adding I would do all in my power to oblige him. In this my firſt excurfion, I did not communicate to him any thing relative to the intimacy between the Queen and the Countefs, much lefs of the Cardinal's, he knew nothing of my having correfponds, in fhort I acquainted him with no particulars, but barely that I had money to remit to Paris. He anfwered that he knew a merchant in the city, named Motteux, that if I negociated it through his means, he would allow me the fame advantage as to traders, whereas Mr. Hammerfley would deal with me, as with a nobleman. He calculated the benefit I

fhould

should reap by placing that sum with Mr. Motteaux: and, as it seemed to me rather considerable, and he persuaded me that Mr Hammersley would not make me the same allowance, I determined to go to Mr. Motteaux, whither he accompanied me. I delivered to him the three thousand pounds sterling, I had already received on the former bargain.

Let us return now to the thirteen diamonds I had left with Gray. I gave him an appointment for the next day. When the Chevalier O'Neil was gone, I went to that jeweller, who immediately sent into the city, to let Eliason know I waited for him at his house. He came, but we made no bargain; eight or ten days passed away in fruitless meetings and considerations. They often told me, they wondered how a gentleman should have such a knowledge of diamonds, as to ascertain the exact value of them; but that I certainly was sensible, that such articles were hard to be disposed of, that they should perhaps be obliged to keep them two or three years upon their hands, during which time the interest of the money was lost, and other things to the same purport. At length, after much trouble and attendance, we came to a settlement for the thirteen stones, at the sum of two thousand pounds sterling, ready money, a ring, convertible into a neck button, valued at two hundred pounds sterling, and for which, I lately got but one hundred, a parcel of very fine pearls for the mounting of a pair of bracelets, valued at a hundred and fifty pounds, another parcel of pearls for sixty pounds, and a pair of girandole ear rings, valued at five hundred pounds. Such were the two bargains I

D d *made*

made with Lhasor, in presence of Gray. Six diamonds, which formed the rose of two oval ones, I exchanged at Gray's for a medallion set round with brilliants, two steel swords, a scent pin, a pair of asparagus tongs, and a cruet syphon. Four more diamonds which were between the rose and the four tassels, were likewise exchanged at Gray's for a ring, still in my possession, a hoop of diamond seeds, a lady's pocket case sattin and gold, with all its furniture, a pair of steel buckles, and a miniature.

I had sixty diamonds left, arising from the tassels, twenty-two from the scollops, and the stone which formed the button. Out of the sixty I selected twenty-eight, which I gave to Gray, to set in drop ear-rings, and two and twenty of the scollops to make into a necklace of one single row. I then had left only thirty-two stones arising from the tassels, and the stone forming the button. I chose the sixteen finest, which I kept unmounted, and the remaining sixteen I parted with to Gray, at the rate of eight pounds the karat, out of which I bought in his shop sundry small matters, not worth mentioning. Thus terminated all my negociations for diamonds in London.

I had still remaining the button stone, which I shewed to Mr Morland, asking him whether he could not find an opportunity of selling it to my advantage; he said he would let an acquaintance inspect it, and let me know his answer in two or three days. He did so, by telling me, he had the stone in his bank, and that one thousand guineas had been offered for it, which he believed might be carried to twelve hundred. He proposed

posed my calling in Pall-mall to take the diamond, and from thence go into the city, to Mr. Duval's, the person who made the offer, but that he believed it was not for himself. We met with Mr Duval, who shewed me several articles in jewellery I told him my design was not to purchase any, since I was on the contrary come to treat with him about a diamond, which Mr Morland had given him to inspect After surveying it a second time, he told me, that the person to whom he had shewn it, offered but one thousand pounds, which he (Duval) looked upon to be its full value. I took back the diamond, and resolved to keep it till I found a means to dispose of it more advantageously. The same day I gave it to Gray to set in a ring. Let us now proceed to those that were sold and exchanged at Paris Before my departure for England, the Countess had delivered to Mr. Tilleux some diamonds, which she had kept privately, that had formed part of the scollops and knots of the tassels · she desired him to sell them for her, and pay her the money, charging him not to make me acquainted with it. He sold the whole parcel to one Paris, a jeweller, for the sum of twenty eight thousand French livres Two stones, part of the scollops, were exchanged by me, for two pendulum clocks, at one Turet's, in St Honore Street, with twenty-five louis d'ors in addition. One diamond in like manner from the scollops, was set in a ring by Regnier my jeweller. I had a chain in small brilliants, which Franks the Jew had sold me that I gave to Regnier, adding a few small diamonds, which belonged to the knots of the tassels, the whole of which he made into a chair, which the Cardinal's counsel valued at *forty thousand livres*. I with much difficulty parted with it for *fifty pounds sterling* in London. It was nearly the same with every particular; they were, in order to obtain their ends, obliged to multiply the price for which every article sold, in a like proportion; and thus, from this false estimation, endeavour to prove that the *whole* of the necklace had been in my possession.

I had now left, in all, sixteen diamonds, which I had brought back to London, four and twenty very small ones, which were on the sides of each oval stone, at the bottom of the tassels, the encircling of the two large oval stones, two small ones on each side of the button, sixteen of the same size, six of which held the two oval stones between the scollops, and the twelve others, which were immediately adjoining to the ribband at top, the roses and what held the tassels were not yet taken to pieces. I delivered the whole to Regnier, out of all which, he selected the best diamonds, and nearly of an equality, to encircle the top of a box, and mount a small pair of drop ear-rings, which the Countess wanted to make a present of. The remainder I directed him to sell, for which he got thirteen or fourteen thousand livres. These made up the number of what I sold, as well at Paris as in London. Let us now recapitulate.

I received in ready money in London, *five thousand pounds* sterling from Mr. Eliason, and fifty or sixty pounds from Mr Gray.

In exchange I received a medallion, a pair of girandole ear-rings, a ring, a shirt-pin, a hoop, two steel cords, a pair of steel buckles, one pound of pearl seed,

two

two rows of pearls forming a necklace, a mount for bracelets, a small parcel of pearls, a neck button, convertible into a ring, a snuff box, a pair of asparagus tongs, a wine syphon, a lady's pocket case, sattin and gold, with appurtenances, a miniature, a pen-case of roses valued sixty pounds sterling. Some few other small articles I had from Gray's shop, as needles, knives, steel forks, spring-pincers, scissars, a pair of silver buckles, an opera-glass, a small steel watch chain.

I sold at Paris to Mr. Pâris several diamonds, to the amount of twenty eight thousand livres, and I received near fifty louis d'ors, for a part of the pearl seed carried from London by Chevalier O'Neil, the remainder of the pearl seed was sold to Mordecai, a Jew, residing in Rue aux Ours.

I have already said, I had delivered to Gray twenty-two stones to set in a necklace, and twenty-six for drop ear-rings. I had acquainted him with the day of my departure, and he had promised the work should be compleated, yet the day previous thereto, he shewed me all the pieces, only sketched, assuring me there was a great deal more work than he had at first imagined, and that if would leave them with him, he had an opportunity of conveying them to Paris within a fortnight, I left him the diamonds with my address, and set out upon my journey on a Sunday morning with the Capuchin M'Dermot, who attended me as far as Dover. At parting with him, I made him a present of a box, with a very handsome painting on the lid, and defrayed his journey back to London

When

When I left Paris, I had taken credit for two thousand crowns, I won at Newmarket near a thousand pounds sterling, out of both which sums I expended an hundred guineas in sadlery, harness and race-horse body-cloaths, a hundred guineas more for a phaeton, a hundred and fifty guineas in English stuffs and cloaths, for myself and servants, the rest was spent in travelling and during my six weeks stay in London, which will not appear extraordinary, when it is known I had taken up my residence at one of the principal hotels in that town, that I kept two servants, a hired coach and two saddle horses, that I often gave entertainments, and that keeping the most fashionable company, I was obliged to play and enter into expensive pleasures.

All I recovered left of the wreck of the famous necklace, were two rings, one for myself, the other belonging to the Countess, a small diamond mounted on a plomb-coloured stone, a pair of drop ear-rings, and a circle on a black tortoiseshell box, and what I had left with Gray, namely, the necklace of twenty-two stones and the ear-rings.

Thus have I given a minute detail of the diamonds I polished, and of the manner in which I had disposed of them.

From the account I have kept, and have just set down, of all the diamonds I had in my possession, or that of the Countess, belonging to the necklace, and by comparing it with an exact representation thereof, engraved on a scale, of the size of the diamonds, it appears that the Queen had kept TWO HUNDRED AND FIFTY-SIX brilliants of the same magnitude THIRTY-EIGHT smaller ones

ones of the same form, and the TWO FINEST DIAMONDS of the first size. The two hundred and fifty-six diamonds were what composed the most beautiful part of the necklace on the account of the assemblage and the regularity of so great a number of stones.

Mr Duval who has retired from business, and left it to his brother, furnished the Queen of England with a number of diamonds like those her Majesty kept, to mount a pair of bracelets. The Queen of France had given orders to the same Mr Duval to procure her some like them, but he told me, he never could get a sufficient quantity together. As he knew the necklace, and had it in his hands, I pointed out to him upon the drawing, what portion I had possessed, and what the Queen had retained, which occasioned him to recollect the order he had received from her Majesty to procure such diamonds. As she had a great desire of having bracelets, counterparts of those of the Queen of England, it is probable, that those she kept will one day be employed to that use. The Countess asserts, that her Majesty having once denied, she will ever deny, and that such is her disposition, that she would sooner cause the diamonds, to be thrown into the sea, than leave tokens subsisting, of an action which has been attended with such horrid consequences to us ----This is possible, the only inference I mean to draw, from this long exposition, is, that our persecutors having never been able to prove our disposing of a single carat, more than what I have stated, they cannot be credited upon that ground, when they slander us so undeservedly, by saying that we stole the necklace, all that they can allege with plausibility is, that we cannot ad-

duce

duce proof of the Queen's donation.----How do they know?-----Her Majesty may perhaps have a reflective, compunctive moment, we await it on her death-bed---- let them do the same

It must be in the reader's recollection, that I departed from Bar-sur-Aube with a hundred louis d'ors, and that I left my family possessed of all my own jewels and those of the Countess, and in general of all the property I had, that circumstance, which evidently vouches in favour of my innocence, and proves how far I was from foreseeing what has occured, has, however, contributed most, to afford my enemies grounds for criminating assertions, the house of Rohan giving out that I was gone off with the remainder of the necklace. Those reports obtaining credit, it was undoubtedly a duty incumbent on my family to produce my diamonds and those of the Countess, the more so, as she had given an exact list of them a few days after her arrival at the Bastile, but calculating and *hoping* that the family of Rohan would prevail over us by our destruction, and that they would consequently be able to appropriate to themselves, not only our jewels, but the greatest part also of our plate and effects, they neglected to take one single step towards altering or weakening the suspicions drawn from my departure,----nor, will their shameful avarice presently be doubted of

Soon after the judgment, seeing in the public papers that they had given up none of our jewels, I sent to them an express, in hopes they would at least deliver to him a part but what did they do? After exclaiming in abusive terms against me, they sent him back,
without

without even giving him wherewith to bear his expences. Rightly judging I should not stop there, and that one way or the other I should force them to a restitution, they determined on making a sacrifice, hoping they might with impunity keep all they had robbed my house of. They in consequence put into the Countess's casket her bracelets, a star of brilliants, a medallion, a pair of girandole earrings, a plume-bearer, a black tortoiseshell box with a circle of brilliants on the lid, a pearl necklace, a pair of garnet bracelet clasps set in gold, and three or four rings, valued at the utmost at thirty or forty guineas. They afterwards pretended to have found this casket in a place where I had hid it, before my departure, and to manifest their own honesty and disinterestedness, they sent it to the police, persuaded, that after that voluntary restitution, no search would be made at their houses, and that they might safely write to me (as they actually did) that all my property having, in general, been seized, it was very astonishing I should daily send messengers to them, to make indiscreet demands that once for all I ought to convince myself they had nothing belonging to me, they concluded their epistle by observing, that as I had disgraced them, I must expect no assistance at their hands. Soon after the receipt of this letter, I received from Paris a statement of all that had been sold at the Hotel de Bullion. Being by this means assured of their knavery, I immediately dispatched another express, with a letter, couched in terms that so alarmed them, as to compel a promise that they themselves would repair to London, and deliver to me, what they had (as they pretended) been " so lucky as to save " The period

E e

they had fixed on being passed, and receiving no letter from them, I sent another messenger with fresh instructors. When they found there was no farther room for tergiversation, they determined upon setting out.

The inhabitants of Bar-sur-Aube, loudly reporting that my relations had kept part of my jewels, and incensed at their behaviour in that respect, and the plundering of my house, (since the alarm that had been given them, had forced a surrender of part of my plate, which they had buried under a dunghill) suspected, that the different persons I had sent over, were come to claim the effects I had left with them. The latter thinking to brave the people of the town, and divert their attention, spread a report that they were going to Paris, but took the road to Boulogne, having the precaution, previously to dispatch the person I had sent to them, and especially to prevent his passing through Paris, apprehensive that he might there say something disadvantageous.

Coming to London a few days after the Countess, (who at the period I am mentioning had made her escape) to whom they had refused 25 louis d'ors as she passed through Bar-sur-Aube, they delivered to me a ring, which had formed the stud of the necklace, a watch chain which I sold for 50 pounds sterling, and a box I had taken in exchange, and which I sold to Gray for sixty pounds. Restoring these three articles, they told me that they were all they had been able to preserve of our jewels. Having had full leisure to invent these falsities, and persuaded that I could not have been informed of their conduct, and the depredations they intended on my property, they spared no pains to convince me of the truth of what they had advanced, which would indeed have appeared reasonable, had my intelligence not been so well founded.

Affecting to be satisfied with what they had delivered me, I, the same day, procured a writ to be issued, hoping thereby to frighten them into a surrender of the remaining jewels; but they imagining, from the enquiries they had made, and the advice they had received, previous to their departure, that I could not by any means molest them, they pretended, to shew the utmost indignation at my conduct, and finally declared they had nothing left belonging to me, that they had sold every article, and that, could they have foreseen the ingratitude I now evinced towards them, for what they had done, they would have given up all my jewels, and even have deprived me of the three articles they had just delivered

Judging from their resolute tone, that something more than words was requisite to bring them to a sense of justice, I insisted no farther, but urged by necessity, put the writ into the hands of a sheriff's officer, who soon after, though much to my regret, arrested my uncle, a man of property, childless, enjoying the first offices in the place of his residence, and possessing the esteem of all its inhabitants, and whom I really respected. The case was otherwise with his beloved consort, a despicable woman, detested by all who knew her, who, I am certain had prevailed on her husband to be guilty of such a piece of meanness and injustice. The moment she saw him arrested, she came to me, urging my acceptance of

bills

[212]

bills to the amount of my claims, still assuring me she had nothing of mine, and that she was going to part with some of her own property to purchase her husband's release. Finding he could not make me accede to the terms she proposed, she concluded on acknowleging every thing, and she actually departed to fetch, what she absolutely affected upon oath, to have been surrendered to government.

On her return she gave up two rings that had belonged to the necklace, a pair of drop ear-rings, out of which she had taken four diamonds (which I only perceived after we parted) a hoop-ring, a neck-button, a hair ring, set round with stones, and another ring of small value. The day after this forced restitution her relations returned to their own home, where they shared the remainder of the spoils, nor have I heard of them since, but to be informed, in a circumstantial manner, of all the havock they have made in my house at Bath-ca-Aube, and of the contempt they have drawn upon themselves by their behaviour towards me.

As they are capable, after all they have done, of saying, that they came over to bring me the remainder of the necklace, I think myself bound to add, that, of all which they restored to me, there were but three stones belonging to the necklace, and of which I have spoken above. Every thing else, as well as what was sold at the Hotel de Bouillon in Paris, was (with one very small matter) our property before we ever heard the necklace mentioned.

I have parted with every article, which they brought to me, to Mr Gray of New Bond-street, for the sum of

two

two thousand two hundred pounds sterling. Thus having explicitly, and with great veracity, stated every circumstance wherein I was particularly concerned, I relinquish the pen to the Countess.

(Here the Countess *resumes the Narration.)*

The Count, my husband, having concluded that part of our history, which, as he was singly concerned in the transactions, he could with greater accuracy relate, I now resume my narrative, and think I may safely affirm, that, whatever prejudices, the iniquitous sentence pronounced against me, resulting from the intrigues both of the Queen and the house of Rohan, may have given birth to, those who feel the strongest impulse, cannot doubt, after viewing our account, supported by so many concurrent and undeniable facts, that we have cruelly been made a sacrifice to pride, ambition, and revenge.

The bare conversation of Count de la Motte with the French Ambassador, by disclosing the machinations agitated by the Queen's party, surely gives a perfect idea of those that have *really been put in practice* by the Rohan party; but I do not expect the public to rest their opinions upon mere assertions. I mean to unfold those intrigues of my adversaries of which I can produce positive proofs, and even in these I shall not be able to display one tenth part of their iniquitous conduct.

Before I enter into these particulars, it is important to observe that, by an unaccountable fatality, annexed to the nature of the circumstances, the Queen, whose wife, in the main, was united with mine, or of whom,

(as

(as Count Adhémar very well observed) I was only the representative, could not be brought forward in the business, as the tenor of the Letters Patent, affording the over-ruling party of the Cardinal, a pretence for confining the enquiries solely to the affair of the necklace, banished from discussion every thing foreign to that subject.

By these means, the baseness of the Queen, as I have observed, not being brought into question, and her Majesty not having an interest in the proceedings, I found myself alone, unsupported, and without fortune, having to struggle against the interest, wealth, and reputation of an illustrious and powerful house, and to aggravate these circumstances, I had singly to struggle against the secret influence of the Queen herself, whom my *forced* precaution, relative to the Cardinal, had incensed against me. Is it a wonder, if I sunk under the combined power of such adversaries?

On the supposition, which is a natural one, that the moment I saw myself involved, in that unhappy affair, (setting aside a regard for the truth, superior to that of my own safety) I had thought fit to have coalesced with one or other of the parties concerned, I should not have been able to have accomplished it. I never had, for a single instant, the liberty to consult either justice, my own inclination, or my real interest, perpetually beset with the agents and emissaries of both parties, I saw nothing but rocks on every side. I could not even open my mouth, nor make the least observation, but I heard it repeated to me "If you do that you are undone!"—alas! gracious Heaven! cried I incessantly, whom must

I listen

I listen to?---whom believe?---More tortured with that uncertainty, than uneasy about the real business itself, I grew tired of everlastingly thinking on one object, and fell into that state of insensibility that produces a kind of torpid indifference to consequences, whether good or evil. On one point only my ideas possessed a degree of stability, because it was what I had long since foreseen. I reflected thus---the Queen is bent upon the Cardinal's ruin---but the Cardinal has been my benefactor:--will it not be monstrous in me to become the instrument of his destruction?---the Queen has also been my benefactress; if I am averse to serving the purposes of her revenge, I ought at least to reverence her secrets---All that might have been reconciled, had discretion been all that was requisite. But what was I to answer to eternal questions, most of them insidious ones? how extricate myself out of that wilderness of interrogatories, cross examinations, &c. capable of perplexing an abler head than mine? The confusion of mind thence arising, is the only reason I can give for the frequent contradictions into which I was betrayed.---" say *white*," one told me, " or you are undone;" I said *white.* " say *black*" suggested another, " or it is all over with you;" and of consequence I said *black.* " Do not speak of such a thing," said a third, " you would ruin all." I was questioned concerning this very thing, and answered incoherently, and little did I suspect that all those inconsistencies would combine to criminate and stand as proofs against me. But, let us pass through some of these gradations, by which I was led to the precipice: *some,* I say, because it would require volumes to particularize to clear them all. From my entrance into the Bastile, until the *day of abomination,* not one step was I permitted to take, not a single word was suggested to me, but what tended towards the consummation of my ruin.

The first thing necessary to be known is, that a few days previous to that, which I just now called the *day of abomination,* I received a letter, which, I to this day, impute to the Baron de Breteuil, the purport of which was, that my safety depended on myself; that I had nothing to do, but to place every thing to the account of the Cardinal and of Cagliostro. (*)

On

---

* A manifest proof that the anonymous letter received by me three or four days previous to the arrest of the Cardinal, was sent me by the Baron de Breteuil, appears from this circumstance. It is well known, that when he entered officially the Cardinal's hotel at Paris, hoping to find there the correspondence, and enraged on hearing that a courier dispatched to the Abbé Georgel, had frustrated him in obtaining that object, as the papers had all been committed to the flames, he cried out, upon seeing the bust of Cagliostro, "I meet every " where with nothing but the figure of that mounte- " bank, but patience, I hope there will be an end of " ... con ----I was at that moment very quiet at Bar- sur-Aube, and he only expressed himself thus, because under a persuasion that I should implicitly follow the counsels he had given me in his letter.

On the 11th of August, when was I carried to the Baſtile, (already incenſed againſt the Cardinal, who, in order to enſnare the Queen and ſave himſelf, threw all the blame upon me,) I perceived the Commiſſary Chénon advancing towards me, who, having had his leſſon from the Baron de Breteuil, aſked me what I ſhould ſay in my defence?----Recollecting then the letter I had received, but unwilling to go as far as the anonymous writer adviſed me I anſwered, that I would ſay, the Cardinal had made me a preſent of a quantity of diamonds, without my having a knowledge whether or not they belonged to the necklace. He adviſed me not to purſue that method, repreſenting that it would prepoſſeſs the King againſt me. That would be acknowledging myſelf a miſtreſs to the Cardinal, and in that caſe it would appear no wonder he ſhould have made me ſuch a preſent, " ſay rather," added he, that " he gave them to " be diſpoſed of by you, to his advantage, and that you " have remitted to him the ſums received for them---- " that will wear the greater air of probability, and be " infinitely more decent for you."

This was the firſt advice, that I confeſs myſelf weak enough to follow, and which, while it produced my ruin, preſerved the Cardinal, becauſe, it was not poſſible for me to prove that I had paid him the money, whereas had I purſued the mode I had planned, and ſaid that he had given me a great number of diamonds, he would have been unable to prove the contrary but it was not till ſome conſiderable time after that I felt the difference of thoſe two declarations The commiſſary, whom I plainly perceived to be the inſtrument of the Baron de Breteuil,

Breteuil, had made it his business to prevent me as much as possible from reflecting on my situation, and in order to fix my whole attention, had given me to understand that the Queen would protect, and speedily bring me out of the Bastile. " An additional reason," said he to me, " for avoiding to speak of any present you have re-
" ceived, because the Cardinal would not fail to an-
" swer, that you had told him, those diamonds were
' presented to you by the Queen, in which case, her
" Majesty would be exposed, a circumstance you must
" take special care to avoid." In vain I represented to him, that did I not comprehend how I could dispense with mentioning the name of the Queen, in a business, of which she had been the essential source. He answered,
' *If you name her, you are undone.*" (*)

The

---

* When I received a second visit from the Commissary Chénon, he communicated a letter, he said he had received from Baron de Breteuil, whose writing I knew again. He gave him notice what Counsel he had chosen, and pointed out the methods of engaging them to undertake my defence. He advised me to write to them, in such manner as to make them sensible, that by pleading for me, they would certainly do what was highly pleasing to the Queen, the Baron de Breteuil, &c. without however naming them. In order to leave no doubt remaining, he persuaded me to add, that they might go to the police, and receive the information of what I had advanced. This appeared to me to be an
excellent

The Lawyer Doillot, whom Mr. de Breteuil in like manner sent me for a Counsel, began also by forbidding me

---

excellent piece of advice, and looking on the Baron de Breteuil as entirely governed by the Queen, I wrote without hesitation what the commissary dictated to me. He took upon him the charge of conveying the letters. Those, to whom they were addressed, did not delay (after they had been to Mr De Crone's) to present themselves to defend me, but the vanity and jealousy of Mr Doillot, made him reject two celebrated Counsellors, and it was at that moment he published his first memorial, which is a mixture of nonsense and falshood. At the same period the commissary Chénon had desired me to give him, in writing, all that I had verbally communicated to him, intending, as he said, to lay it before the Baron de Breteuil, who being informed of the whole connexion, would be the more concerned for me. As I was one day employed in that business, which I had almost brought to a conclusion, Doillot came in, I related to him what was passing between the commissary and the Baron de Breteuil, and showed him the memorial I was preparing for him. He began to exclaim against me, called me *child*, persuaded me, from several circumstances which he related, that the commissary sought to deceive me, and concluded, by prevailing on me to permit no more of his visits, a piece of advice I punctually followed. At his leaving me he took up and pocketted the memorial.

me ever to utter the Queen's name, assuring me, *from good authority, that she would protect me.* On the other hand, the Cardinal's party sought to engross me to themselves. De Laune, Governor of the Bastile, devoted to the house of Rohan, had placed near me, a certain Abbé Lecuve, Chaplain to that horrid prison, whose principal employ was to pass from the Cardinal's apartment to mine, from mine to the Cardinal's, and to concert our respective answers against the time we were to undergo our examinations.

It may readily be supposed, those answers were so calculated, that, without my perceiving it, mine had always a tendency to confirm the probability of the Cardinal's. I indeed sometimes experienced moments of distrust, but that villain of an Abbé was so dextrous, shewed so much concern, and affected so much regard for me, that I acquiesced in every thing he proposed. He was informed of every thing, brought me messages from the Cardinal, and was always apprising me of the objects to which the examination would be pointed. "To-morrow" he would say to me, "you will be "brought face to face with the Cardinal, he will per- "haps be brought to say to you, such and such things; "beware

---

The King my require of that lawyer to produce the memorial, as also the one he made me afterwards write; he may judge, by the resemblance, that I never varied, when I spoke the truth, and that the circumstances I this day relate, are absolutely the same as those I committed to paper at the periods I am speaking of.

" beware of contradicting him, all that, is only matter
" of form, the trial will never be brought to issue, it
" is impossible it ever should,-----the Pope is in-
" terested in it,---the Chapter of Strasburgh is moving
" heaven and earth,----you will perceive, and the Car-
" dinal charges me to assure you, that this affair will
" terminate without a judgment, and the Queen will
" be non-suited. (*) The misfortune is, that he cannot
" expose

---

* Since I have been in London, I have read, in the journal of a writer, intitled " *Secret Memoirs for the History of the Republic of Letters in France,*" a letter from Abbé Georgel to the Princess of Marsan. I deemed it so much the more necessary to insert it here, as the reader will judge by its contents, that Abbé Lequele drew his information from the same source as Abbé Georgel, and that in lieu of Baron de Planta, I unfortunately was pitched upon for the victim to be sacrificed to *disgraced power*.

Sept. 18, 1785.

MADAM,

CEASE to be uneasy concerning our dear Cardinal. He bore with all the dignity of a Rohan, the unthought of blow aimed against him. His health continues good, in his confinement, the severities of which are moderate, and his soul is at peace, as much as that of an illustrious man, under such accusations can be, who foresees he never shall be judged. But if authority recedes,
will

"expose her without endangering the loss of his own
"head----I am persuaded, that after the services he has
"done

---

will not that be a justification? The King with the advice of his council has just referred the matter to the Parliament. The letters-patent are registered. The whole procedure may very likely terminate there, for in short, the trial of a mere clerical person cannot be carried on but before the Ecclesiastical Judge. Have a Bishop, a Cardinal his immunities? The history of France presents us with seven Cardinals impeached by our Kings, not one could personally be brought to trial, the Chancellor d'Aguesseau himself allows, that out of these instances, there are eleven in behalf of the church, nor can we doubt being the first body in the state. In 1652 the trial of Cardinal de Retz was referred to the Parliament by letters-patent, which unquestionably served as a precedent to those of 1785. But three years after, a solemn declaration repealed the decree, confirming the ancient right of Bishops, to be tried only by their own metropolitan.

The crime was a one of high-treason, and all the pretension on the part of the Crown was, that a crime of that nature suspended all immunities. So that when there is nothing that concerns the King or state, no court but the common-law is in its full force. You may see, Madam, what all the bustle of the day may come to. Do not however think, that there is any unsoundness in the Keeper of the Seals, and the Count
de

" done you, you could not without a heart-breaking sorrow
" bring him to the scaffold." " What am I to do then?"
answered I keenly, " if I can neither impeach the Car-
" dinal nor the Queen, it will all fall upon me!"----
" In

---

de Vergennes, they both know what they are about, the one is conversant in the French law, the other understands the Roman politics, they alone could afford light, but *they are our friends*. They are actuated by the *same views*, the *same aversions*. They know that the Elector of Mentz will demand a revocation, that Rome will lay claim, that the clergy will remonstrate, that even the empire will murmur. They have hitherto been silent, and paid a seeming deference to the apparent equity of committing the matter to a national tribunal. If the clamours are not sufficiently powerful, the proceedings of the Parliament will continue, but in such a manner as to operate neither against the accusers nor the accused, if difficulties increase, the King will retract, which will be so much the more in our favour, as there will be greater *perplexity* in the carrying on the business. *There will then no longer be but one victim requisite to sacrifice to offended power.* Why should not the Baron, who was only an agent, be dismissed as the principal? We should completely triumph, all interests would be reconciled, revenge would be gratified,----and respective enmities would cease. Madam, I have communicated facts, let those facts be a secret for your life

" In your situation *I would tell the truth, I see no harm*
" *in having received diamonds of the Queen.*

" No,—but there is danger in telling it, because it
" is telling that she received the necklace, and that is
" what she wont allow.'——Generally speaking, at that
time I saw no one but the Abbé Lequele, who often
came, and told me, the Cardinal grew very weary of the
protraction of his trial, and that his health declined
daily. I, complaining on my side, and with greater
reason, asked him, if there was no possibility of putting
a period to the business? A thought that instant occurred to me of writing to the Queen, I imparted to him
my idea, which met with his approbation, he, even
charging himself with the delivery of the letter. I wrote
therefore in his presence nearly in these terms.

MADAM,

NOTWITHSTANDING all the severities of my
situation, not a single complaint has escaped me; all the
insidious methods that have been practised to extort
confessions from me, have served only to strengthen me
in the resolution, of never saying any thing, by which
you may be brought into question, yet, persuaded as I
am, that my fidelity and discretion ought to facilitate
my being extricated from my difficulties, I own to you,
that the efforts of the family of the " *Slave,*" make me
fear I shall become a victim. Three months examination
of anxieties of every kind, the despondency of seeing
myself accused (I, who am innocent) has greatly weakened

ened my fortitude, and makes me apprehenfive I fhall not be able, much longer, to be fteady in that refolve. You have it in your power to put an end to this unhappy bufinefs, by caufing it to be negociated by B. He may give to the *Minifter* what turn his intelligent mind may fuggeft to him, avoiding particularly to bring you into queftion. The dread I am under of feeing myfelf forced to a full difcovery, drives me to the meafure I now adopt, perfuaded Madam, that you will give orders to have this unfortunate matter brought to a conclufion.

I am with the moft profound refpect,

Madam's moft obedient fervant,

COUNTESS DE VALOIS DE LA MOTTE.

April 13, 1786.

I gave him my letter to read, which he approved of, and propofed my communicating it to the Cardinal As the latter was at leaft as much interefted as myfelf, in having the proceedings terminated I faw no impropriety in fo doing I delivered to him my letter, and pointed out the manner of conveying it fafely, by inclofing it under three covers He put it into his pocket, and after an hour's converfation on various topics, he pretended to go, then ftopping for a confiderable time, as if full of thought, and at laft obferved to me, that, upon mature reflexion, it was not poffible for him to deliver

[226]

...such a letter, without rendering himself liable to be ... furnished with an apartment in the Bastile, for ... generally known, that he was the only person I conversed with, people would naturally turn an eye of suspicion upon him, as to the delivery of such a letter from me. He therefore returned it, saying he would speak of it to the Cardinal, and that some person should be thought of, that might undertake the commission, without incurring the same degree of danger.

Thus it was that wretch, by buoying me up with hopes, found means to induce a conversation with me, and to take advantage of every unguarded word that might escape me.

The examinations being ended, I had the precious permission to see counsel Doillot, who, if not naturally ..., was seduced by the Baron de Breteuil, consequently full of no other consideration than that of bringing the Cardinal to the block, and preventing the Queen's being, in any manner whatsoever, betrayed and exposed.

His first visit to me, after the conclusion of the examinations, will evince by the account he brought how many shifts and stratagems had been used to circumvent him, and prevent his giving up his second memorial. Wishing to be informed of the result of his own motion, he went to Mr. Laurencelle's, deputy to the Attorney General, who after much tergiversation, and pretended impossibility for him to communicate any thing further, that I had made a full confession of ... and proven in writing, that the ... I had been put to, for having made
such

such declarations, had rendered it impossible for me to be seen, that a few days before, I had bitten off the thumb of my turn-key, St. John.

Doillot, stunned with this information, answered that he could not believe it, after all I had told him, and the writings I had given to him. The deputy seeing him in this state of uncertainty, and looking upon him, as already disposed to believe whatever he might suggest, imparted to him the examinations, wherein he read the confession I had made. Stupified with amazement, incensed at having been so grossly deceived, he walked hastily about the room, cursing those who had prevailed on him to undertake my defence, &c. Growing somewhat calm, and recollecting all the methods used to impose on me, as well as himself, he requested to look over the examinations a second time, and particularly to ascertain my signature, as also those of the other parties, which Laurencelle absolutely refused his assent to. Suspecting therefore a design to deceive him, and prevent his coming any more to me in the Bastile, he withdrew, determined to search into the truth. He in consequence of what had passed, paid me a visit, in spite of all opposition to his family and friends. His serious and inquisitive countenance, on entering the apartment, appeared to me so much the more extraordinary, from having written down and recapitulated all that passed during the whole time of the examinations — I could not imagine what had produced such an alteration. At length, after signifying his surprise at my chearfulness, he acquainted me with all that had happened at Laurencelle's, with the reports that were circulated, with the pretended confession I had made, and particularly with my fit of rage, in which I had bitten off my turnkey's thumb. Poor St. John, who was present at this story, cou'd not contain himself, but after bearing testimony of the truth, said, that "the Governor, who was "sold to the family of Rohan, was the fabricator of "those calumnies, and that he was ready to stand be- "fore his face, and reproach him with his infamous be- "haviour from the very beginning of the business." He added, that "far from my being outrageous, as it "was pretended, I had been too mild; and that in my "place, he should not have been able to bear with "those villains, but would have torn their eyes out."

I then delivered to Doillot my examinations, which I had taken care to write down at each sitting, and after reading them over, and being delighted with them, he required me to sign my name at the bottom of every page, in order to leave no doubt of their authenticity; then went out triumphantly, promising to have all the particulars I had been relating to him immediately printed. Before I let him depart, I told him of the snare which the knavish Abbé had laid for me, to which he answered, that "I must be good indeed, to "puzzle my brain with such a parcel of pitiful stuff, "that he was glad my letter had not been conveyed to "the Queen, as it could not but have produced a bad "effect, and indisposed her to be inimical to me, "that in a word, once for all, I ought to be persuad- "ed, I should come off with flying colours." He was all this time drawing up memorials, writing briefs, void of common sense, shapeless assemblages of absurdities

and

and falshoods, making me declare in every page, that I had never seen the Queen, and forcing me to affirm it before my judges: whereas my natural and sure defence was, to say (what was inceſſantly in my heart and on my lips) that the Queen had loaded me with favours, ever since the period, when through the accident I before mentioned, I had been so happy as to intereſt her Majeſty in my behalf.

When Doillot was departed, Abbé Lequele came to know whether I had not charged him with the letter I had written to the Queen? I anſwered I had not.—" You did very right," replied he, " I have talked the " matter over with the Cardinal, who thinks it would " have paſſed through the hands of Baron de Breteuil, " who would not have failed making his advantage of " it, by hindering it from reaching the Queen."

I preſerved the letter to the moment of my appearing before the Parliament, determined (if I diſcovered an intention of ſacrificing me) to drop it as I went out, which would neceſſarily have brought on an explanation, that I would have entered into, by divulging the whole affair.

Unfortunately for me, I ſaw myself encouraged and applauded, and in conſequence of the hopes all along given to me, during the trial, I went back, perſuaded I ſhould gain my cauſe. On my entering the keeper's parlour, I related to his wife, who was very kind to me, all that had juſt been tranſacted, imparting the circumſtance of the letter, which I ſhewed her, ſhe called in her huſband, who, terrified beyond meaſure, ſhut the door upon us, and immediately burnt the letter.

From

From everything I have related, it appears that I was nearly in the case of a patient, to whom one physician says " If you eat you will die of indigestion," another, " if you do not eat you'll perish through mere " want." The fact is, that die I must, for seeing before my eyes the *food* or *poison*, in cafe I mentioned the Queen's name, I took care not to do it, but then by not naming her, I fixed upon myself the guilt of purchasing the necklace.---And indeed, from the moment it was apparent the Cardinal would extricate himself, either through the treachery or inability of my counsel, it became clear, that a victim must fall, and that I was destined to be the sacrifice. It is at once shocking and remarkable, that both the judges and evidences united to aim the mortal blow at me. The epitome of the examinations (which the public never had knowlege of, but through the *unfaithful* narrative of the imprudent lawyer Target) would impress the mind with horror, if the records that contain it, were exposed to every eye. I will adduce a few passages, which I cannot have forged.

We must not lose sight of a fact I have already mentioned, and which is now universally known, that is, as well in the previous interrogatories, as in the examination, neither the Cardinal nor myself ever uttered one word of truth, the reason of which is very plain that is, and we came so, it was *under penalty of forfeiting our lives.* Neither the Cardinal nor myself were to name the Queen, what therefore cou'd we say, that should bear reference to what the truth really was?---Secondly, as I have already previously observed, both of us being

being prepared to utter nothing but untruths, our depositions, declarations and various speeches, were a ready calculated game, in which it is evident, that, seeing the immense inequalities of our stations, the advantage could not be on my side, for I played the weak hand against whom? a great Queen and a powerful Lord! Was it possible that evidences, of the cast of those who appeared in this affair, should waver a moment between me and either of my adverse parties?--- and indeed, what was the consequence? Why, that in all the affidavits, obtained at a vast expence, marks of bribery and corruption stare me in the face? I ask pardon of Monsieur Dupuis de Marce, solicitor in the iniquitous prosecution, but I can prove him to have prevaricated to a scandalous excess. Let us refer only to one circumstance, the iniquity of the sentence, which crowned all the iniquities practised against me. Her Majesty was a powerful Queen, the Cardinal as powerful a Prince. I had nothing but the *name* of VALOIS to render me of any consequence. It has been seen that, being equally made the victim of misfortune, from the advice dictated by the malice of my enemies, and the interests which I had occasioned, I was led astray by the counsels of both friends and foes. There remains for me to prove the corrupt evidence produced against me, and the prevarication, with which I charged the Solicitor, and by quoting instances of the former, I shall furnish some of the latter.

First, having unhappily entrusted that villain Lequele with the particulars of the affair, who, a spy of the Governor's and a creature of the Cardinal's, was

necefnecessarily a most dangerous confident, it is made manifest by the event, that he at the same time communicated to the Cardinal's counsel, and to his own patron, what I had communicated relative to Villette and the girl Oliva, and that it was pursuant to that imprudent step of mine that the Rohans stimulated the authority of their friend de Vergennes, to have those two persons taken into custody, in order to instruct them, and make them depose whatever should be judged suitable to their purpose.

Scarce had Villette entered the Bastile, when they ensured him his safety, and furnished him with the means, by suggesting the idea of writing to Count de Vergennes, who, certainly must be supposed to have personal interest in the business. He therefore wrote to that minister, that he had matters to impart of the utmost importance, which he could entrust to none but himself. The wily statesmen, who had advised this plan of proceeding, but would not appear the least concerned in the prosecution, caused him to be told, it was impossible for him to grant Villette an audience, but that he might with equal safety "entrust every thing with the Governor." He might as well have said "to the Cardinal and his counsel."

Villette having objected to disclosing himself, he was advised to write a second letter to Mr de Vergennes, with a free confession of all he knew, to which he answered, he would willingly comply, but for the fear of exposing the Queen. "Well" said they to him, "do not expose her, cannot you omit her name, and tell every thing else you know?" As he seemed perplexed, they saved him the trouble of arranging his depositions,

and

and the very first day they were given to him ready prepared. They pointed out to him the nature of those confessions he was to avoid, and suggesting such as he was to substitute in lieu of them, and in the same manner as the Baron de Breteuil, Count D'Adhémar, the Commissary Chénon, and others, calling themselves partisans of the Queen, had dictated to my husband and me, " Lay all to the Cardinal's account " the partisans of the Rohans said to the witnesses whom they instructed, " Lay every thing to the charge of the Countess de la " Motte." But it will be said to me, " What proofs " have you for these assertions?---they may be slander- " ous"---what proofs? I could bring many, but one only is sufficient. It is this in whatever light the affair is considered, Villette, by his own confession, was at least guilty of a species of forgery, which if not deemed of a nature to incur a capital, at least deserved some kind of punishment. Was he punished? No,---on the contrary his circumstances were rendered easy, he had a settlement made upon him, in a word he was rewarded! ---for what?---for the docility with which he complied in being silent upon the Queen's account, and in placing every thing criminal to mine. Needs there any farther proof of flagrant corruption?---Informed as I am, to the minutest particulars, how that scene of iniquity was carried on, I regret that I am obliged to declare from whom my intelligence was received, but whatever I do not reveal in these Memoirs, will be through want of recollection. I say therefore, that my author, for those particulars, is the CHEVALIER DU PUGET, *the King's Lieutenant of the Bastile,* who was present at all those

[234]

vile cabals carried on by the Governor. The indignation he conceived in consequence of them, determined him to inform me, that I might make my advantage of them. Accordingly on a cross examination with that Valette, I made him confess the matter, and then, observing to him there were, exclusive of the Governor, other persons who prevailed on him to make depositions concerning such and such particulars, he had the honesty to say, "It is true, it was those two Gentlemen, pointing at the same time to the Solicitor and the Recorder."---How wonderful the integrity of that Solicitor!---I know not what it brought him in, but the sum must have been large, if proportioned to the infamy he had brought upon himself. I shall return to him more than once. I beg permission to say a few words concerning poor Olive. I shall first observe, that she was so simple, so very simple, that all the wilyness of the de Launay's (*), of the de Puis de Macé's (†), of the French (‡), never cou'd make her say *yes*, instead of *no*, *black* in lieu of *white*; and indeed for that reason all her depositions and examinations remained buried in the Bastile. She never could be diverted from the native simplicity of her narrative, ingenuously relating the adventure of the green-arbour, and maintaining to the very last, the Queen's being present. In vain do they observe to her, that timidity had made her see one object instead of another, that she might be deceived

---

* Governor of the Bastile.   † The Solicitor.
‡ The Recorder.

deceived through the darkness of the night in short that she was pur-blind, Oliva not apprehending that her answers were prompted to her, in order to bring her off, persisted stoutly, and her last word was: " I am very " certain that I both saw and heard the Queen, and that " she spoke to me" It must be readily conceived that when they came to confront her with me, they spared no pains to bias her, there was no possibility of burying the words she spoke before me, as the interrogatories might be for that reason they dreaded to let her speak. To obviate this positive inconvenience, the Solicitor thought to surmount the difficulty, by putting the questions to her, in such a manner, that she had nothing to do, but answer by a mere negative or affirmative I did not let that escape me, but desired Mr Dupuis de Marcé " to suffer her to speak, and not to be her mouth- " piece " (a trivial expression, which occurred to me I know not how) He blushed---was stung with rage--- and getting up like a demoniac, put an end to the session!!! Apropos, of this session so hastily put an end to, it is now time for observing, that he never did otherwise, but, daily, had recourse to that artifice. Whenever the Cardinal was in a dilemma, and that the worthy Solicitor, or the Recorder Fremin, could not by their significant looks and glances, either silence him, or suggest his answers, they immediately quitted their seats; at other times, when they saw me grow warm, and appear ready to convict the Cardinal by some unanswerable argument, they would sooth me, would affect to pacify me, to make me lose the thread of my discourse; which I could not recover again, either because the

flurry

flurry of my spirits threw my ideas into confusion, or that they did not allow me leisure to recollect myself --- The case was not the same in respect to the Cardinal, they would stop him short in the middle of a sentence. I have often seen the Solicitor, and the Recorder Freman, as red as fire, rise up with emotion, and say to the Cardinal, "Hold your tongue---you have no memory,---you are contradicting what you deposed on 'such a day.'" Those gentlemen had still another resource. Whatever was said in favour of the Cardinal, was committed to writing with incredible eagerness and punctuality, but if they came to any circumstance that tended, the least in the world, to expose him, I was forced to exert myself, even passionately, to make the Recorder take it down, who still found ways to baffle me. It is a fact that upon a second perusal of the depositions, or personal examinations before each other, of the preceding day, I several times perceived them to' be altered, and obtaining no redress when I made mention of it, I frequently arose and declared "I would " attend no more, and that since those gentlemen were " bent upon finding me guilty, they might as well pass " judgment on me ahead, my presence being use-" less."

At one time I held my resolution for a whole week, nor could be prevailed upon, but by pressing solicitations of our hands, to return to what I called the *den of mystery.* It was in these scenes of iniquity that those vile men presumed to call me a "*wicked wo-*" *man,*" and I am indebted to them for a name, which people, seeing them their conduct has too often attached

tached to me. Surely that epithet muſt revert to my accuſers, to thoſe who not content with all the prevarications and artifices I have been diſcloſing, had moreover the *villany* to alter and interpolate the records, by adding or ſuppreſſing on their ſtamped paper, as beſt ſuited their purpoſes, by omitting what operated againſt them, or by introducing ſpeeches that were never ſpoken. I once very diſtinctly overheard the *horeſt* Dupuis de Marcé ſay to the Recorder, "*Set your lines a little wider from one another*" Another legerdemain trick I beg leave to expoſe I had one day ſtoutly inſiſted on ſomething conſequential, that had dropped from the Cardinal, being taken down The Recorder anſwering, "*he had no room left, but would add it on the next leaf,*" I would not leave him till he had noted it in the margin, (*) which he did, but they took care that day, not to require my ſignature to it. Two days afterwards

I was

---

* The Cardinal having maintained on ſeveral occaſions, that he uſed to ſend me by his Swiſs porter and his valet de chambre *four, five* and *ſix louis d'ors* in cards. Being one day terrified with the ruſtling I occaſioned by various papers I had in my pocket, and unmindful of his former depoſitions, he ſaid he was ſure I had received at *two inſtalments,* FIVE HUNDRED THOUSAND LIVRES which had been placed in the hands of his notary I permitted him to proceed to the end, not failing afterwards to make him obſerve the contradiction, pointing out to him, that ſince he was ſure, I had

received

I was presented with a paper to sign, at the same time with the examination of the day; on my perusing which, I discovered it was the very same, on which I had caused a note to be set down in the margin, but that note was no longer to be found there. I exclaimed against such a piece of perfidiousness, I was answered with prevaricating arguments, and the note was *not* restored.

Another day, I was in reality "*wicked*" as those gentry were pleased to call me. They confronted me with Cagliostro, and that Mountebank, as rude as he is shameless, took the liberty to treat me with unbecoming language, which proved wonderfully entertaining to Mr. Dupuis de Marcé. I quickly put an end to the scene, by throwing a candlestick at the *quack's* head, and turning towards Monsieur the Solicitor, I told him, that the better to put perfection to heighten the *dénouement* of the farce, I requested he would supply me with a broom-stick. It was on that occasion I discovered a fresh piece of villainous intrigue. Cagliostro enraged and foaming at the mouth, said to me—"He will come, thy Villette, he will come, it is he that will speak."——From whence did he know that?——How did he know it?——Who could have told it?——It was then the time for interro-

---

received five louis and the said times, it was not probable he should further have lent me *five or six louis*. I ordered the Recorder to write down that deposition, on his replying he had no more room, and that he would do it next time, I caused it to be put in the terrogatories and examinations----I saw no soul living, and that knave Cagliostro knew every thing! Can there be a more striking proof of the scandalous confederacy that reigned between the accused, the prosecutors, the evidences and the judges? (*)

I know

---

* My *rencounter* with Cagliostro originated from a circumstance rather ludicrous. He obstinately denied the cabalistic scenes acted at the Cardinal's, particularly the one in which HE HAD CAUSED MY NIECE TO SEE THE QUEEN IN A BOTTLE, ACCOMPANIED BY THE GRAND COPHTI, AND THE ANGEL MICHAEL, WHO WERE DECLARING TO HER MAJESTY SHE SHOULD BE DELIVERED OF A MALE CHILD, &c. On that occasion, as I had seen the letter No XXXII, I told him, I knew how much the Queen despised him, that she called him a meer mountebank, an impostor, in short I acquainted him with those terms of disdain, in which she had refused the Cardinal her consent to see Cagliostro ----" apropos," said I to him, " Grand Cophti, " has your prayer produced its effect? If it has so much " efficacy, why don't you use it to get out of this " place?" It was on that account he flew into a rage, and talked to me impertinently. The Solicitor asked what the purport of that prayer was, but as I had already entertained him sufficiently, I did not think proper to afford him farther satisfaction. I answered, that Cagliostro perfectly understood me, and that was sufficient, but I will shew more complaisance to the public.

The

I know not whither my recollection would carry me, were I to yield to all the suggestions, with which my mind is full. At the present moment, when I am sensible I must have exceedingly wearied the reader with the dull details of so complicated an examination, I see myself

---

The truth is, that at the period when the Queen wrote to the Cardinal, the subjoined letters in which she complained of the " vexatious behaviour of the Polignacs, &c." Cagliostro, whom he consulted, if his fingers did but ache, told him, " he had a secret for getting rid ' of people who gave umbrage," and at the same time ' gave him two prayers with the manner of using " them." The Prince's first care was to send them to the Queen, recommending to her the use of them, and to put faith in them. As I had the charge of delivering those precious amulets, the Queen imparted them to me in a loud fit of laughter, and asked whether the Cardinal was going out of his wits, or if he took her for a simpleton? I do not remember the very words of those prayers, but perfectly well their use. One was to be applied below the left breast, the other in the pocket on the fore side, and when the Queen had a mind to make any one of her set, she needed only to place her hands on the two prayers while she recited them, at that instant all were to be proftrate, all were to be otherwise confirmed, and perform her will ----a circumstance which, after exciting her mirth, made the Queen say to me, ' I am very likely to make trial of it."

myself surrounded with a croud of perverse witnesses, who, however disgraceful it may be to them, seem to solicit a little corner in my memoirs.

I cannot withstand the temptation of saying a word, concerning the part assigned to the QUEEN DOWAGER, the immaculate DU BARRE of monastic memory. The evidence of that woman set forth, that I had been at her house to solicit *her protection!* and that I had left with her a memorial signed *Mary Antoinette de France.* The fact is, that I only went to her house out of curiosity, in a good coach and four, that at that period I stood so little in need of her protection, that their Royal Highnesses MADAME, and MADAME COUNTESS D'ARTOIS, had taken me under theirs. Upon her signifying to me, that she thought the branch of VALOIS had been extinct, I gave her a memorial to which was annexed my genealogy, signed " MARY ANTONY D'OZIER DE SERIGNY, JUDGE OF THE NOBILITY OF FRANCE." This she was pleased to transform into " MARY ANTOINETTE OF " FRANCE," saying, that that was my signature. When she was confronted with me, she took it into her head to assume towards me an air of haughtiness and insolence. I hastened to set her in her proper place, by making her sensible of the distance between her birth and mine, upon which she cried out, " It is very hard I " must be brought hither to be humbled by Madam." The Solicitor then said to her, loud enough for me to hear him, " Well well, Madam, never mind, you will shortly be revenged." Hence it is plain the scheme of those gentry was no secret.

I ask Madame du Barry's pardon, if I name her with such bad company, but in truth, without affectation, the name of De Brugniere, is that which occurs next immediately after hers.

That exempt of the police deposed, "that he had "seen in the hands of a Jew, (whose name I do not "call to mind) some diamonds which the Sieur Villette had carried to him for sale, and which were, he "said, at least *as large as his thumb!*" Take notice, that the Sieur Brugniere's thumb is as broad as a half crown piece! those are the very diamonds that were sold to Pâris the jeweller, for the sum of fifteen thousand livres. The *honest* De Brugniere was convicted, by the Jew's evidence, on that circumstance.

As I had given in an exact account of all my own diamonds, and those of my husband, there had been one required of my waiting woman, hoping it would differ from mine. The Solicitor vexed to see them tally so well, sought, artfully, to make her magnify the size of several diamonds, belonging to my husband, but she, acting on principles of honesty, which the exempt of the police was not master of, refused compliance, and described all our jewels as they really were.

To those I have mentioned let me add another honest man! Regnier, my own jeweller, had been brought over to give a list of diamonds bought of me, which he had valued at a large amount. Seeing through the knavery of it, I required his books to be produced, but this satisfaction I never could obtain.

Grenier who had come to me with La Porte, about the project of finance I have mentioned in the former part

part of these Memoirs, has, as well as the Capuchin M'Dermot, given in a very long deposition, manufactured by the lawyer Target, which was still more shocking, and discovered a greater degree of collusion. Grenier is a man of very circumscribed intellects, and by no means equal to the producing of so well written a performance. It laboured especially to prove that I had told him I was accustomed to see the Queen; and that, while in my bath, I had shewn him letters, which I said I had ceived from her Majesty, directed " *to my cousin the Countess de Valois.*" What a piece of absurdity!

La Porte's evidence except in a few instances is exactly the same. Baron de Planta, in order to prove also that I visited the Queen, said, he accompanied me as far as her Majesty's apartment, that he waited for me at the bottom of the back stairs, whence he saw me come out, he added, that he had knowlege of several considerable sums, I had received from her Majesty. I took care not to make any comments on the Baron's deposition, who did not perceive that it flatly contradicted what the Cardinal had deposed. The Solicitor and the Recorder were silent, imagining that my memory was not more tenacious than that of the Baron, but when they saw that in spite of their representations, I insisted all he had said should be taken down in writing, then it was they ruled against the Baron, and refused me the satisfaction I required. Incensed at this behaviour, I withdrew in a rage, saying, that since they were determined at all events to find me guilty, they might as well condemn me unheard, that most assuredly, they should see me no more. I above related the Governor's promises and solicitations to get me again to the council hall, which would be better denominated the hall of desolation.

Bohemer in his first memorial to the Queen, makes no mention of my name; his deposition rather tended to exculpate than to criminate me; but what I have to charge him with is, that he did not relate all that he knew. He was one day taking with him to his country house, a man whose name was Pagan; as they passed before the Bastile, he made him take notice of the place where the Cardinal used to walk, saying to him, " The " Cardinal's life was in my hands, his fate depended on " me, but I said nothing; people owed me a grudge " for it yonder, (meaning at Versailles) I thought for " a while I should lose my place, but you know every " thing is at last forgotten."

Father Loth, a Minim friar, another notorious villain, who was under the greatest obligations to me, and to whom (when I quitted Paris) I had left the management of all my concerns, was the man who evinced the most zeal for the house of Rohan. His project, as well as the Capuchin M'Dermot's, was to get himself secularised, which he thought he could not more readily obtain, than by running about in quest of false evidence, and himself making depositions shocking to common sense. Hearing that he had been endeavouring to prevail on a young person who had lived with me, to make a false affidavit, I required her to be sent for, she came accordingly, and made affidavit of the circumstance. Dupuis de Macé could not forbear testifying his indignation, especially when informed of the services I had done him. I believe he has before this time repeated his

infa-

infamous behaviour, for from that moment he has been despised and forsaken by every body.

Of the whole body of witnesses, that were collected together against me, none, [except the Sieur de Villette, who accused me of prevailing on him to sign *Mary Antoinette of France*, of which I have related the particulars) pretended to have any of the necklace; why therefore was I condemned as having stolen it? what proofs were there to maintain such an accusation? ---none. Mr. St James, whose depositions contained very pointed facts, and Bohemer, were two dreadful evidences against the Cardinal It was given out that one was a *fool*, who did not know what he was saying; the other deaf, and had misunderstood one thing for another, yet the Cardinal shewed those two individuals (who gave evidence of it) letters from the Queen, and said he had seen in her Majesty's hands SIX HUNDRED THOUSAND livres, which he would not take charge of. If pains had not been taken to stifle the truth, on the very lips that strove to utter it, would circumstances so material have been passed over so slightly as they were? ---what is the use then of evidence?---let us examine what those exculpatory writings were, which the Cardinal published, in order to eradicate the impression he dreaded, and which must naturally result from such a multiplicity of facts. We have seen, that one Jefferys a jeweller in Picadilly, to whom my husband had first delivered a quantity of diamonds, had made him an offer of " four thousand guineas," payable by installments, which offer he declined This Jefferys, vexed to hear that he had struck a bargain with Mr. Gray,

embraced

embraced the opportunity to be revenged, as he imagined, of his *ffc* jeweller, by laying, at the instigation of Carbonnieres, an information as false as could be made, with a view to make Gray pass for a man of little probity, in having purchased, as he termed them, stolen diamonds. Jefferys in the first place said, that immediately on having the diamonds in his hands, he went to the office and gave information, that he had returned the diamonds, being unwilling to purchase them, from suspicion of their having been stolen. This was the declaration sent to Paris, and signed by an *honest* French notary, named *Duvergig*, who from that time to this, never would communicate the original declaration, though he was sent it to Paris, and "never "kept duplicates of the said writings." A notary, and not keep the testimonials of the business transacted!!!(*) As soon as Jefferys had heard that my husband had concluded a bargain with Mr. Gray, he renewed his application to him, telling him, " he would have made him " greater allowance, had he known he would have ac-
" cepted

---

* This Dubourg, whom the family of Ronan ought not to have abandoned after his ready compliance with their instructions, has lately been obliged to solicit Mess. D'Aignan and B. Jeremy for two guineas, to convey him to a convent of Monks where he is to take the cowl. It is on the testimony of that Infer-wolfey Friar, that the family of Ronan has presented justificatory writings, accused of mere their falsehoods, and drawn up by the same Dubourg.

" cepted of jewels in exchange, and asked, whether he " had any more diamonds?" Mr. de la Motte produced what he had left, which Jefferys took away with him for examination, but my husband finding he had carried them to the person with whom he had made the former bargain, took them out of his hands, and concluded a bargain with the same person himself.

When Count de la Motte came back to London, Jefferys went to him and assured him, that his declaration had been interpreted quite otherwise than he had intended, and concluded by asking, whether he had any more diamonds; saying, that in order to prove the falsity of what had been asserted, he was ready to purchase them. The Count, designedly, gave him a ring of the value of about one hundred guineas, which Jefferys took with him, and a few days after returned to make an offer. As my husband did not purpose parting with it, and only made it a pretence to ascertain his conduct towards him, he dismissed the jeweller, paying him a bill of two guineas for buckles he had bought of him.

Such has been the consistent behaviour of that first furnisher of " justificatory writings,' let us proceed to the second.

Gray, in giving an account of the various bargains my husband entered into with him, said, he was persuaded the Count had never sold for the account of any other person than himself, and that he never uttered either the Queen's or the Cardinal's name. That declaration, though consonant to truth, made, at that time against us, in consequence of my having been advised to say, that the Cardinal had delivered diamonds

to

to me, to be sold for his emolument; and had I had paid him the price arising from the sale of those two declarations, that of the Capuchin M'Desnot, and they contain the entire substance of the justificatory writings, on which so much reliance has absurdly been placed.

I have declared my apprehensions of never coming to a conclusion; my memory now suggests a few important facts, out of which I shall select the most striking; happy, if, while I spare the reader the perusal of the rest, I ever can myself forget them.

During the last interrogatory, Monsieur Titon de Villotran took me by the hand, and said to me, " My " dear Countess, believe me, speak the truth; it is the " only way you have to save yourself, we have un- " doubted proof, that you used to see the Queen, why " will you not confess it? Be convinced therefore, that " what I say is for your good."---My counsel and every person about me, had so terrified me, and at the same time persuaded me I ought above all, to avoid uttering the Queen's name, that I had the weakness to yield an implicit compliance to their counsels.

As to Mademoiselle Dorvat, shortly after my misfortunes commenced, she was sent out of the way, to the farthest part of a distant province. Such is the reward bestowed by the Queen, on persons the most intimately connected with her.

I will save the reader the relation of a greater number, of the like particulars, which might prove tiresome, without any of them separately taken appearing a sufficient means of conviction. It would be very
difficult

difficult for me to diffuse a clear and intelligent light, that could pervade through a heap of intrigues, which so many powerful and complicated interests, served to render a mass of confusion, but the attentive and impartial reader will discover, in the artless simplicity of my narrative, the leading truths, which have been attempted to be obscured, and enveloped in darkness. Such readers will perceive, that if I am compelled to bring forward circumstances, which appear so strange and unaccountable, that they must be thought to run counter to all probability, yet what they have previously had exhibited to them, was equally extraordinary, and more unaccountable. Who has yet been, or perhaps ever would be able to penetrate into this labyrinth of intrigue, had I not removed the cloud of obscurity with which it was enveloped, and produced a clue to trace the paths of intricacy, which lead to its inmost recess?

How is it possible to reconcile the certainty of the very *secret* and very *intimate connexion* which subsisted between the Queen and the Cardinal, with the resolution, suddenly taken, of bringing him to the scaffold?---How would it be supposed that the Cardinal could be so simply weak, so much a dupe, to a woman like me, to have been guilty of such a number of senseless, mean, inconsistent follies, as he has been charged with, in order to exculpate himself, and criminate me. What construction can be put upon the romantic adventure of the girl Oliva, the use made of the forged signature, the absolute disappearance of the principal parts of the famous necklace, and the strange manner in which the Queen is involved in both adventures? In short how can it be thought natural, that having first been kindly countenanced by the smiles of Majesty, afterwards arrested, but treated with particular caution throughout the whole legal procedure, alternately practised upon by promises and threats, that I should, in the end, prove the only victim, selected from a number, who were accused, to be given up to the severity of justice, and, am I doomed to say it, that the hand of the executioner should be the remuneration for that silence, so strongly recommended to me?

I have produced the key which unquestionably solves these ænigmas, it is the real, since it is the only one, and it is impossible to find another. There could not exist such extreme perverseness without some powerful motives, such violent party intrigues, without uncommon causes. I have made apparent those motives and those causes, by barely relating my history; and unskilled in the method of giving a polished gloss to proofs, I trust to the impression, which the perusal of my plain and simple narrative, may produce in unprejudiced minds.

The evil which may ensue, must rest on those who have compelled me, for the preservation of my honour, to produce persons and circumstances in their native form and colour. I wish it were in my power to conceal, what I have been under a necessity to reveal. I am far from thinking, that the august Princess, whose victim I am become, would have doomed me to the infamous treatment I have undergone, or that, from her own heart, she would ever have proceeded to the extremities to which a chain of concurring circumstances reduced her. Let what my pen has dropped without restraint, upon the paper, be collected together

and

and placed in order, and it will be seen, that notwithstanding the disorder of my ideas, and artlessness of my manner, the origin of that series of events may be traced, and causes be discovered from the effects they have produced It has been seen, that born of the blood of the VALOIS, *poor*, *proud* and *ambitious*, I blindly gave myself up to every means of obtaining the support I hoped for, that my intimate acquaintance with the Cardinal de Rohan, the man the best suited to serve my views, soon led me on to an intimacy of another kind with the Queen that the Cardinal, long since aiming at ministerial omnipotence, imagined from my intimacy with the Queen, I should prove a medium, by which he would obtain the fruition of his wishes, and conciliate all differences which subsisted, from the recollection of those indiscretions, that had drawn upon him the frowns of Majesty. It has also been seen, that he did not depend solely on that support, that the politics of the Emperor, with whom he had kept up an intercourse, were coincident with his views, but by what means I am at a loss to conjecture, unless by his inducing the Emperor to believe he could be very useful to him, if his Imperial Majesty would assist him in procuring for him the reins of government It has further been seen, that the Queen, from an unjustifiable partiality and attention to her brother's interests, concluded she ought to sacrifice her resentment against the Cardinal, to the prosecution of every plan for the promotion of their interests, and even cherished this unpardonable crime to such an excess, as *to receive to her arms* the man whom she had, in her mind, previously intended to decapitate, as unrelentingly, as she has since

carried

carried on the shocking prosecution, aimed at his life, the whole weight of which, and its horrid consequences, have artfully been contrived to be the lot of female weakness, of the unhappy VALOIS DE LA MOTTE.

The reader must have noted that the Cardinal, "*ruined*" (as a creature of the Queen's observed) "*both in a moral* "*and physical view*," adding to his other faults an unpardonable indiscretion, that of proclaiming every where those secret interviews of gallantry, which men of honour ever hold sacred; and even speaking in terms of regret of the moments in which he was indulged with favours of so peculiar and tender a nature, by relating to me, to the Prince of Soubise, the Duke of Lauzun, the Prince of Luxumbourg, the Princess de Guémeneé, Madam de Brionne, the Baron de Planta, to the Jewellers, and to twenty other people, how, when and in what manner he had those marks of favour conferred upon him at Trianon, and this to some persons, accompanied with the most indelicate and shameful anecdotes of the conduct of himself and his friend, counsellor and *chymist* CAGLIOSTRO. In short, all those monstrous reports having reached the Queen's ear, a very short time after the delivery of the necklace, his ruin was irrevocably doomed; and, indeed, was a circumstance at which no person seemed surprised. But what would appear astonishing beyond measure, in a private individual was, that the Queen, before she took any steps towards her revenge, did not return the necklace. The astonishment, I confess, is natural, but her prudence is on a parallel with her sensibility, her pastimes, her affections, a mind for ever wavering without consideration, without stability.

It

It may be recollected, that the Queen was taken by surprize, when the Baron de Breteuil, having wrested the secret from the Jewellers, made a merit of imparting his discoveries to her Majesty, who, in that moment, exclaimed, "*I never heard a syllable of that neck-lace*"---It is not astonishing, that she should think herself bound to abide by that false assertion. The answer of the Cardinal, on the same subject, was very similar, who, at the moment, when overawed by the presence of Majesty, also exclaimed---"*I have been deceived*." He could never afterwards assert any thing of a different tendency, so that those two assertions, however inconsiderately made, equally concurred in giving credit to the charge which was brought against me (*) But, if the alledged *theft* had been proved, as any person unacquainted with the facts would be tempted

to

---

* The Cardinal found no other way to extricate himself, but by accusing me of having stolen the necklace; had he been convinced that there was a shadow of truth in his malicious charge, he could have expressed nothing but contempt and indignation for me, that he held, apparently, sentiments of a different nature, I am about to prove. I have already said, that Abbé Lequelle was commissioned by him to visit me every day, and enquire after my health, and to explain to me the reasons that compelled him to be my accuser, as he could not introduce the Queen in this mysterious scene, without exposing himself to the chance of having had administered

to believe, since I have undergone the punishment due to such a crime, why then was so much gold, so many favours lavished away, to prevent my innocence from being proved? Why that subornation of witnesses, who, instead of being committed, some to the house of correction, others to the galleys, according to their differ-

---

ministered to her a mess of *Veja lles soup*,* or perhaps something worse——— Imagine to yourself," said he, "that if
" it were proved the Cardinal had been on such secret
" terms of intimacy with the Queen, he would first be
" tortured, and afterwards lose his head on a scaffold,
" &c."

Our first interview, in presence of the Solicitor and the Recorder, has something remarkable in it, and will enable the Reader to judge, whether the Cardinal thought we guilty or not. When I entered the Council-chamber, he came up to me, took me by the hand, and said, "Good morrow, Lady Countess, how fares it with you?" Then joining his hands, and lifting them towards Heaven, he exclaimed, "*Ah! how unfortunate we are!*"———
Several times after the sessions were ended, the Cardinal went aside with me, from those gentlemen, to converse privately. The Chevalier Dupujet, the King's Lieutenant of the Bastile, having perceived us thus in close conference, upon opening of the door, signified to me his astonishment at it. He will not be backward (in case those gentry should chuse to deny it) to relate the circumstance.

* A dose of poison.

ent deserts, have been caressed, rewarded, provided for, and protected? Wherefore that connivance, fully proved, between one party accused, the accusers, the witnesses and the judges? Six of us were equally involved in the accusation, why, out of those six individuals, more or less guilty, is the *Countess de la Motte* alone judged to be so, alone condemned to punishment? I flatter myself, that every body will answer, in my behalf---" Because the prosecution really existed between the Queen and the Cardinal only; and that I having had the fatal misfortune of being their confidant, they respectively found it their interest to make me the sacrifice, in order to preserve themselves." " *I don't know that wo-* " *man De la Motte,*" said the Queen, " *That woman De* " *la Motte has deceived me,*" said the Cardinal, and the obsequious herd, implicitly obedient, became the lying echo's of the Queen, and of the Cardinal, as their various interests directed the sound ---One question more--- If the Queen *never knew me,* and if I *deceived the Cardinal,* why was such particular caution used, never to have the Queen's name uttered in the course of the proceedings? and why, when after it was decreed, that the business

was

---

cumstance. On many occasions, Mr Dupuis de Marcé caught us making mutual signs to each other, and as he had observed to the Cardinal, such behaviour was reprehensible, and no ways consonant to his assertions, the latter concealed himself from him, and gave me to understand, by winks and nods, the motives of his constraint.

[256]

was to be renewed, a new trial to take place, and a complaint to be preferred against the Cardinal, by the Attorney General, for an attempt made on her Majesty---wherefore, I say, did the Queen recede?----Wherefore had she the littleness to say, on such an occasion, where her honour was so intimately concerned, that she would confine herself to divesting the Cardinal of his ribband, his offices and his liberty? It was, because *she could not take away his life, because she dared not attempt it* it was, because, all the volumes, which will only be brought to light, at the moment these memoirs appear before the public, would have been divulged by bringing on that second trial. It was not in order to prevent its being proved, that *I had deceived the Cardinal*, that the Queen quashed the second impeachment, it was to conceal her own intrigues with the Cardinal and me, that she demeaned herself so far, as to decline the interference of the Courts of Justice. Now, if from these circumstances, the natural inference is drawn, that the more the Queen insisted on not knowing me, the more manifest it appears that I actually *knew her*, from the moment that this Royal falsehood is ascertained, that, which the Cardinal was guilty of, when he said, that I *had deceived him*,' becomes still more apparent, and it most plainly appears, that I have had inflicted on me, the punishment of a *pretended crime*, which the artifice and power of my adversaries procured me to be convicted of, in order, if possible, to obliterate the traces of a one, of which they had *actually* been the perpetrators.

If

If a reflection upon my unhappy and unmerited sufferings could influence the mind of the Queen, could teach her to regret the cause, and create in her a wish to recompence me, what is there, even in the power of royalty, which could possibly make me ample amends? Could she efface those horrible reflections, which must, during my life, inevitably occu----could her utmost munificence remove from my " mind's eye," by day, by night, nay almost every instant of my wretched existence, the hideous picture of the minister of her revenge? I may, however, be mistaken, perhaps, the orders they had received were less savage than the mode in which they executed them. I was once induced, from the attempts that were made, to imagine they had received secret instructions to destroy me between the prison doors, but the monsters were certainly frustrated in their intentions, so that, in lieu of an instantaneous death, which would have been my wish, they inflicted on me a lingering dissolution, of which I daily see the approach. From the consequence of being crushed, as it were, under a press, between the massy doors of my infernal mansion, suddenly and violently closed upon me, by the unfeeling and savage ferocity of my gaolers, I find I have, in the midst of continual pain, a wretched existence, to which I have incessantly wished that Providence had put a period. Never have I, however, indulged that wish so ardently as at this day, at the moment I conceive myself a-dying,---yes I now shall die in peace---nay I could receive the awful summons with pleasure, if I might be allowed to indulge the fond flattery idea that the powerful of my Me-

L l

[250]

more, has, in any manner, served to eradicate those impressions, which my silence has too long suffered to take root——no——would that pleasure be enhanced, with … rapture could my soul fly to the regions of eternal peace and mercy, if my unhappy fate, related with the strictest regard to truth, should have occasioned the tear to fall from the eye of … , should have created for me one string pang from the feeling heart, and produced a sigh from those, to whom I was once endeared … …

All I have now left to do, is to form my accents by those of the Royal prophet, to direct to my sovereign, the humble supplication which David addressed to God, and to … hands uplifted towards him.

" … I have … led my cry up to thee, O … … … hear my … !"

Yes, humane sovereign! righteous monarch! patience … … … aside your attention for an instant, from the immense concerns which claim and urge it, … people will forget a momentary absence in consideration of the motive … eign to bestow one gracious … … honour with one condescending look, the most unfortunate of your subjects. She has a claim to … … … Sire, from the very reason that people have sought … found successful methods to … her from … Your Majesty has long been uninformed, … … … … … … … to be made acquainted … the … … … … which have been prac‑

tified, to conceal from you the knowledge of those dreadful truths contained in these Memoirs.

I am not ignorant, that at the period of the ministerial examinations, your Majesty vouchsafed to command that all the records of the proceedings and depositions, should be laid before your royal presence, had these commands been faithfully fulfilled, I had been saved, my innocence had been victorious. But what, Sire, has been the conduct of my enemies? (and who alas, is the *female enemy* who takes precedence of them all!) they pretended, that the original records, blotted and disfigured, were not fit to be presented to the eyes of majesty, and then substituted for them, copies, in which the facts were falsely stated, apparent proofs of my guilt were adduced, and even a fictitious confession of it was added to the lying scroll, in which was forged such indecent, such dishonest, such shocking expressions, said to have proceeded from me, that, after perusing part of them, your Majesty, spitting upon those supposititious writings, said, " FYE UPON THE FILTHY CREATURE! " I'LL READ NO MORE OF IT"

O Sire! can the most just of King's, thus permit the dæmon of intrigue, to compel an act of injustice, so foreign to his native benevolence? But, Sire, you, in your wisdom well know, that it is not the first time, the sanctity of princes has been imposed on. Had not the knowledge of all the facts that must have concurred to prove my innocence, been secreted from your Majesty, if even the Minister, who in those detested times, enjoyed the largest portion of your confidence, had not stood up between the truth and your Majesty, you

would

would have known that Count de Vergennes stirred heaven and earth, to prevent my husband's appearing, to tear off the veil that shrouded the real culprits, and you would have commanded that unfortunate man, whom they meant to associate with me in my ignominy, to be confronted with my oppressors.

Then, Sire, would truth have been victorious! then would the miscreants mentioned in these Memoirs, the perfidious Dupuis de Marcé, Laurencelle and his abettors, have trembled; then would they never have dared to present unfaithful copies of the proceedings, which had they not been falsified, would, by overwhelming my adversaries, have born solemn testimony of my innocence.

Vouchsafe, Sire, to measure back your steps, vouchsafe to have the genuine records laid before you, if they exist, if they do not, the fraud committed by my foes is ascertained. Be graciously pleased of your royal bounty and justice, to order that the lawyer Doillot humbly submit to your Majesty's perusal the papers that I had entrusted to his care, the only vouchers to the truth; be pleased likewise to command that defender of my cause, visibly prevaricated, to declare, wherefore, being furnished with these writings and all the documents I was able to afford him, he allowed himself the licence of drawing up memorials, filled with improbabilities, lies, and fooleries, without attempting a single mode of rational justification.

Perhaps, Sire, the day of retribution is come.——I would not say *passed*, were I certain that these Memoirs

mous will appear in your auguft prefence, I would then cry out---" *I am now avenged*"

In this hope, which I am fond of indulging, I caft myfelf at your Majefty's feet.---Let not my approach alarm you, Sire: innocence cannot fade away, even under the malignant blafts of malice, you are able, with a breath, to reftore it to its wonted bloom, a fingle word from you would reinftate me in my *honour*, before I quit your knees, command only, THAT MY CAUSE MAY AGAIN BE PLEADED, AND THAT IT BE SUBMITTED TO THE DECISION OF STRICT AND IMPARTIAL JUSTICE.

My hufband is ready, Sire, to perform what he has not ceafed to petition for the liberty of doing, to furrender himfelf to the prifon of the Concergerie; I will accompany him thither, order its gates to be opened to us, let there be produced before us, ALL the perfons more or lefs involved in this dark tranfaction.

Then, Sire, your Majefty, being informed of the firft impofition on your goodnefs, will happily be guarded againft a fecond.

Then the truth, which your juftice and clemency fought for in vain, at the time of the firft trial, will appear to you triumphant! then fhall the unhappy DE VALOIS, cafting herfelf at YOUR MAJESTY's feet, prefume to petition a laft favour. THE FORGIVENESS OF HER ENEMIES.

London, *January* 1, 1789.

(Signed) *Comtefse de Valois de la Motte*

Affidavit of Mrs. Costa.

MIDDLESEX,   *London, December* 9, 1788.
TO WIT.

I, the under-written Benjamina Costa, depose and assert as follows That on the third of April, 1786, I departed from Edinburgh, in order to deliver at Paris, a packet of letters and papers from Count de la Motte, to a lawyer of the name of Doillot that after performing the said commission, I took my way back to England, with the aforesaid lawyer's answer to the Court: that at the town of Aire, in Artois, I was taken up by people dispatched after me from the police at Paris, and carried back to the Bastile, whence, after two days confinement, I was taken out and carried before the Baron de Breteuil, one of the Ministers of State, who told me he had received a letter from my husband, "who," he added, "has great confidence in you," then referred me to the Lieutenant of the Police, who was to give me one hundred louis d'ors, which the latter accordingly did, after taking, in my presence, a copy of the letter which I had from Mr Doillot the lawyer, in answer to Count de la Motte that I was then dismissed under the escort of Bailiffs of the Police, who took me post down to Calais, where I passed the sea, and on my arrival in London I had an audience of Count d'Adhemar, to whom the Police at Paris had referred me for my instructions His Excellency bid me tell my husband to take a house near Newcastle-upon-Tyne, to facilitate the conveying off the Count de la Motte, and that my fortune should be made, adding that d'Arragon should set out next day for Newcastle Being myself arrived there, I heard from my husband, that he had received one thousand guineas from the Secretary d'Arragon, of

which

AFFIDAVIT OF MRS COSTA

which sum I saw in notes to the amount of nine hundred and forty guineas in my husband's possession, sixty guineas having been defalcated by the said d'Arragon for his own use. That my said husband informed me he was to receive moreover, ten thousand pounds sterling, for delivering up the said Count de la Motte to the French Ministry, the Sieur d'Arragon reserving to himself also one fifth part of the said sum; that my husband had been solicited by the said d'Arragon, to administer to the said Count de la Motte, the contents of a certain phial, which were to put him to sleep for the space of four and twenty hours, during which they should put him into a sack, and convey him to a ship lying ready in the harbour, the Captain of which was one Subois, an exempt of the French Police; that my husband absolutely declined administering the draught contained in the said phial. That the pretence for the said vessel's (of which the whole crew were a swarm of retainers to the police, in disguise,) sailing to Newcastle, was to make experiments on pit coal. That my husband having all along discovered to Count de la Motte, the whole machination, the latter, unwilling that Mr Costa should lose the money promised him, suffered him to act as if in concert with the people sent to apprehend the Count, in consequence of which we all came up together to London, where my husband had a meeting in a hackney coach, with Count d'Adhemar, and his Secretary d'Arragon, apparently on the subject of betraying the Count de la Motte. In witness whereof I have signed the present attestation.

BENJAMINA COSTA.

Sworn before me,
the 5th of December, 1782.
    Wm HYDE.

No. I.

JUSTIFICATORY PIECES.

MEMORIAL.

Concerning the House of Saint Remy de Valois, sprung from the natural son, whom Henry the Second, King of France, had by Nicole de Savigny, Lady and Baroness de St Remy.

Arms of the House de St. Remy de Valois. Argent with a fess azure, charged with three flower de luces or.

HENRY the Second, King of France had by (*) Nicole de Savigny, Henry de Saint Remy, that follows. The said Nicole de Savigny, styled High and Puissant Lady, Lady of Saint Remy, Fontelle du Chatellier and Noez, married John de Ville, Knight of the King's Order, and made her last will on the 12th of January 1590, in which she declared " That the late King Henry the Second had made a donation to *Henry Monsieur*, his son, the sum of 30,000 crowns sol, which she had received in 1558."

Henry de Saint Remy, called *Henry Monsieur*, is styled High and Puissant Lord, Knight, Lord of the Manors, and Baron du Chatellier, Fontette, Noez and Beauvoir, Knight of the King's Order, Gentleman of the Bedchamber in ordinary, Colonel of a regiment of horse, and of foot; and Governor of Chateau-Villain; married by contract October 31, 1592, articled at Essoye, in Champaign, Dame Christiana de Luz,(†)styled

II DEGREE. *Fourth Progenitor.*

(*) Genealogical History of the House of France, by Father Anselme, vol. 1. p. 136.

History of France, by the President Henault, 3d Edition, in 4to. p. 315

(†) The two younger sisters, Marina and Magdalen de Luz, were married, the one to Francis de Choiseul

A Baron

[2]

High and Puissant Lady, relict of Claud de Fresnay, Lord of Loupy, Knight of the King's Order, and daughter of Hon. James de Luz, also Knight of the King's Order, and of Lady Michelle du Fay, Lord and Lady of Bazoules, died at Paris on the 14th of February, 1621, and had of his marriage the son who follows.

III Degree *Great Pr...* Renatus de Saint Remy, styled High and Puissant Lord, Knight, Lord and Baron de Fontette, Gentleman in Ordinary to the King's Bed-chamber, Captain of a hundred men at arms, died March 11, 1663, and had married, by articles entered into April 25, 1646, at Essore, Jacquette Breveau, by whom amongst others, he had the following son

IV Degree *Great Grand-Father* Peter John de Saint Remy Valois, styled High and Puissant Lord, Knight, Lord of Fontette, Major of the regiment of Bachevilers horse, was born September 9, 1649, and baptized at Fontette, October 12, 1653, married first to Demoiselle Reine Margaret de Courtois, and a second time by articles passed on January 18, 1679, at Saint Aubin, in the diocese of Toul, to Demoiselle Mary de Mullot, daughter of Paul de Mullot, Esq. and of Dame Charlotte de Chaslus, died before the 14th of March, 1714, and of his second marriage had a son who follows

V Degree, *Grand-Father* Nicolas Renatus de Saint Remy de Valois, styled Knight, Baron of Saint Remy, and Lord of Luz, was baptized at Saint Aubin-aux-Auges, in the diocese of Toul, the 12th of April, 1678, served the King during ten years as garde-du-corps to his Majesty, in the Duke de Chaost's company, quitted the service to

Baron de Ambouville, and the other to Benjamin de Sanciere, Lord and Baron of Tenance.

marly

marry by articles of the 14th of March, 1714, Demoiselle Mary Elizabeth de Vienne, daughter of Nicolas Francis de Vienne, Knight, Lord and Baron of Fontette, Noez, &c. Counsellor to the King, President, Lieutenant-general in matters both civil and criminal, in the Royal Bailiwick of Bar-sur-Seine, and of Dame Elizabeth de Merile, died at Fontette on the 3d of October, 1759, and of his marriage had two sons. first, Peter Nicolas Renatus de Saint Remy de Fontette, born at Fontette, June 3, 1716, received in 1744 a Gentleman Cadet, in the regiment of Graffin, where it is assured he was killed in an engagement against the King's enemies, and second, James, who follows.

James de Saint Remy de Valois first called de Luz, and afterwards de Valois, styled, Knight, Baron de Saint Remy, was born at Fontette, December 22, 1717, and baptised January 1, 1718. In his baptismal attestation, which contains his name and condition, his father, thereat present, is called and styled, " Messire " Nicolas Renatus de Saint Remy de Valois, Baron de " St Remy." and his aunt, who was one of the sponsors, is therein called " Demoiselle Barbara Theresa, daughter of late Messire Peter John de Saint Remy de Valois." Both of them signed their names to it, Saint Remy de Valois. He espoused, in the parish church of St Martin, at Langres, on the 14th of August, 1755, Mary Joffel, by whom he already had a son, who follows and died *at the Hotel Dieu, in Paris*, February 16, 1762, according to the register of his death, in which he is called and styled " James de Valois, Knight, Baron de Saint Remy."

VI DEGREE
Father.

James

VIIDegree Precreating

James de Saint Remy de Valois, born February 25, 1755, and baptized the same day, in the parochial church of St. Peter and St. Paul, in the city of Langres, acknowledged and baptized by his father and mother in the act of their espousals of the 14th of August, of the same year.

Jane de St. Remy de Valois, born at Fontette, July 22, 1756.

Mary Anne de Saint Remy de Valois, born also at Fontette, October 2, 1757.

We, Anthony Mary d'Ozier de Serigny, Knight, Judge at Arms of the Nobility of France, Knight, honorary Grand Cross of the Royal Order of St Maurice of Sardinia, do certify unto the King, the truth of the facts certified in the above Memorial, by us drawn up from authentic records. In witness thereof we have signed the present certificate, and caused it to be counter signed by our secretary, who has put to it the seal of our arms. Done at Paris, on Monday the 6th day of the month of May, in the year 1776. *(Signed)* D'Hosier de Serigny *(lower down)* by Monsieur the Judge at Arms of the Nobility of France Duplessis, *(and sealed)*

We the undersigned Judge at Arms of the Nobility of France, &c. do certify that this copy of the present Memorial is conformable to the record preserved in our repository of nobility, in witness whereof we have signed it, and caused it to be counter-signed by our Secretary, who has affixed to it the seal of our arms. Done at Paris, on Thursday the 13th day of the month of October, in the year 1785. *Signed* D'Hosier de Serigny.

By Monsieur the Judge at Arms of the Nobility of France *Signed* Duplessis.

No II.

LETTER FROM THE CARDINAL TO THE QUEEN.

March 21, 1784.

Madam,

"THE charming Countess has imparted to me, how much you seemed affected with the account she gave you of the little services I have rendered her. The concern alone which she inspires, induced me to seize every opportunity of obliging her, for certainly I was very far from foreseeing she would one day be in a capacity of mentioning me to you, in such a manner as to remove the evil impressions which my enemies have ever given you of my disposition. Chance has therefore befriended me, more than my own endeavours, for you know all the efforts I have made to speak to you, only for one instant, without ever being able to compass it Persons whom I imagined my friends, and who were possessed of your confidence, have availed themselves of the desire I had of terminating my disgrace, to make me commit acts of imprudence, take false steps, and almost surely to work my ruin, and were it not for a circumstance, as extraordinary as that which this day affords, I should always have appeared a monster in your eyes, without even an opportunity of establishing my innocence. But hope begins to shine in my heart, and I presume to think you will not disdain to hear me. Let but your beauteous mouth pronounce the word *yes*, you will behold your slave at your feet, and this day will be the happiest of his life

---

No III.

LETTER FROM THE CARDINAL TO THE QUEEN.

March 28, 1784.

MADAM,

'WITH sorrow I am informed, that you will not vouchsafe me a private interview, till I have produced the most authentic proofs of your having been imposed upon. You require of me, in writing, a compendious plea towards my justification. Although secure of the person through whose hands it would be conveyed to you, I must own, that as yet not knowing what degree of confidence you repose in her, I would not lightly entrust a writing, containing anecdotes in which your Majesty should be brought in question. As I cannot possibly employ the hand of a third, I ought (especially after all that has befallen me) to be extremely cautious. I presume to believe, that your Majesty will not look upon this act of circumspection as a refusal to comply with your will. I wait for further commands, and in consequence of the conversation I have had with

[7]

Countefs (which fhe will impart to you) I hope, that in order to avoid any thing's falling into unfaithful hands, you will permit me to lay before you, by word of mouth, the particulars you require of me. I remain, in expectation of your ultimate will and pleafure, the moft fincere and moft devoted of your fubjects.

No IV.

LETTER FROM THE CARDINAL TO THE QUEEN.

April 3, 1784.

" I am bound to fubfcribe to the will of my Mafter, and look upon myfelf as too happy in his condefcending to liften to any thing relating to his flave. The dear Countefs raifed me to the fummit of happinefs, by telling me, that you could wifh to find me innocent. Yes, I am fo, and can give you the moft convincing proofs of it. So great is the joy which that idea produces in me, that every object to me no longer wears the fame appearance. You will difcover by my ftyle, that my imagination is exalted, I could wifh to defcribe to you all the fenfations I experience, but my ideas fucceed each other fo rapidly, that I find it impoffible to write coherently. This moment

[3]

of bliss has obliterated all the pangs I have endured, and I the more willingly forgive the authors of them, as I conceive what sacrifices may be gladly made to merit and preserve your kindness.----I no longer delay sending you part of what you ask of me, reserving for a verbal explanation what was the aim of the Princess of Guémenée, when she wished to puzzle you with a story, in which the Duke de Lauzun, and the Prince of Luxembourg were brought in as parties concerned.-----Discoveries which I have since made, have let me into the knowledge of my dear niece's disposition. I know that it was she who contributed most to my disgrace, and raised me enemies, who have been but too successful in continuing it. She has, however, been punished for it, and the contempt she inspires you with persuades me that you will easily perceive the falsity of all the slanderous tales she has devised, in order to effect my ruin.

" I at this instant receive a note from the Countess, who tells me she is setting off for Versailles, I send her this letter, and to-morrow will dispatch a courier, who will deliver to her what you require.----The matter is settled.------Your faithful slave.

LETTER

No. V.

LETTER FROM THE CARDINAL TO THE QUEEN.

April 4, 1784.

MADAM,

" PERUSE me attentively, judge of my desire to be again favourably received, by my recent behaviour, and do justice to him who has suffered all undeservedly

Madame de Guémeneé, to remove from my mind every suspicion which her conduct might raise, and to draw me into an unbounded confidence, told me, that she was almost persuaded you was acquainted with the various letters I had written, in order to raise an obstacle to your marriage with the Dauphin, that those letters had been forged at Madame du Barry's, and afterwards by her shewn to Lewis the Fifteenth, in one of those moments when she knew how to make him believe what she pleased, that this first discovery was the motive of the hatred and contempt you had conceived for her and for me that in the next place you had been assured, that I, stimulated by revenge for the little regard paid to my counsels, had written to the Empress, to inform her of your intimate connection with the Count d'Artois, that the letter was written in the plainest terms, and that probably the Chancellor, the Duke d'Aiguillon, and Madame du Barry, had improved upon the expressions, as the difference of style evidently shewed those personages were concerned in it. That is, said she, the information I have gained. If in reality those writings ever existed, and you were the author of them, you must never expect forgiveness, nor shall I, by any means, take a single step towards obtaining it for you; but if, on the contrary, you was barely the agent in that transaction, and that Madame du Barry, to whom you could refuse nothing, (after the services she had done you) prevailed on you to lend your name to that odious villainy, it will be easy for me, by some well timed observations, to reconcile matters. but previous to my taking the first step, I require of you a sincere account of all that passed. This account, which I shortened considerably, threw me into a state which I cannot describe; astonishment, indignation, rage seized on my spirits, and made me pour forth against those monsters, a torrent of epithets they well deserved, but which respect forbids me to repeat. Grown somewhat calmer, I said to Madame de Guémeneé, it was impossible such detested falsehoods could ever have been, that I had absolutely no knowledge of them, and that I could not persuade myself any one had been daring enough to use my name, as a vehicle to information so base and injurious. I cannot think, continued she, that you acted a feigned part, or that the discovery of these monstrous dealings, leads you to such violence of passion in order to persuade me that you are innocent. I know your disposition, and that you are incapable of such deceit; but that those guilty writings have existed, as also that the Queen is come to the knowledge

of

of them, is a fact, but to tell you in what manner, is more than I know. It is your interest to help me in discovering the authors, I may possibly facilitate you the means; but let us have a little patience.----The entrance of the Prince de Guémenée put an end to this conversation, and shortly after I took my leave, fearing lest he should observe my emotion. Several weeks elapsed, without a possibility of finding an opportunity to renew the conference, I was only transiently informed there was nothing new stirring, and that a favourable moment was watched for, to enter upon an explanation, though matters were not to be hurried on, but that great reservedness must be used in bringing on the tapis anecdotes, that had occasioned many disappointments, and that an able courtier should never stir up disagreeable recollections, that I might depend on her desire of serving me, and live in hopes of seeing my disgrace brought to a speedy conclusion. Those flattering promises contributed a little to restore me to my tranquility, for, from the period of my first interview I had ceased to exist, and I own to you, that I was thrown into so great an agitation, by the machinations that had been put in practice against me, that I was repeatedly tempted to throw myself at your knees, and beseech you to hear me, but a short reflection, and the fear of making an éclat, prevented me. Above all, the hope Madame de Guémenée gave me, every time I met her, allured my resolution to such a degree, that she managed to make me believe whatever she would. I was one Sunday evening with the Prince de Soubise, who was waiting for his carriage to return to Paris,

when

when a groom of the chambers to Madame de Guémenée, came to desire my attendance on her, while you were at the card-table, intimating, that she had something to communicate. The satisfaction I discovered in her countenance, on my entering her apartment, proved to me a good omen; nor was I mistaken in it. I have good news, said she, to impart to you, sit you down and you sh—— ——I saw the Queen yesterday, and by an unexpected piece of good luck, the conversation turned upon you, without my bringing it about. I eagerly seized the opportunity to tell her, she had been cruelly deceived by the reports that had been conveyed to her; that for the time of your having incurred her displeasure, your existence was the most wretched that could be, and that were it not for the hopes you entertained of one day justifying yourself, you would ere this have left the court, and retired to Save ne. If what you tell me were true, answered she, he would have sought the means of justification, yet hitho to I do not perceive he has taken any method whatever to effect it. This gave me an opportunity of relating to her the conversation you and I had together, to which I added several other circumstances, which could not fail to persuade her of the fallacy of the facts reported to her; but I perceived by her answer, that more than one conference would be requisite to convince her; for which reason I did not think it expedient to carry things any farther, or to propose a premature explanation which might have ruined all.

"I have an infinite —————— —— will second me, I make no doubt of succeeding in the enterprise.

She

She has for some time past wished to have a small, white spaniel dog: I know that the breed is frequently met with in the Upper Alsace, if you could, through means of your acquaintance there, procure me such a little creature, I would make her a present of it, reserving to tell her it came from you, as opportunity shall serve.

"I was so lucky as to procure the charming little dog which you was so fond of, and took so great a liking to. Madame de Guémenée failed not to apprize me of it, assuring me that she had told you, that I, hearing of the desire you had for a little Alsatian dog, had made all possible enquiry after one and that having been successful, I had brought one to her with an Arabian name, the meaning of which was " faithful and unhappy," that this account, far from lessening your fondess for the little unfortunate being, had encreased it. from which she drew the most favourable omen, and hoped that I shortly should be obliged to change the name of my representative.

"I knew not in what words to express my gratitude to her, she was sensible of the excessive joy she gave me, and availed herself of it, to request of me the loan of a pretty considerable sum. I would have parted with my whole fortune, thinking myself too happy in being useful to a woman to whom I was so greatly beholden. The easy compliance she had met with, enticed her to make farther demands, which I could not refuse, she always knowing how to accompany them with hopes, with soothing promises, and at the same time with difficulties she would find ways to overcome, all which she did in order to gain time. But my finances being greatly deranged, by the sums I had been obliged to borrow for her, and finding my resources exhausted, since I had been several times obliged to give her a denial, she imagined, that to throw a mask over all her iniquities and falsehoods, the only way for her was to ruin me entirely in your opinion. She knew that the Princess de Marsan had spoken to me concerning your little dog, telling me she should be glad to see me come into favour again; that I ought to depend on your indulgence, since you had accepted of what came from me. Fear of my discovering the truth, made her contrive a very sure way of rendering me odious. You are acquainted with the imprudent steps I took, they were her work; and at the moment I thought I was complying with your commands, she was persuading you it was a rashness to be condemned in me, that I only acted thus to expose you, and that I was in confederacy with two or three other persons, whom she named to you. Thinking her work imperfect, she wished to put a finishing hand to it, and to give me the fatal blow. To compass this she must first assign to me the reasons why I still proved unsuccessful. She is fruitful in expedients, infinite are the resources of her imagination. I was subdued to her will, I implicitly believed every thing.

"You was to give an entertainment at the Little Trianon, but the time appointed was yet distant. During the intervening space, I prepared all things necessary for my disguise. The long wished for day being come, and following my dear niece's instructions, I

slipped

flipped into the gardens, where I was not long, before I was surrounded and pursued, like an owl that had intruded into that enchanted grove. The shouts of Monsieur l'Abbé, and other very mortifying epithets, made me see clearly that I had been pitched upon to serve for sport to the whole assembly. Irritated at having been dismissed in such a manner, I withdrew, rage and despair filling my breast, fully determined to be revenged as soon as I found an opportunity. This scene caused in me so great a revolution, that I had a severe fit of illness. The authoress of my misfortune made moreover a handle of my unhappy situation, to spread a report that I walked in my sleep, and that my night rambles in the gardens had brought on my disorder. She used every method to turn me into ridicule, and to raise me fresh enemies, who since have not ceased to persecute me

" These are events which you have ever been ignorant of, and will serve to shew how far I have been the dupe of my sincerity

" As to the disappearing of your little dog, I will tell you what I have heard concerning it, as also many other stories laid to my account, and in which I never had any share· having sought, through all the unfortunate periods that ensued, every opportunity to afford you instances of my respect, and sincere attachment.

" These are very tedious particularities, which have made me forget the hour. I hope, however, that my courier will arrive time enough to deliver my letter. I wait with great impatience for the Countess. Heaven grant she may bring me good news.---Ever faithful and unhappy "

*C 2

LETTER

No VI

LETTER FROM THE CARDINAL TO THE QUEEN

April 10, 1784

M D*m*,

'I EASILY conceive, that after all that has passed, it would be a contradiction in your conduct towards me, if you were seen to grant me openly, and so speedily, a protection, which those about you have persuaded you I was undeserving of. It would doubtless be sounding an alarm for all my enemies, who would not fail to come together on that occasion. But all their efforts would prove unavailing, if my dear Master has a desire to pardon his Slave. Sovereign, equally powerful and respected, your will must ever be a law, which your attendants will be too happy in submitting to. If, however, you have particular reasons for acting with reserve till a certain period, I will conform to whatever may be pleasing to you, and will, to the utmost of my power, remove whatever might disturb the quiet and happiness of my dear Master.

I ceace to hope, that to indemnify your submissive Slave for all the contradictions he will be forced to experience, you will condescend again to enable him to kiss that benefactress hand, and hear that charming mouth pronounce his pardon.'

LETTER

No. VII.

LETTER FROM THE QUEEN TO THE CARDINAL.

April 28, 1784.

" I READ with indignation the manner in which you have been deceived by your niece I never had any knowledge of the letters you mention to me, and I question whether they ever existed The persons you complain of have in reality contributed to your disgrace, but the methods they used to effect it, were very different from those you suppose. I have forgotten all, and require of you never to speak to me of any thing that has reference to what is past. The account which the Countess has given me of your behaviour towards her, has made a stonger impression on me, than all you have writtten to me. I hope you will never forget that it is to her you are indebted for your pardon, as also for the letter I write to you. I have always looked upon you as a very inconsistent and indiscreet man, which opinion necessarily obliges me to great reservedness, and I own to you, that nothing but a conduct quite the reverse of that you have held, can regain my confidence and merit my esteem.'

No VIII

LETTER FROM THE CARDINAL TO THE QUEEN.

May 6, 1784.

" YES, I am the happiest mortal breathing! My Master pardons me, he grants me his confidence, and to compleat my happiness, he has the goodness to smile upon his Slave, and to give him publickly signals of a right understanding. Such unexpected favours caused in me so great an emotion, that I for a moment was apprehensive lest the motive should be suspected by the extraordinary answers which I made. But I soon recovered, when I saw my absence of mind was attributed to quite another motive, upon which I assumed an air of approbation, in order to divert observation from the real object. This circumstance is a warning to me, to direct henceforth my words and actions in a more prudential manner.

" I know how to appreciate all the obligations I am under to the charming Countess. In whatever situation I may chance to be, I shall be gratefully mindful of all that she has done in my behalf.----So much for that.---All depends on my Master.-----The facility he has of making beings happy, makes his Slave wish for the means of following his footsteps, and being the echo of his good pleasure.'

LETTER

No. IX.

LETTER FROM THE QUEEN TO THE CARDINAL.

May 15, 1784.

" I CANNOT difapprove of the defire you have of feeing me, I could wifh, in order to facilitate you the means, to remove all obftacles that oppofe it, but you would not have me act imprudently to bring about more compendioufly a thing which you muft be perfuaded you will fhortly obtain. You have enemies, who have done you much differvice with the *Minifter*, (the Countefs will tell you the meaning of that word, which you muft ufe for the future) The turning of them out cannot but be advantageous to you I know the changes and revolutions that are to happen, and have calculated all the circumftances which will infallibly bring forward the opportunities which I defire In the interim be very cautious, above all difcreet, and, as there is no forefeeing what may happen, be referved, and greatly perplexed in what you hereafter write to me."

No X.

LETTER FROM THE QUEEN TO THE CARDINAL.

May 23, 1784.

" MENTION was made of you to me yesterday, in a manner that induces me to think there is a suspicion of some intelligence. I cannot conceive what can have given rise to such a supposition. Whatever the intention was, it was not gratified, I give you notice of it, that you may be upon your guard, and avoid all surprize. I shall go this week to T----n, and shall there see the Countess, to whom I will communicate a scheme that will certainly be pleasing to you."

No XI.

LETTER FROM THE CARDINAL TO THE QUEEN.

June 2, 1784.

MADAM,

THE Countess misunderstood what I said to her relative to my request of entreating from you an interview. I should be very unjust, and truly

remain

indiscreet to solicit that favour, whilst those obstacles remain which you so kindly acquainted me with. This is exactly what I jestingly said to her, not thinking she would report it to you " Charming Countess, you
" are very amiable, and doubtless deserving of the at-
" tachment that is conceived for you-----How happy
" are you! You will to-morrow see my dear Master,
" you will be at his feet, whilst his faithful Slave lives
" under a continual restraint, deprived of the only plea-
" sure he could have of seeing, admiring, adoring him,
" and swearing at his feet that his respect, his attach-
" ment, his love, will only end with his life You have
" it in your power to crown all my wishes, it depends
" greatly on you.----Hear me----I should indeed be
" sorry, did my Master imagine, that my whole con-
" duct had no other tendency but towards ambition,
" and the desire of being avenged of my enemies.-----
" The request I preferred to him of receiving me, may
" have raised those suspicions in him, which, in order to
" remove from his mind, and persuade him that I have
" no other aim, or desire, but to please him, tell him
" that I would very willingly consent to pass for ever in
" the public estimation for a man in disgrace, and
" who richly deserves it, if he would vouchsafe me
" the favours he grants to you This confession is as
" sincere as the desire I have of seeing my wishes ac-
" complished "-----The Countess laughed heartily at the notion, and made her account of entertaining you with it. The manner in which she related to you our conversation, is no doubt what occasioned your reproaching

* D

me.

...re. My crime is very pardonable, and indeed I rely much on your indulgence. You are so kind, so ready to relieve the wretched, that your slave cannot persuade himself you will much longer debar him from embracing your knees."

No XII

LETTER FROM THE CARDINAL TO THE QUEEN

June 12, 1784

' The Sage is delighted---he has just mentioned to me with rapture, the signal of intelligence and kindness which he received from the Master---I, in order to perplex him, endeavoured to insinuate, that it was to the Countess, and not to him it was directed, which threw him into a violent rage. You see how jealous people are of pleasing you, and obtaining a single look from you. From that instant the savage has been happy, and I am persuaded there is nothing in the world he would not undertake to merit your esteem and countenance. He hopes you will become reconciled to his figure, and that his qualifications will make you regard him with a more favourable eye.

' I was in hopes of hearing from you before my departure, but the Countess has just told me, that your toilet and the etiquette of the day, had not left you one moment's ment's leisure. I am highly pleased with the Minister, I don't despair of seeing him one day act as my mediator"

No. XIII

LETTER FROM THE CARDINAL TO THE QUEEN

July 29, 1784

"MY adorable Master, permit your Slave to express his joy for the favours you have conferred upon him ---That charming *rose* lies upon my heart---I will preserve it to my latest breath. It will incessantly recall to me the first instant of my happiness ---In parting from the Countess I was so transported, that I found myself imperceptibly brought to the charming spot which you had made choice of. After having crossed the shrubbery, I almost despaired of knowing again the place where your beloved Slave threw himself at your feet ---Destined, no doubt, to experience, during that delightful night, none but happy sensations, I found again the pleasing turf, gently pressed by those pretty little feet---I rushed upon it, as if you had still been there, and kissed with as much ardor your grassy seat, as that fair hand which was yielded to me with a grace and kindness that belong to none but my dear Master ---Inchanted, as it were, to that bewitching spot, I found the greatest difficulty in quitting it and I

should

[24]

should certainly have spent the night there, had I not been apprehensive of making my attendants uneasy, who knew of my being out. Soon after my return home I went to bed, but pressed for a considerable time a restless pillow. My imagination, struck with your adorable person was filled, during my slumbers, with the most delightful sensations.----Happy night! that proved the brightest day in my life!---Adorable Master, your Slave cannot find expressions to describe his felicity!---you yesterday witnessed his embarrassment, his bashfulness, his silence, the natural effects of the most genuine love! you alone in the universe, could produce what he never before experienced ---Enveloped in these pleasing sensations, I sometimes imagine it to be only a visionary felicity, and that I am still under the influence of a dream, but combining all the circumstances of my happiness, recalling to mind the enchanting sound of the voice which pronounced my pardon, I give way to an excess of joy, accompanied with exclamations, which if they were overheard, would argue distraction. Such is my condition, which I deem supremely happy, and wish for its continuance the remainder of my life.

I shall not depart till I have heard from you!

LETTER

No. XIV.

LETTER FROM THE CARDINAL TO THE QUEEN.

August 9, 1784.

" I THINK I have found out the opportunity and pretence the Master is wishing for ---Not long since I imparted to him the fears of his Slave, and the dangers he is exposed to, in consequence of the suspicions which his assiduities have raised A discovery would undo him for ever, by the insinuations which would necessarily ensue, and the Master, spite of his authority, would find himself forced to sacrifice his Slave, lest himself should be exposed, through an endless circulation of tittle-tattle.

" We are sometimes under a necessity of bestowing our confidence upon persons who are placed near us, on whose fidelity perhaps, we can but little depend, and who often avail themselves of circumstances to draw us into inconsistencies, which we are not at first aware of Their aim is to become possessed of weapons, which they know how to turn against us, in order to preserve their sway, and incapacitate us from acting in conformity with our wishes Such is the situation of the Master---thwarted in his views, his projects, his very conduct he sees, but too late, the danger there is in giving one's self up without reserve especially to the wicked, who know how to make their advantage of every thing. Not knowing as yet the reasons of the reservedness he is to put on, nor the nature of his confidence

dence, I can give him no counsel, nor investigate the means of avoiding what might prove displeasing to ———— you comprehend my meaning.---I must then confine myself to pointing out the method of sending open-[ly] for his Slave, without the *Master*, the P. the V. the B. &c. being able to pass any reflection on that proceeding. That first step being settled, nothing will be more easy than to continue visits, which will be sanctioned on one side, and a matter of indifference on the other.

' You have at the present moment a young person who works under your immediate inspection---I know that that person's works have been pleasing to you, and that you wish to patronize her. She has made a clergyman, a relation of hers, to whom she is under great obligations a partaker of your bounty. The latter is come to consult me, and ask whether he might hope to obtain a vacant place, which would be demanded of me by you. Being made acquainted with all the particulars, I directed him to draw up a memoir, which will be delivered to the little one with all instructions requisite. You will find the petition at the bottom of your basket, and will perceive by the contents of it, that the Slave must necessarily be sent for, to receive his orders from the Master, to whom this unaffected transaction, and the ——— of complying with his will, must undoubtedly afford an opportunity of shewing his indulgence, and of sensibly forgetting what has passed.

' The Counsel waits to be told I consider that she may —— receive either your determination or your commands —— E S C D---You comprehend my meaning.

LITTLE.

No. XV.

LETTER FROM THE CARDINAL TO THE QUEEN.

August 13, 1784.

"THERE is a proverb which says, "no good fortune ever comes alone"---my sad adventure will prove the proverb false. Do not be alarmed, prepare, on the contrary, to laugh heartily, and to make game of me at our next meeting. After the most complete happiness, I was stealing away to the passage you know, when passing along a quick-set hedge, a loud noise made me apprehensive some body wanted to surprise me ---terrified to the last degree, I made but one jump to get out of reach. My hastiness having prevented my taking the usual precautions, and still less noticing that the rain had made the ground slippery, I found myself, I cannot well say how, in the very middle of the ditch. The Savage, who was waiting for me on the other side, perceiving in my comical fall, nothing more than an excess of clumsiness on my part, burst out into an excessive fit of laughter, holding his sides, and writhing himself in the most whimsical manner. A few significant words stifled, for an instant, his immoderate risibility, and he helped me out of the mire, into which I had sunk pretty deep. You know the serious turn of the Savage, would you ever have thought, that after I had apprised him of the cause of my fright, he would have

fallen

fallen a laughing afresh? Undoubtedly not. Well, off he goes, twisting himself about, rolling upon the grass, unable to utter a single word. Seeing nothing move on the opposite side, I waited with tolerable composure to see the end of this extraordinary merriment. When he was grown a little more sedate, I told him somewhat seriously, that I would be careful never after to take him along with me, since, in so delicate an occurrence, he behaved with equal folly and indiscretion. "Do not " condemn me unheard," answered he, " hear me---It's " a rabbit or a partridge that has frightened you---you " thought you saw the whole gang at your heels, and " without reflecting in the least, you came and played " the dipper to avoid being seen by them.---Suppose " yourself in my place, as I neither perceived nor " heard any thing that could occasion so precipitate a " retreat, my first motion was to laugh. You relate " your fright, I guess at the motive that gave rise to it. " I then survey you, behold you all over mud, with " your breeches torn from one end to the other---who " the Devil could forbear laughing?"---I myself look, and see the truth of his account, our eyes meet, and we join in chorus. So far all was right, except the tearing of a pair of breeches, and a rather filthy masquerade---- but the discovery of my thumb's being out of joint, brought on a little gravity in our progress. Having stolen in unperceived at home, the Savage performed the office of a surgeon thanks to his balsam, I am in much less pain to day. The Countess, whom I saw this morning finding me with my hand muffled up, naturally asked what had happened to me. Though sure she would run her jokes upon me, I told her my said mishap, at which she laughed so immoderately, that she was forced to leave me, and go into another apartment. The marks she had left in the drawing-room of her excessive risibility, making me apprehend a second shower, I withdrew without seeing her again.-----The charming laugher will not fail of telling you what she calls my aukwardness, but I hope that for this time her mirth will not terminate in the same manner

---

No XVI.

LETTER FROM THE QUEEN TO THE CARDINAL.

August 15, 1784.

" LAST night I received the packet, the instructions, and reflexions thou sendest me concerning Calonne. I know him to be a man who would not miss an opportunity of setting himself off at the expence of any person whatever, but I likewise know, that when I have recommended to him any matter whatsoever, he will pay regard to it, and not seek to thwart me. The object of which thou speakest to me relative to the Countess, has no manner of reference to this, I am well pleased with thee for thy demand upon him; but the matter of fact is, that at that period I only knew the Countess by sight, and for having heard her spoken of by Madame, who was her well wisher. The encomiums she passed on her, and the circumstances of the 2d of February did all the rest. A minister is often forced to contrive falsehoods and be guilty of injustice, especially when sure of impunity; he was ignorant at that moment of my concern for her, nor do I wonder at his using my name, or that of the *Minister*, in order to avoid all farther solicitations from thee. Moreover as it is an affair of the first magnitude, and that requires mature deliberation, we will take all necessary measures not to meet with any obstacles, and at the same time revive the saying of the Doctor. All is for the best. Farewell."

No XVII.

LETTER FROM THE QUEEN TO THE CARDINAL

Aug. 16, 1784.

" ... observation made to me yesterday with an air of curiosity and suspicion will prevent my going to day to ———— but will not forbid us to deprive me from ... Sire. The Minister sets out at ... to go a hunting ... R————, his return will be very late, or to speak more properly, next morning. I hope being his able to make myself ... for the ... I have experienced

perienced for thefe two days paft. Imprudent conduct has brought me to that pafs, that I cannot without danger remove objects that are difpleafing to me, and who haunt me. They have fo thoroughly ftudied me, and know fo little how to feign and diffemble, that they attribute my change to nothing but a difcretion, which to them appears blame-worthy, it is therefore very effential to be on one's guard, to avoid all furprize

"The daring queftion put to me, perfuades me that my confidence has been abufed as well as my good nature, and that advantage has been taken of circumftances to fetter my will. I have a way of coming at information concerning it, but I will firft confult thee. As thou wilt play the principal part in the fcheme I have devifed, we muft needs agree as well on this point as we did laft Friday on the S——. This comparifon will make thee laugh no doubt, but as it is a juft one, and I defire to give thee a proof of it to night, before we talk of ferious matters, obferve exactly what follows. Do thou affume the garb of a meffenger, and with a parcel in thy hand be walking about, at half paft eleven, under the porch of the chapel. I will fend the Countefs, who fhall ferve thee for a guide, and conduct thee up a little back ftaircafe to an apartment, where thou wilt find the object of they defires."

LETTER

No XVIII

LETTER FROM THE QUEEN TO THE CARDINAL.

August 18, 1784.

" SINCE the step I directed the Countess to take with the President d'Aligre, concerning your affair of the Quinze-Vingt, I suspect (from his astonishment) that he has endeavoured to pry into the motives which actuated me, and that unable to make any discovery, he has spoken of it to *certain persons*, who are supposed to be ignorant of nothing, and who, perhaps, on this occasion, have dissembled their behaviour to shew they still possess my confidence. The restraint I am under, by their redoubled assiduities, the continual chit-chat with which I am plagued, their anxious and inquisitive looks when I answer a question, in short, every thing persuades me, that they suspect our secret intelligence, and that they are using every method to acquire the certain knowledge of it.

" This morning the M——s conversed with me concerning these with airs of kindness, which induces me to believe he has received some information. As it is not the first time it has happened, and I never failed to acquaint and consult those persons I suspect as the authors, whose views are to pin me down still more, I shall not fail to impart to them my astonishment, with such circumstances, as will enable me to judge whether my suspicions are well or ill grounded.

" Thou

" Thou art much in the right in telling me, that I am in a wood, surrounded with whatever is dangerous and venomous on the face of the globe, but, in short, we must howl with the wolves till we have muzzled them. As to the *Minister*, I know his coarse spun finesses, and his foible for me; they know his brutality, and what account is to be made of the first stroke from his tusk, and that is what gives me spirits; they know, that in circumstances more delicate than the present, I have chained up the lion, and have made him see and believe whatever I pleased.

" Thou knowest what it is prevents my getting rid of my leeches, help me to find out the way, and to deprive them of the means of hurting me, and thy desires shall soon be gratified

" I expect thee to night at the same hour and place; I hope before that happy moment to have got all out of the *Minister*

    J t. R t. B. a. V. C S   Adieu.

No. XIX.

LETTER FROM THE QUEEN TO THE CARDINAL.

August 18, 1784.

" I WRITE to thee in haste, to give thee notice that it is impossible for me to receive thee to-night, I have gained more information than I could wish, and though enraged at the scene I have just had with

[34]

with la P———, I will conceal my resentment, and carry my dissimulation to the utmost. I know that anger is of no service, and therefore take the resolution most suitable, though contrary to my own inclination. I will not leave the Minister till I have wrought him to my purpose, which object accomplished, I am not at a loss to find a future, and the bomb-shell bursts, I shall be able to make the splinters fall on those who set fire to it. Do not depart till to-morrow at one o'clock, and fail not to be this evening in the walk to T——— as I doubt not (from what I have heard) but all thy steps are watched, it is a material point to perplex the inquisitive, and render it impossible for them to realise their suspicions.

"The Countess will stay here to-morrow, and inform thee of all that has passed. Depend on my attachment, and be persuaded that I shall know how to treat, as I ought, ungrateful people, who are become thy enemies, because thou wast not introduced by them. Above all be discreet, I rely on the Countess as on myself."

No. XX.

LETTER FROM THE CARDINAL TO THE QUEEN.

August 21, 1784.

"IT would indeed be unjust, after the confidence you have granted me in the present circumstances, if I did

not

not adopt the line of conduct you have prescribed for me. Be assured that I will sacrifice every thing to the quiet and happiness of my dear Master. Whatever may occur during my absence, (which is become necessary) he will call to mind my sincerity, my zeal to serve him, and my most tender love. I am not superstitious, yet, shall I tell thee? I have forebodings which I dread to see realized; the more I reflect on the secrets thou hast communicated to me, the more I perceive the possibility of a reconciliation. The absent are always in the wrong.----When once I am got to S------ a thousand ways will be found to do me prejudice. I shall not be at hand to clear myself---slander, aided by anonymous letters flying from all sides, will be the weapons used by my enemies,---and then, to support them, will come the handsome F------. He is not, I grant thee, an ambitious man, he is young, amiable, and aspires solely to the happiness of pleasing you----but the C------ is an old flager, whose affairs are greatly involved, and who is susceptible of no attachment, any farther than the gratification of his interest and ambition. Such are, I am sure, part of their attempts, and the terms in which they will address you; if insufficient to sway you, they will have recourse to the last contrivance.---I confess to you, 'tis there I dread them most----it would be an unpardonable villainy, but from their indecency, and their extreme carefulness in laying hands upon and preserving those writings, it is plain they did it only with an intent to make an ill use of them. However, from all the reflections I have made, I think that with resolution supported by authority, they might be compelled to a restitustitution. If that method be dangerous, there is another which appears to me infallible, and that agrees perfectly well with their selfish disposition, I will impart it to thee in my next letter.----Since this discovery, my mind has been anxiously bent on finding out the most speedy and best expedient, and I own I still recur to my first opinion.

" I shall depart on the feast day, and not appear at V------ but on receipt of a particular order. Meanwhile my thoughts shall be occupied with the great object.-----The packet will go off to-morrow night.----- The caution I shall use will prevent all confidence that might prove dangerous, and if unfortunately any surprise should happen, the bearer will be able to give no indication nor token of intelligence.

No. XXI.

LETTER FROM THE CARDINAL TO THE QUEEN.

August 24, 1784.

" THE courier set out last night at half past twelve. The Countess will tell thee how I contrived the delivery of the packet. I have given all instructions necessary for the arrival and departure of my

two

two couriers, by which means I shall hear from thee at least once a week, and if any thing extraordinary should occur, I shall always have a confidential person in readiness to dispatch ------All my equipages are ready ----To-morrow is the fatal day, when I must part with all that is dear to me. This reflexion depresses my spirits, and occasions me to feel an uneasiness, which I cannot overcome, yet I know that my absence is necessary here, and my presence indispensible at the place of my destination.------I think I am jealous, a dreadful malady! The personage in question disturbs my brain, and makes me dread my departure ------Have a little compassion on me, seek to calm my uneasiness, and persuade thyself that I should not outlive thy infidelity. Farewell--- be careful of thy health, live happy, and sometimes bestow a thought upon the Slave"

No XXII.

LETTER FROM THE QUEEN TO THE CARDINAL.

September 8, 1784.

" IT is very astonishing that the courier is not yet returned; it gives me uneasiness, as I required the quickest dispatch. If on receipt of this letter he is not yet arrived, dispatch immediately a

* F courier

courier with the inclosed note, tell him by word of mouth, whom he is to deliver it to

"Thy departure has silenced every tongue, whether out of discretion or policy, thy name has not been pronounced. People redouble their dutiful attendance, and strive to make me forget the scene, as well as the motive that gave rise to it. The advice thou givest me is impracticable. They never told me they were in possession of----I only surmised it from behaviour, reproaches and speeches which I have overheard. I am fully persuaded, that let what will happen, they will never expose themselves to convey any writing into the hands of the *Master*, but I should always be uneasy to know they had in their possession what could disturb my tranquillity. I am fully resolved to take a decided part, but I have made so many sacrifices for all those people, and the M------ has so often accused me of inconstancy and fickleness, that I must absolutely have a reason to assign to him; not that he loves or values them, quite the contrary; but he pretends that it is for my sake, and that it is always extremely expensive to have new favourites.——A well placed system of œconomy truly!————to-morrow I set off to T---- where I shall remain a few days to have greater liberty to see the Countess. Hadst not told me the Savage --- --- at Paris a very useless thing."

No. XXIII.

LETTER FROM THE QUEEN TO THE CARDINAL.

September 8, 1784.

" YOU muſt have received a parcel which I ſent you, I am ſurpriſed I have not had an anſwer to it You may judge of my uneaſineſs by its contents I hope for the future you will uſe more punctuality

---

No. XXIV

LETTER FROM THE CARDINAL TO THE QUEEN

September 13, 1784

" THE Maſter will ſee by the packet I ſend him, that his object is attained, and his note become needleſs The courier before this laſt, was entruſted with a letter, ſomewhat long, relative to his attendants ------After the deepeſt reflexion, the Slave thinks that the Maſter may without danger, follow the counſel which he gives him, for after all, he is the Maſter. I have ſent the Countefs a ſmall phial for you, which con-

tains

tains a liquor that may be written with, and nothing appear, but being shewn to the fire, or light, grows black, and disappears again afterwards. In case of any thing particular, leave a wide space between your lines, that you may interline with that liquor ----I saw the day before yesterday, the person in question, whose answer appeared to me to be evasive ---He is to call again in the course of the week, to make known his last determination If he refuses, I have another person in my eye The Countess will communicate what I am prohibited doing in this paper.

(t. C. E. I. M. A. b)

No XXV.

LETTER FROM THE CARDINAL TO THE QUEEN.

September 20, 1784

IF the Slave is happy to contribute to the success of the grand object, undertaken by the Dame, he thinks it will be necessary before, the execution, that he should remove to a less distant situation. The most impenetrable veil being necessary to cover the author of the project, there must be an immediate return of writing to the source, in order to be doubly guarded against contingencies ------I have perfectly considered the latter reflexion.------There is nothing permanent

permanent in the world ----In confequence of this truth, the Mafter's policy is plainly feen, for in cafe of a revolution, he is fure of receiving a *fupport*, which will validate his claims, and prevent the triumph of his enemies. Divided between hope and fear, my fituation is the moft cruel, and my exiftence wretched----Yet when I make reflexions on the paft, and bring into confideration my degree of confidence with the Mafter, I fee the injuftice of my fears. The hopes of feeing myfelf foon within his arms, gives a frefh fpring to my joy, and reftores me to my fecurity."

No. XXVI

LETTER FROM THE CARDINAL TO THE QUEEN.

Nov. 22, 1784.

"THE defire I feel of being ferviceable to the Countefs, and to remove all obftacles that ftill oppofe a public reception, makes me practife every poffible method to fulfil thofe two objects. The Mafter will judge by the proceedings which I have directed one of my dependants to adopt, whether the fuccefs of his folicitations can ferve as a pretence to the mutual defires, and remove all difficulties. The Abbé de Befaryes is to refign his office of Mafter of the Oratory, to the Abbé de Phaff, by extraction a German, whofe friends live at Bruffels, in the retinue of the Archduchefs. As a difficulty exifts which you alone can remove,

move, I have advised him to go to Bruffels, to ufe all methods with the Archduchefs, to obtain from her a letter of recommendation to you. As the bufinefs cannot be tranfacted without me, fince 'tis I who furnifh the funds, it will be an additional motive for bringing me into recollection.---I had projected a fcheme to accelerate and prevent a denial, but as that might have brought you into queftion, and raifed fufpicion, I judged it moft prudent to decline it. So much for that---you will allow that events fucceed fo rapidly on both fides, that it were dangerous to proceed too far. So politic an anfwer from an afpiring fpirit, aftonifhes me the more, as the æras, fpoken of, are yet very remote. I forefee many difficulties in bringing that to a profperous iffue---*that's underftood*---I fhall always be ready, fcrupuloufly, to perform the commands of the Mafter: the moft pleafing would be, no doubt, to be recalled near his divine perfon."

No XXVII.

LETTER FROM THE QUEEN TO THE CARDINAL.

Dec. 12, 1784.

"Had I followed the maxim that fays 'in all things make flow hafte,'" the accident when befel my laft letter would not have happened.
The

The earnestness, the eagerness of reading, urging me to put the letter too near the light, it took fire, and in spite of all my endeavours to extinguish it, could save only some part of it. To him that understandeth, greeting ---The first packet was gone off when the courier arrived Being pressed for time, I could not answer with regard to the Abbé, had I been forewarned, I would have saved him a needless journey. We have made an agreement, never to grant any person whatever a request of that nature, assuredly the Abbé will not be an exception to the rule, besides, suppose the scheme could have taken place, it is clear the object could not have justified the proceeding The situation I am in, will infallibly bring on a more favourable opportunity. The most speedy dispatch will shorten the exile of the Slave *I believe it is understood.*"

No XXVIII.

LETTER FROM THE QUEEN TO THE CARDINAL

Jan 15, 1784.

" IF it had not been my intention there should be a mystery in the purchase of the jewel, I certainly should not have employed you to procure it for me I am not accustomed to enter thus into treaty with my jewellers, and this way of proceeding is so much

much the more contrary to what I owe to myself, as two words were sufficient to put me in possession of that object. I am surprised that you dare to propose to me such an arrangement, but let there be no more said about it. It is a trifle that has occasioned me to make a few reflections, which I will impart to you when opportunity offers. The Countess will deliver to you your paper. I am sorry you have given yourself so much trouble to no purpose."

No. XXIX.

LETTER FROM THE QUEEN TO THE CARDINAL.

January 29, 1785.

"HOW is this? affectation with me? Why, my friend, ought people in our predicament to act under restraint, to seek for shifts, and deal with infrece it? Dost thou know that thy reserve, and thy false pride, drew upon thee the letter thou hast received, and that but for the Countess, who has told me all, I should have attributed that pretended arrangement to quite a different motive. Fortunately all is cleared up. The Countess will deliver thee the writing, and explain the motives by which I have been actuated in this matter. As I am supposed ignorant of the confidence thou hast shewn her, as also of the token of trust that thou wilt give her, by laying before her our particular engagements, that is a more than sufficient reason to make thee secure, and remove all difficulties. Thou wilt keep the writing, and deliver it to none but me.

"I hope, notwithstanding my disorder, to see thee before the holiday I expect the Countess to-morrow. I will tell her whether I shall be able to receive from my Slave, the object which had nearly set us at variance."

No XXX.

LETTER FROM THE QUEEN TO THE CARDINAL

July 6, 1785.

YOUR fears are groundless, the coolness and dislike for you, which you surmise, is by no means the effect of inconstancy. Put the question to yourself I long to speak to you. the steps I cause to be taken towards you, must needs convince you of it. The *Minister* returned from the chase much sooner than I expected him, he was still with me, as also Madame E.----- when I dispatched the confidential person to you. do not depart to day, be at ten o'clock with the Countess, and believe that no one desires more than I do the explanation you request"

* G   LETTER

[46]

No. XXXI.

LETTER FROM THE QUEEN TO THE CARDINAL

July 19, 1784.

" I BELIEVE I have informed you of the disposal of the sum, which I destined for the object in question, and that probably I should not fulfil the engagements till my return from Fontainbleau. The Countess will remit to you thirty thousand livres, to pay the interest. The privation of the capital is to be taken into consideration and this compensation will make them easy.

" You complain and I say not a word. a very extraordinary circumstance, time will perhaps acquaint you with the motive of my silence I do not love suspicious people, especially when there is so little reason for it. I possess a principle I never will recede from. Your last conversation is very opposite to what you related to me at a preceding period. Reflect upon it, and if your memory serves you faithfully, by comparing the *arts* you will judge what I am to think of your pressing solicitations.

LETTER

No. XXXII.

LETTER FROM THE QUEEN TO THE CARDINAL.

February 12, 1785.

"FROM all that I have heard concerning that extraordinary man thou tellest me of, I cannot look upon him but as a mountebank. It may be prepoffeffion in me, and I know by experience, that one ought never to judge of any body from the report of others, but I have many reafons for not yielding to thy entreaties. I am not fuperftitious, nor is it an eafy matter to impofe upon me, but as thofe fort of people have fometimes things that aftonifh, and thereby difpofe one to fee and believe whatever they fay, I am not in a fituation for fuch trials. Befides, it would be very difficult, nay, even impoffible to receive him as myfterioufly as I could wifh, and thou knoweft the cautioufnefs with which I muft act in the prefent moment. The Countefs made me laugh heartily, by relating the laft fcene, it has fomething of prodigy in it, and raifes in me the greateft defire to fee the grand Cophte. Yet, if I muft believe the Countefs, it requires a perfon to be very innocent, in order to behold the myfteries of that great man though, to judge from the circumftances of all his apparatus, I believe he looks upon thee and the Countefs as two fimpletons, and treats you as two dupes. Don't be offended at my franknefs, I promife thee I will judge of him in my own perfon.

"The

[48]

' The M____r leaves me as little as he can, I do not yet guess at the reason of it, but shall not be long before I do. Luckily I have not to deal with an Egyptian like thy Cagliostro, who guesses the past, and foretells the future. He is not possessed of the Talisman that gives utterance to the ladies toys, and indeed I am at ease, and dread not any indiscretion from mine.

" Excuse my foibles, for some time past I so seldom allow myself any diversion, that thou wilt no doubt be delighted with having afforded me the opportunity of a moment's recreation."

FINIS.

Lightning Source UK Ltd.
Milton Keynes UK
UKHW020908270422
402094UK00007B/1433